# BY MY OWN RECKONING

Smyth & Helwys Publishing, Inc.
6316 Peake Road
Macon, Georgia 31210-3960
1-800-747-3016
©2008 by Smyth & Helwys Publishing

*Library of Congress Cataloging-in-Publication Data*

Sherman, Cecil E.
By my own reckoning / by Cecil Sherman.
p. cm.
ISBN 978-1-57312-506-2 (alk. paper)
1. Sherman, Cecil E. 2. Baptists--Biography. 3. Southern Baptist
Convention--History--20th century. I. Title.
BX6495.S469A3 2008
286'.1092--dc22
[B]
2008010551

# CECIL SHERMAN

## By My Own Reckoning

To our daughter, Eugenia Sherman Brown,
our son-in-law, William Douglas Brown,
and our grandson, Nathaniel Brown.

This book is dedicated to them.
They are God's good gifts to Dot and me.

*Cecil E. Sherman*

# CONTENTS

# FOREWORD

Bill Leonard says being Baptist is messy. Bill Hull says being Baptist is an experience. So it should follow that what you have in hand is one Baptist's narrative of a messy experience. Not so! What you have in hand is an ordered chronicle, a unique story, of a solitary human being—a man who arguably has been the most important Baptist of his generation, the most formative Baptist Christian of the past sixty years.

Cecil Sherman, in sharing his autobiography, has written about some things he had rather forget. Much of this has been dredge work, a labor of mind, heart, emotion, and will. Yet, who better than he can share a view from the inside of the Baptist family in this country since the 1950s? So with moist eyes and set jaw, Cecil bids you join him for "his story"—amazingly, a slice of our own free-church history as well.

Here is joy and here is pain; memories sweet and bitter, emotions tender and rugged, dreams realized and dreams shattered, and throughout a tough love for the people called Baptists.

Cecil Sherman would never admit to heroism, but if medals of honor were ever pinned on husbands and fathers for their battles, he would wear a few. Family has always been his passion, while his fierce love for Dot during her years with Alzheimer's surpasses all his struggles with pastoral problems, SBC politics, Gatlinburg gangs, Peace Committee futility, CBF coordination, or the birth pangs of a dozen new theological schools partnering on his watch.

One personal note: Cecil was present when my seminary president colleagues and I went to Glorieta, New Mexico, in 1986 to meet with the SBC Peace Committee. He listened in silence to our ill-fated attempt at placating that incorrigible group. The next morning, he and I had breakfast together. Through tears he told me, "You fellows have sold the store." Later that day he resigned from the committee. Now I know more than before the truth in the adage, "Even a dwarf on a giant's shoulder sees farther of the two."

So, welcome! Climb upon a giant's shoulders and read along. Remember too: Life isn't about how to survive storms, but how to dance in the rain.

Cecil Sherman is one Baptist who has danced.

— **W. Randall Lolley**
President, Southeastern Baptist Theological Seminary, 1974–1988

# INTRODUCTION

Several years ago Mark McElroy of Smyth & HelwyPublishers asked me to write an autobiography. I was reluctant on two counts: I did not see that my life is different from the life story of a thousand other pastors. And I did not see a broad market for my autobiography. Why write if no one is likely to read? I did not take Mark up on his offer.

Five or six years passed. From time to time friends mentioned that it would be good to have a full account of Moderate political efforts in the SBC controversy of the 1980s. Others expressed regret that there had been no record of the work of the Peace Committee from a Moderate point of view (little has been revealed about the internal life of the Peace Committee from either point of view). Jim Slatton and Tom Graves spoke of the need for someone to write. I still did not want to open those files or recall some of those conversations.

Then in 2006, my daughter, Eugenia Sherman Brown, entered the conversation. She is a historian. When she weighed in on the side that I should write, I was persuaded. She argued that in a few years there would be no one living who could fill in pieces of the story that were bedded in my memory, for I was a participant in events and conversations that ought not be lost. One part of Genie's argument for an auto-biography always included Dot's Alzheimer's story. She believed a reading public might be sensitized to the Alzheimer's plague that devastates so many in our senior population. All the while, with every accidental contact, Mark McElroy continued to urge that I get to work on an autobiography. I told him I thought Smyth & Helwys would lose money on the venture, but he insisted that I get to work. So in the summer of 2006 I began to write.

There is nothing remarkable about most of my life. Remembering stories from my childhood and youth was pleasant. Recalling years at my churches was delightful, and the story moved quickly. A thousand other pastors have gone through similar experiences, but the process of organizing "my story" was good for me. When I was busy in the daily, I did not see the gracious hand of God. The next appointment or sermon consumed my mind; I saw the trees but not the forest. When I looked at the whole of my life, I saw that the boundary lines have fallen for me in pleasant places, I have a goodly heritage" (Ps 16:6 NRSV). There have been disappointments, but on balance the good far outweighs the bad. "Our side" lost the Southern Baptist Convention to organized Fundamentalism, and at the time I grieved, but that is past, over and gone. God has not put "all his eggs in one basket"; I shouldn't, either. It has been more than twenty years since I resigned from the Peace Committee. That was the time I de facto resigned from the SBC. Writing this story has let me know that I really am past that sad experience. I've been able to step back, see the story whole, and know I'm at peace with those events and the consequences of them. But for one thing I am glad: If I had tried to write my story in 1990, it would have had an edge. Time has given me more balance. This is not an angry story, nor have I tried to settle scores.

A conversation with Walter Shurden, both a friend and one of our best Baptist historians, gave me a way to think about the balance of the book. Shurden said that I should move quickly through the pastor years, but I should slow down and tell a detailed story of three things: Moderate politics, the Peace Committee and the start-up years at CBF. That made sense to me. If there is a part of my life that is unique, those three parts are it, and so I tried to do what Walter Shurden said. There is a sense in which my story is an attempt to explain Moderates and give some order and justification to what we were trying to do.

I worked at being fair with those who opposed us. Rough exchanges, and there were a few, have been compressed. Some "war stories" have been omitted. I tried to quote my opposition often enough to give insight into what Moderates were up against; I did not detail every messy confrontation. Some of those people are dead now; others will take issue with my interpretation of events. Those who read history years from now will reach their own conclusions. But not all the story was put to paper. I tried to give a gentle judgment of "the other side."

My life has been more than the SBC controversy. By far most of my years have been spent as a pastor. I hope that comes through in the story. I have a life-wish for the Church. I long for my best students at the seminary to become pastors. It is a need, and there is great satisfaction in the pastor's life. The friendships I've made with wonderful lay-people, bringing churches to health, working through the growing years with young people . . . that has been the stuff of my life. Controversy makes headlines; it does not make ministry. Controversy makes for confrontation; the majority of my life has been about reconciliation. And I'd like to be remembered so.

The last chapter describes what it is like to see your wife slip into Alzheimer's Disease. There is nothing clinical in that chapter, and I do not argue that my experience will help another husband/wife who is suffering the same loss. But if you can catch the pathos, the helplessness that has been mine for the last ten years, the story will have served a useful purpose for millions of people are facing the same predicament. This autobiography does not fully describe the beauty and goodness of Dot, but I pray a part of that beauty and goodness will leak through all the story. She has made my life good. She has been a moral compass. Often she spoke for God to me, and I am the better person for having spent my life in her company. A shadow of that Christian woman remains, and I give thanks. My daughter argued that Alzheimer's is so pervasive in our older generation that Dot's descent into that awful disease is reason enough to write the story.

The construction of my story is not chronological at one point. For several years I was doing two things at once. While a pastor at First Baptist Church, Asheville, North Carolina (1964–84), I began doing Moderate politics. For me to try to tell the Asheville story and then jump over to the political story seemed to me to make for hard reading. So I artificially divided my life: I told the pastor story at Asheville, and then in a separate chapter I told the political story. The same was true of Broadway Baptist Church in Fort Worth, Texas, and the Peace Committee. The two were happening at the same time. To dart from one to the other and then back to the one seemed to me both a story that would be hard to write and a story that would be hard to follow. So I tell the story of my pastor years at Asheville in two chapters. Almost no mention is made of the SBC controversy. I tell of the Broadway years in a chapter. Then I wrote several chapters about the controversy and its aftermath.

I need to thank people who helped me write. My daughter read each chapter; in this task she was performing as her mother before her. She edited my material, and it is cleaner copy for her gift of time and skill. She made editorial suggestions that uniformly improved the story and made it easier to read. Bill and Veta Sherman (my brother and his wife) read other chapters and made helpful suggestions. I've already mentioned Walter Shurden's contribution to my arrangement of materials. Jim Slatton read the chapter on Moderate politics and made helpful suggestions. Then the people at Smyth & Helwys have been patient and uniformly helpful. To all of the above, I am in your debt.

It has taken me about eighteen months to write this story. While writing I took care of Dot, taught part-time at Baptist Theological Seminary at Richmond, wrote commentaries for Sunday school teachers, and served two churches as interim pastor. It kept me busy. Now that I am finished, I want to thank Mark McElroy for pressing his point. Age is a time for reflection. This assignment has made me recall things I would not have remembered had I not written. Looking back on my life, I see the guiding hand of God more clearly in retrospect than I did in the doing of it. There have been disappointments along the way, but there have been more sunny days than gloomy ones. God has been gentle. When I was seventeen years old, I answered a "call" to ministry. God did not "call" me and drop me. He has been a Presence all along the way, and it has been an interesting journey.

—Cecil E. Sherman

Richmond, Virginia
October 2007

# Chapter 1
# BEFORE I WAS BORN

I come from Americans. At a time unknown to me, Shermans, Brannons, Brownlows, and Cooks came to America, but I don't know when or from where they came. I wish I did, but none of my forebears thought it necessary to leave a marked trail. Stories have been passed down the generations that give glimpses of who those people were.

Peter Sherman was my great-great-great-grandfather. He came from Fonda, New York. When he was a teenager, he enlisted in the first New York Infantry, Continental Army. For more than six years he served the American Revolution as a private. For his service the New York legislature awarded him six hundred acres of land in the New York wilderness. That grant was in Onondaga County. Today the city of Syracuse sits on part of that grant. Promptly, Peter Sherman sold half his six hundred acres for forty dollars. From then until now, Shermans have had a way with money.

The man could neither read nor write. I've visited the Onondaga County courthouse in Syracuse. Since he was the executor of several of his neighbors' estates, he had to sign his name in probate court. His "mark" appears on the records. He was a farmer and had the good opinion of his peers, else they would not have named him to be their executor. He lived a long life, surviving until 1848.

Peter's son had the unusual name of Peter Will-Comeback Sherman. I know nothing about him except his name, but the son of Peter Will-Comeback comes into clearer focus. That son was my great-grandfather; his name was Charles Wesley Sherman. Though

born in Tompkins County, New York, in 1823, early in life he went
west. He and a beloved wife named Maria settled in Decatur County,
Indiana. He was a farmer, and, given his name, he had to be a
Methodist. When he was thirty-eight years old, the Civil War broke
out. He enlisted in the Union Army; quickly he became a sergeant.
Records in the General Services Administration in Washington, D.C.,
tell of the times he answered roll calls and the times he was sent back
to Indiana to enlist more troops. At dawn on December 31, just outside Murfreesboro, Tennessee, he was caught in a surprise Confederate
charge. The Union troops were dressing and making coffee when out
of the woods came the rebels. The Battle of Stones River had begun. A
ball entered my great-grandfather's leg just below the knee, broke both
bones, and left him bleeding and unable to move. He nearly bled to
death. The day was raw. A cold rain gave way to sleet and then snow.
The wounded soldier waited for help, but others with less serious
wounds were taken from the field first. Finally a stretcher-bearer recognized Sherman as one of his order and took him to a field hospital.
There the wounded were divided into two groups: those who were
expected to live and those who were not. Sherman was put in the not-
likely-to-live group. The next morning he was still alive, and a surgeon
cleaned the wound by running a silk handkerchief straight through his
leg. Amazingly, the wound did not fester; he healed. Two years later in
Indianapolis, the grotesque, maimed leg was removed at the knee.
From that day he walked with a peg leg. He could no longer be a
farmer.

Back in Indiana he was made a jailer; it was something a one-
legged man could do. The spoils of war were available to soldiers from
the North. Charles Wesley Sherman was offered a job as postmaster of
the hamlet of Brighton, Missouri. By wagon they crept across Indiana
and Illinois, took a ferry over the Mississippi River, and then made
their way to Brighton, a little place twelve miles north of Springfield.

Charles Wesley Sherman's first wife died; he then married Caroline
Brace. She would bear his children, all eleven of them. Seven died
before they reached adulthood. I've been to his grave. Caroline lies
alongside him; then seven little markers tell the sad story of the want
of public health and of the pain of burying your children. Charles

Wesley remained postmaster of Brighton until 1903. One day when he was eighty years old, he came home from work, ate his noon meal, said he would take a twenty-minute nap, and quietly died. After coming to Missouri, Charles Wesley Sherman had "seen the light" (that's the way his obituary put it); he became a Baptist. Four children survived him.

One of the survivors was George White Sherman, born 1866. George and his brother Frank became Baptist preachers. George graduated from Carson Newman College in Tennessee. The way he met and courted his wife was unusual. George and Frank Sherman drove mules from Springfield, Missouri, to Columbia, Tennessee. Columbia was famous as "the mule capital of the South." The mules were sold in Columbia; then the riders would return to Missouri. But riding from Missouri to Middle Tennessee is a long way; one could get saddle sore. So the men lingered in Columbia for a couple of weeks to recover. During those two weeks, George met Sally Brownlow. They began a correspondence that lasted all through the year. The following year when the time came to lead mules to Tennessee again, George was ready to go. This time he stayed in Columbia for a month; at the end of that month, George and Sally were engaged. They were married and moved to Louisville, Kentucky, so that George could attend the Southern Baptist Theological Seminary. George graduated from Southern in 1892.

Sally's father was Joseph Polk Brownlow. The man had quite a life, and he alone of my ancestors took the time to tell his story—in seventy-two handwritten pages. During the Civil War he was a Confederate cavalryman. He rode with Nathan Bedford Forrest; the war produced no one who was more colorful or controversial than Forrest. After the war, Brownlow sold mules for a while; then he saw the need for a bank and started the Farmers and Merchants State Bank in Columbia. The bank prospered and so did Brownlow. He was a deacon in the First Baptist Church. At the time of his death in 1915, he was treasurer of the Tennessee Baptist Convention.

Four children were born of George Sherman and Sally Brownlow; my father, John Franklin Sherman, was the youngest (born November 1901 in Hartsville, Tennessee). The last church George served was the

Polytechnic Baptist Church in Fort Worth, Texas. One Sunday night in October 1921, he complained of chest pain. In less than an hour he was dead. My nineteen-year-old father became the caretaker of his near-invalid mother. His carefree days were over, and so was his formal education. My father met my mother at the Poly Church. All of this prefigured my life as a child; I was reared in that church. I never knew my paternal grandparents, as they both died before I was born.

My mother's people were of the South. The earliest entry in the Brannon family Bible is for Bridger Brannon, my grandfather's great-grandmother. She lived in the Edgefield District of South Carolina. I don't know when the Brannons moved to Georgia and Alabama. It had to be after Andrew Jackson defeated the Indians at Horseshoe Bend (March 27, 1814). I know nothing of them until after the Civil War. To my knowledge, none of them owned slaves; they probably couldn't afford them. Strangely, they fought for those who did. Lewellen Brannon (my grandfather's uncle) never owned a slave, but he died with an Alabama regiment outside Richmond in 1862. Another Brannon was killed at Dover in Tennessee. My grandfather was born in 1882; as a boy he was taken to Confederate reunions with his uncles.

My grandmother, Effie Cook Brannon, was not alive during the Civil War, but she was reared in the South. Her father was sheriff of Cleburne County, Alabama. The sheriff was a colorful character who dispensed rough justice. Several times he was involved in shootouts; once he was wounded for his trouble. One of my grandmother's brothers, Grady Cook, was a county judge.

Farming the Coosa River bottom was hard; two years in a row the Coosa flooded and my grandfather's crops were washed down the river. All of this happened when my grandfather was a young man. His father had died young. He had the charge of his mother, brothers, a wife, and a daughter (born 1905). That daughter became my mother. She was named Annie Mae Brannon.

Distant relatives had "gone to Texas." They wrote letters telling of "a land of milk and honey." It sounded like a better place to farm than the Coosa River bottom. My grandfather and his mother sold their holdings in Alabama, boarded a train, and went to Texas. I can't imagine it. All arrived at Handley Station (east side of Fort Worth) on December 20, 1906. They started over again. It was a hard life. For a few years my grandfather was a sharecropper; then he bought sixty acres of his own, paying $1.25 per acre. Finally he had his own "place." He kept it until he could farm no more.

Dad Brannon, as we called my grandfather, went to school only two years. He was a good farmer and a hard worker. He rose early, milked cows, ate a big breakfast, and was off to the fields. At noon my grandmother would go out on the porch, ring a bell that could be heard all over the farm, and then it was time for "dinner" (the noon meal). As a child, I was often sent to the farm for a week. I watched my grandparents make do on a nineteenth-century farm. The mules pulled the plows and wagon. The cows were milked by hand. The water was in the well. The "outhouse" was beyond the chicken house. The barn had hay and corn for the mules. It was a self-sustaining place that is my window into life before electricity.

My grandfather was tight with money; he had to be, for he didn't have much of it. One summer day I was at the farm. I must have been eight or nine years old. A stranger walked up from the gap (the entrance to my grandfather's farm). The man wore a straw hat and a white shirt with tie. Obviously he was not a farmer. The man was from the government. An electric power line was going to run along the northern border of my grandfather's place. If Jim and Effie Brannon wanted power, they could pay $60 a pole and have electricity in their house. My grandfather asked how many poles it would take to get power to his house. The government man said it would take three. Then the stranger asked, "Will you take it?" To my surprise, my grandmother replied without waiting for my grandfather. She said, "We'll take it." I was startled. That is the only time in my life I ever heard my grandmother make a financial decision. But Bama knew her mind. She wanted an electric stove instead of a wood stove. She wanted lights in the house instead of kerosene lanterns. She wanted to do the wash with a machine instead of in the backyard in pots over an open fire. Electricity came, and life changed for my grandparents.

Farming and electricity were not all there was to life on the farm. The Brannons were members of the Tate Springs Baptist Church. Dad was a deacon; his youngest brother, Henry Brannon, was the pastor. From before I was born until after I finished my education, Uncle Henry was the pastor at Tate's Springs. I was taken to "protracted meetings" at the church. After the revival, there was usually a baptizing in Village Creek. Church was an important part of life. My grandmother played the organ, pumping it to make music.

Next door to the church was Little School. There were only eight grades at Little School. If you wanted to graduate from high school, you had to move to town (Fort Worth) for the last three years of high school. My grandparents were determined that their children would get an education. Though my grandfather had limited education, he was on the Little School Board. He recognized education as one way to escape poverty. He wanted that for his children. So when my mother was fifteen, she was put in a rented room on the southeast side of Fort Worth so she could attend Polytechnic High School. She stayed in the home of Mrs. Young. To help with expenses she worked in a bakery. Mother graduated from Poly High in 1924. While living at Mrs. Young's, she attended Poly Baptist. There she caught the eye of the pastor's son; my sister, brother, and I are a result of their courtship and marriage. They were married October 15, 1926.

I've reflected on the people who emptied their blood into my veins. Though I knew few of them, they marked me. Since they were the way they were, I am the way I am. It is not as simple as that, but they have formed me. Several patterns emerge from these generations of Shermans, Brownlows, Cooks, and Brannons:

- Most of them were farmers. People close to the land are dependent. No one can control rain, frost, or hail. Because they can't control such events, they see life as gift. That idea makes room for God.
- Most of them were English, Welsh, or Scottish. Shermans were shepherds who sheared sheep. They were "sheermen." Family lore says they came from south of London. Most were of the Puritan tradition. Presbyterians, Methodists, and Baptists are in my line.
- With the exception of the Brownlows, all were middle class or poor Southern farmers. Work was required to survive. A commitment to

work was more than cultural necessity; it was theology. Laziness was a sin.

• Most of them took their religion seriously. Preachers were honored. Church was more than a membership; it was a commitment. Preachers, deacons, Sunday school teachers: all are in my background. In one sense, I am what my family made me. I am not a preacher because my family conditioned me to be, but all the parts of my family approved ministry as a vocation. When God called, my family approved and encouraged.

I had nothing to do with who these people were, what they believed, or the way they went about their lives, but all of them are a part of me. For the most part, they have blessed me. With the psalmist I can say, "The lines have fallen unto me in pleasant places; yea, I have a goodly heritage" (Ps 16:7 KJV).

Chapter 2

# FAMILY, FAITH, AND SCHOOL

Once there was a house numbered 2818 East Rosedale. It was on the southeast side of Fort Worth, Texas. In that house was a life-laboratory called a family. I am a product of that lab. I lived in that lab for the first seventeen years of my life. It was my family, my home, and I have never escaped the long shadow of the place and the people who lived with me.

Life was uncomplicated. There were three institutions that shaped me. They were family, church, and school. Two outside influences affected everyone in my generation; they were the Great Depression and World War II. Should you read those old, yellow newspaper headlines, they will tell of depression and war, but my name never appeared in the newspaper. The direct influences on me were family, church, and school.

## FAMILY

The house was plain and ordinary. There were hundreds of houses just like it all over Fort Worth. White clapboards, a straight-line roof, one bath, not well insulated, a 1920s kitchen, a gas space heater for warmth in winter that heated only one room, a sleeping porch that was not heated at all (going to bed in winter was an adventure) . . . that's the place John Sherman and Annie Mae Brannon Sherman lived out their marriage and reared their children.

The neighborhood was called Polytechnic. Before I was born a small school started on a hill that rose above Sycamore Creek. A community grew around the school. The school was Polytechnic Institute; by the time I was a boy, that school had become Texas Wesleyan College. Across the street from the college was a strip of stores, a post office, gas stations—all the things needed to do life. I lived in that neighborhood; we shortened the name to Poly. Sometimes I would not go outside Poly for months at a time. The place could be self-contained. I went to school and church there. Except when we went to my maternal grandparents' farm, there was no need to roam. I saw the world through Poly glasses. It was a small world, and I was a small boy.

For me, life began on December 26, 1927. I was the first of three children. Mother had a job at Montgomery-Ward department store. When I was born she became a full-time mother. Two years later my sister, Ruth Hester, was born. And in another two years my brother, Billy Don, was born. With the passing years he has become Bill. That was the family.

The core of our family was Mother and Daddy. In some ways they could not have been more different in temperament. Daddy was hardworking. Most mornings he was gone when I wakened, and until I was eight, he worked late at night. He ran a blueprint shop that bore his name, but he did not own it. His pay was $160 a month. Soon after the stock market crash of October 1929, the owner came to my father and said, "John, I've got to cut your salary; from now on you will make $90 a month, take it or leave it." Since 20 percent of the American work force was unemployed during the Great Depression, Dad had no choice. He worked for $90 a month. To make $90 a month house, clothe, and feed a family of five for a month was more than difficult; it was nearly impossible.

Mother was the answer to the survival riddle. Mother brought two things to the table that were essential for our family:

• Her parents lived on a sixty-acre farm nine miles from where we lived. My grandparents made their living on a "truck farm." Tomatoes, peas, corn, cantaloupes, watermelons, okra, peaches, pears, plums: all were grown on the farm. Our grandparents allowed us to take what we needed. In the summer we ate well. One job of summer was "putting up" or canning food for winter. The farm kept us healthy.

- The other piece in the financial puzzle was Mother's ability to manage money. She was a genius when it came to stretching Dad's pay. Dad worked hard, but he could not organize his socks. He had little capacity to anticipate. So managing money fell to Mother, and she worked wonders. My mother could have managed a store, a factory, or a school. She gave Dad an allowance each payday; he bought tobacco for his pipe and gas for the car. Mother took care of the rest.

This severe financial strain was relieved in 1936, when my father was offered a job with Gulf Oil. He managed a "reproduction room" where blueprints and photostats were made for Gulf's operations all over West Texas. It was a good job, and the financial tension in our family went away. Dad worked for Gulf until he retired in 1960. I always had a soft spot in my heart for Gulf. Gulf paychecks fed me when I was a boy. I am a child of the Great Depression; I remember the way my parents struggled to "make it."

Though the Great Depression hit our family hard, I did not consider our family poor. We were like everyone else. What I mainly remember is that we had a good time growing up. My sister and brother were always with me. We played games on rainy days. Monopoly was a favorite; we bent the rules. If you went broke, you could borrow from the bank. I'm convinced the three of us learned arithmetic from the enormous debts we ran up in Monopoly. We laughed, argued, asked each other for favors. We bought and sold, went in debt, got out of debt . . . and the hours flew by.

My grandfather gave the family a cow; we named her Beauty. By the time I was eight, I had learned to milk Beauty. Always there was plenty of fresh milk, and Mother poured it into all three of us. Homemade ice cream was a delight in the warm months, and when fresh peaches were added, that was *living*! When Bill became eight or nine, we alternated milking the cow. Bill and I slept together; we would waken and have long discussions. "You milk this morning, and I will milk tonight." Then the reply, "No. It's your turn; I milked last night. Besides, it's cold this morning. I'm not going to trade with you."

The lot on which our house sat was wider than most in the neighborhood. That meant there was more room for grass, and when we were ten or twelve, that yard became the playground for the kids on our block. We had football games, played "catch," and set up a basketball goal—all in our yard. We had no trouble "getting up a game." Early on it became apparent that Bill would be the athlete in the family. He was coordinated and quick. Competitiveness was in all three of us; we wanted to win.

We all were given music lessons. Daddy played the violin and wanted his children to play instruments. I started on the violin, graduated to the clarinet, and was never very good at either. Bill and Ruth were different; both showed real aptitude for music. Bill still plays the trombone, and Ruth plays the piano. Both play well. My father was always ready to display the musical gifts of the three of us. Sometimes he insinuated us into the Sunday night worship at our grandparents' church (Tate Springs Baptist where Uncle Henry was pastor). The three of us were placed at the front of the church; we tried to play a hymn or two. I never thought we were very good, and usually we weren't.

By the time I was ten, my father was working at Gulf and had regular hours. He would come home from work and join in our games. Daddy had a lot of kid in him. He was a good athlete, had a muscular body, and enjoyed playing with us as much as we enjoyed having him. On Saturdays he took Bill and me fishing at Lake Worth.

One Saturday Daddy, Bill, and I went to the lake to fish. Daddy had bought a boat, a three-horsepower Sea King motor, and each of us had a rod and reel. We pulled the boat and gear in a little trailer Daddy built. When we got to the lake, we put the boat in the water, parked the car and trailer, and off we went for a day of fishing. When our outing came to an end, we went back to the landing. To our surprise, some pranksters had jammed matchsticks into the valves of the tires on both the trailer and the car. Six tires had to be pumped up with a hand pump. Fortunately, the tires were not damaged.

There was nothing to do but get to work pumping. Daddy jacked up one wheel then slowly pumped air into the tire. When that tire was inflated to enough to bear the weight of the car, he moved to the next tire. The pumping was hard work. On the second tire, he was sweating. On about the third tire he exploded, "If I could find the sons of bitches who did this, I'd . . ." and some threat followed (this was not approved language at our house). I knew the phrase Daddy had used; I'd heard it at school, but Bill was four years younger. He had never heard that expression before. More pumping, and finally there was enough air in six tires to move car and trailer to the nearest service station to get full air pressure. With all that done, we made our way home.

We arrived late. Daddy said, "Bill, you go tell your mother why we are late; Cecil and I will put up the boat and trailer." Bill went into the house. Daddy and I were putting things in their place when Bill came from the house crying. Daddy said, "What's wrong, Bill?" Bill said, "I told Mother some sons of bitches let the air out of all six tires, and that's why we are late. She slapped me." Daddy sat down on the running board of that '29 Chevy, and with an agonal groan said, "That's all I need." Things were a little tense at supper that night. Mother was a Puritan.

Lake Worth was the family vacation retreat. A tiny cottage was rented. The family moved to "the lake," and we stayed for two weeks. It was cool on the north side of Lake Worth. Winds blow from the south in the summer. Our cottage was on the cool side of the lake; it was God's air conditioning, and we reveled in it. We swam, fished, boated, and ate the fish we caught by "tight-line fishing."

I remember the heat. Fort Worth was not air conditioned for ordinary people until after World War II. Fort Worth gets hot in the summertime. The windows were opened to let any breeze move through the sleeping porch, but sometimes at 10:30 and 11:00 at night it was still ninety degrees and not a whiff of wind. A small oscillating fan tried to cool us, but that was small relief. We just had to bear it. In September the nights became cool again. We longed for September.

Mother was the one who took the time to give the three of us a religious education. Every day she would read to us from Hurlburt's *Stories of the Bible*. Usually Bill was in her lap; the book was cradled round him. Ruth and I sat nearby. Samson was real. David and Goliath came alive. The friendship of David and Jonathan was to be imitated. Abraham almost sacrificed Isaac, and that made me afraid. Moses was larger than life. Peter and Paul were as near as the storybook. Jesus was our friend. He did wonderful things. Every meal we gave thanks for our food in his name. I don't remember when Mother started reading Bible stories to us. It goes back further than my memory.

The religious education given me by my mother arranged my mind. Until this day it informs me. Where did I come from? God made the world, made Adam and Eve, and made me. Who am I? I am a child of God. God knows me, and I am a little bit like my Heavenly Father ("the image of God"). What is right and what is wrong? The Bible is authority; it lays out great principles that answer the right-and-wrong question. Why are there bad people? The reason given was "sin." God didn't make us bad. We sometimes make bad choices. What will happen to me when I die? There will be an accounting/judgment, then heaven or hell. Mother was not concerned about damaging our psyche; she gave us basic theology. All later theology has been a refinement of the primer given me by my mother.

## FAITH

When I was very young, my father was occasional at church. Until he worked for Gulf Oil, he was worn from too much work. Mother took us to church. By the time I was a teenager, Daddy was active in church. We attended Polytechnic Baptist Church. Both Mother and Daddy worked with Juniors (children ages nine to twelve). Mother was the superintendent of the department; Daddy led the singing and taught one of the boys' classes. I went through that department. One year Daddy was my Sunday school teacher.

The leadership of our church was extraordinary. I remember three pastors: Baker James Cauthen, E. D. Dunlap, and Floyd Chafin. Cauthen baptized me; he was at Poly six years. He was intense and intelligent. He suggested by his every move that church deserved our best. My father became active in church again under the ministry of Cauthen. Floyd Chafin was pastor during my teen years. He played on the church softball team with us; he was the catcher. He was a good player and he played under control (not all who played church softball acted like church people ought to act). The pastor of a neighboring church was loud, quarrelsome, and an umpire-baiter; Chafin was a model citizen. I noted the contrast between Chafin and the other fellow. Both were pastors; one was a combative jerk and the other was somebody I wanted to imitate. I had good examples.

When I was eleven I was sent to a Royal Ambassador Camp (a missions study group for boys) at Latham Springs, an encampment outside Waco, Texas. At that camp I heard "Bullet Bill Patterson," all-Southwest Conference tailback on the Baylor University football team. It was at Latham Springs that I first had the impression that God was "calling" me into Christian service. I didn't tell anyone; I wasn't sure enough of what had happened to make an announcement. That idea didn't go away, though.

The Bible was the textbook at our church. Vacation Bible School, Sunday school, Royal Ambassadors: all worked with the Bible as their source. I learned the names of the sixty-six books of the Bible. We had "sword drills"; the purpose was to see who could find a verse in the Bible first. I was not a champion, but I became pretty quick at the drill.

Though we made a game of learning to use our Bibles, all of us knew the Bible was more than a ball or glove. Our pastors told us the Bible was inspired. It was the record of the way God moved upon his people in history. None of my pastors were flippant or casual when using the Bible. All were reverent, and their reverence was contagious. We memorized Bible verses. By the time I was in high school I had developed the habit of Bible reading. Each night I read the Sermon on the Mount or Paul's letter to the Philippians. I repeated this reading each night for months. Philippians remains a special text to me. When life gets hard, I turn to Philippians for encouragement. If Paul could write that letter from jail waiting trial by Roman Emperor Nero, I can buck up and face whatever is on my plate. Bible reading was encouraged by parents and church. By the time I left home for college, I had a layman's knowledge of the Bible. My home and church had done their job.

## SCHOOL

Three children were born to my mother in four years and three months. Rearing the three of us was hard, hard work. When I was six (December 1933), Mother entered me in first grade. I was sent to school, but I'm not sure I was ready for school. I would have been a better student had I been a few months older. The semester began in the mid-term, in January. It was called "low first." The following September, I was in "high first." In that irregular fashion I went through eleven years in the Fort Worth public school system.

The first few years I was an average student. Since I was the oldest child, I brought home all the childhood illnesses. In the first grade I had measles, whooping cough, and periodic tonsillitis. I was absent more than five weeks while I worked my way through one illness after another. My first report card was all C's. When Mother inquired of Miss Alexander (my first grade teacher) about my grades, Mrs. Alexander said, "He's been sick. I didn't know how to grade him." In the summer after my first half-year of school, I had my tonsils removed. I did not miss another day of school until I was graduated from high school. I had good health, and in a few years I caught up with my peers. There were flashes when I would excel, but in the main I was average. That did not please Mother; therefore it did not please me. She helped me with my homework. She instilled in me the idea that school was important, and doing well in school was the doorway to opportunity. I had no consuming curiosity for learning. Mother expected me to do well; I wanted to please Mother. Sometimes her expectations were burdensome when I was a boy; years later I would give thanks for Mother's push. I needed it.

My first "straight A" report card came in sixth grade, my last year at Poly Elementary. Then it was off to William James Junior High School. In elementary school one teacher had a class all day; at William James the bell rang and everybody changed classes, pushing and shoving in the halls. I got lost in the shuffle. I was not as big as I would become; I was skinny. I wanted to be athletic, but what athletic skills I have came later. Junior high was a difficult time for me. By far the most notable thing that happened came in my very last month at William James. On Sunday, December 7, 1941, the Japanese bombed Pearl Harbor. At school the next day the principal brought the entire school together in the auditorium, sat a round-top Philco radio on a chair on the stage, and announced that President Roosevelt was going to make a speech and we ought to listen. For a change, the assembly of rowdy students was quiet. Soon the unmistakable voice of FDR came over the radio: "Yesterday, December 7, 1941—a date that will live in infamy—the United States of America was suddenly and deliberately attacked by naval and air forces of the Empire of Japan." Roosevelt proceeded to ask Congress to declare war. Miss Andrews was my homeroom teacher; she sat beside me as we listened to the president, crying quietly as he spoke. World War II was upon us. The next month I was in high school. The Great Depression and World War II were the external forces that shaped my generation.

There was nothing unusual about my years in the Fort Worth Public School system. In a steady, unspectacular way, I moved through the eleven years (a twelfth year would not be added until after I was graduated). One teacher took a special interest in me. Her name was Patricia Edwards. Mrs. Edwards taught English in high school. She was a graduate of Rice Institute, and she took her job seriously. Mrs. Edwards would stay after school and talk with fifteen or twenty of us. She encouraged us to go to college, gave us tips on how to study, made time to listen when we talked about dating, had advice for us on manners and etiquette; she became a parent substitute just at that time when we were least likely to take advice from our parents. She was a woman of good sense and high standards, and she had a heart for kids who were trying to find their way. I wasn't sure I was college material; neither of my parents had been to college. I confided this self-doubt to Mrs. Edwards. She took my fears seriously and helped me through them. Her love for the English language, for both grammar and literature, and her high standards rubbed off on me. She was the best teacher I had. She got me ready to go to college.

In that group who clustered around Mrs. Edwards were four boys. J. Fred Davis, Bill Evans, Donald Jarvis, and I were classmates. All of us were good students. All took the hard courses offered at our high school. The four of us attended class together, went on dates with girls together, and planned for college together. All my high school education took place during World War II. Gas was rationed. Our family had an A card (that meant four gallons a week). The four of us solved our problem; each got the family car once a month. We went on dates most Friday nights. I recall the times eight kids (the boys and their dates) piled into our 1933 Plymouth and went to some high school party. The four of us stayed in touch after high school. Several times in our adult years we assembled and maintained our friendship. Those fellows and Mrs. Edwards made high school what it was for me.

By the time I reached high school, I had caught up with my peers in academics. I did not excel, but I was in the top quarter of my class. In high school my grades improved. One day I brought home a report card that was all A's and one B. That sounds pretty good, but always my card was compared with my sister's. She constantly made all A's. Bill and I did okay, but not as well as Ruth. Mother questioned me about that B for ten minutes; I was irritated. It seemed to me she should have some kind word for the A's. Dad saw my irritation, and an hour later, out in the yard where only the two of us were present, he said, "That was a pretty good card, son." That incident is a window into my parents. Mother pushed; Daddy encouraged. I resented Mother's prodding when I was young. I thought she was severe. Of course I appreciated Daddy's more gentle approach. In retrospect, I got exactly what I needed. I needed a push and a lift. Mother and Daddy were the balance I needed. I'm in debt to both.

I graduated from high school in May 1945. By not taking a required American history course, I was allowed to stay in high school the spring semester. That spring FDR died and Germany surrendered. All through high school I was in Junior ROTC. I wore the uniform, learned the drills, and profited from the discipline. Two summers I went to a four-week camp sponsored by ROTC for Dallas and Fort Worth Public Schools. Every boy faced the prospect of military service. My friendship with J. Fred, Bill, and Donald made me open to a career in the sciences. I had done well in chemistry, physics, and math in high school. A career in engineering was attractive. I enrolled in Texas A&M College in College Station, Texas. My friends were going to A&M; it seemed the thing to do.

In July 1945, Baker James Cauthen came home from China. He was the pastor who baptized me and involved my father in church again. He and his family had gone to China as missionaries in 1939. They had suffered much in the Japanese invasion of China. China was free, and the Cauthens were home on furlough. Dr. Cauthen was asked to preach to our church for a week. I sang in the choir. During that week, Cauthen began to predict what the post-World War II world would look like. He said we had more scientific knowledge than moral discipline. Our real problems were spiritual in nature, and there was a shortage of laborers to do God's work in the post-war world. I heard what he said. I was planning to go into engineering; Cauthen said there was a glut of people in that field. The shortage was in the realm of the spirit. I had never gotten the idea of a "calling" out of my system. It was suppressed but it would not go away. My decision to change my vocational target was not made on impulse. I wrestled with it for several weeks, and then I committed to a life in ministry. I've since been grateful to Baker James Cauthen for being God's voice. On a Sunday night about the first of August 1945, I told my church family of my "calling." They were pleased, and always they have encouraged me in my decision.

I had a conversation with Floyd Chafin, my pastor. He counseled that Baylor University in Waco was a better place to study for a life in ministry than Texas A&M College. He recommended that I ask entrance into Baylor. The next day, I hitchhiked to College Station, went to the registrar and got my registration file, and told the lady why I was leaving A&M. She was most sympathetic; she gave me the $10 registration fee and said, "Take this $10 and your file to Baylor. Everything is in order. I believe they will accept you." Then I went back to Highway 6, put up my thumb, and hitchhiked to Waco. I walked to Baylor and presented my file to the registrar. I was accepted on the spot. The lady said, "What will be your major?"

I said, "Bible and chemistry." She said, "That's unusual." She was right. As I learned my way, I chose courses that made sense for one going into ministry. Chemistry was not one of them. I was green as grass. The folks at Baylor had seen kids like me before; they were understanding.

Around the first of September 1945, Mother, Bill, and another boy from Fort Worth (Jack Robinson, who would become an All-American basketball player and still later become pastor of First Baptist Church, Augusta, Georgia) put our things in that '33 Plymouth and drove down to Baylor. I was assigned space in room 204 of Brooks Hall. Jack and I took our things into the dorm; then I went out to Dutton Street to tell Mother and Bill goodbye. It was a bittersweet moment. I knew I wanted to be at Baylor; I knew I was leaving a home where people had loved me and done all they could to help me grow up. We said the right words. Mother and Bill drove down to Fifth Street and turned right to go back to Highway 81. I stood on the curb for several minutes. It was a strange feeling. All at once I was very glad and very sad. I had left home. Mother and Daddy, Ruth and Bill, Poly Church and Poly School . . . all that was in the past. I was on my own.

Dwight Eisenhower's last book was titled *At Ease, Stories I Tell to Friends*. The dedication in *At Ease* is to his parents and to Mamie's parents. He said, "To our parents, who loom larger with the passing years!" As I write, it has been nearly sixty-one years since I left home. So deeply etched in me are those memories that I can still see, hear, and smell the scenes of my childhood. They marked me, and I'm still trying to live up to the standards set for me in that house on Rosedale.

## Chapter 3
# GETTING AN EDUCATION AND
# FINDING A WIFE

I've never lived in a world more insulated than Baylor University in fall 1945. The university was small (1,700 students) and friendly. We were a "hot house" of piety and energy. Most of the students were devout, Protestant Christians. A sizeable number were at Baylor preparing for ministry as I was. Students had their own mid-week religious service, Baylor Religious Hour. Friday nights were given over to "missions." We went to the poor children of Waco and taught them Bible stories and choruses. On Sundays we were in Waco churches. We were a religious bunch.

Looking back on those days, I remember the goodness of the people and the warmth of the company. It was as if my family had swollen to several hundred. We all knew each other by name. Dorm rooms were left unlocked. Only two students had cars. We lived there. We had to get along, and we did.

Baylor was on the Dartmouth quarter system (three quarters made a school year). I knew I was at Baylor only until the army called. When I reached eighteen, I would be allowed to finish the quarter, and then I was off to the army. I knew this, and the certain knowledge that I was soon going into the army did nothing for my study habits. Truthfully, I was not very interested in my studies. The heady independence that came with living away from parents for the first time, and the press of religious and social appointments all distracted me from my first purpose for being in college. We were not a wicked bunch. There was no gambling (that I was aware). We were cold sober and only a few were into cigars. We were pious; we were not studious.

I had been a better than average student in high school. When I got to Baylor it became clear to me that I was not nearly so smart as my high school grades suggested. I looked bright in high school because I was in the company of some lazy, dull people. The people who made me look smart in high school didn't go to Baylor (or any other college). The poor study habits I had used in high school were not good enough for a faster academic pace.

Night-before-the-final cramming got me C's. Even frantic efforts to "bone up" for a chemistry final produced a D. My only A was in band. As I look back on the boy I was, I see enough self-control to keep me from harm and evil. I did not have enough self-discipline to take advantage of educational opportunity. I had not grown up.

I turned eighteen December 26, 1945. The winter quarter ended about the end of February. I reported to Fort Sam Houston in San Antonio, on March 11, 1946. I was in the army.

The stay at Fort Sam Houston did not last long. A "troop train" took a crop of eighteen-year-olds to Little Rock, Arkansas. Basic training was good for me: in thirteen weeks I gained weight and strength. The first time our basic training class was asked to run two miles, I thought my lungs would burst. By the end of the thirteen weeks, the two-mile run had become routine. My plans in high school were to go to Officer's Candidate School when army time came. The end of the war dashed those plans. Armies scaling down don't need more officers; they have too many. So I was a private with a group of draftees in the last class of basic training in an army camp that was closing down as soon as our basic cycle was ended. I knew how to march from high school ROTC. I learned to fire a rifle. By two points I missed being an "expert rifleman"; I had to settle for being a sharpshooter.

The people in the army were different from the people at Baylor. At Baylor we were excessively religious; the army was excessively irreligious. Living with people who lifted "raising hell" to an art form was a new experience for me.

At the end of basic training, a few of us were kept at camp to close the place down, and then my orders came. I was given a seventeen-day "delay in route," and then I was off to Camp Carson in Colorado Springs, Colorado. Camp Carson (now Fort Carson) sits at the foot of the Rockies; I had never seen mountains. The army moved me by train. I boarded the train in Fort Worth just after lunch. Dinner was served in Amarillo, and then I went to sleep. When I wakened I looked out the window and saw the majestic Rockies. This Texas boy had never seen mountains; they were rugged and beautiful.

I reported to Camp Carson on July 5, 1946. The 2nd Division was part of the European campaign in 1944–1945. They had taken casualties. By the summer of 1946, the 2nd was back from Europe. Eighteen-year-olds were filling the gaps created by those casualties. I was one of them. One regiment of the division was given mountain training (the 38th Regimental Combat Team). I was assigned to Company K of the 38th. The division was Regular Army; these men were in for twenty years. They had been through combat together. When I moved into the barracks at Carson, I was a boy among men. Years later when I saw the movie *From Here to Eternity*, I recognized the kind of army described in that film. I had been there.

During the summer months we conditioned. In September and October we learned to do rock climbing. By November we were moved to Cooper Hill, outside Leadville, Colorado, to learn cross-country skiing. I was issued a pair of seven-and-a-half-foot wooden skis, snowshoes, a rucksack, and all sorts of clothing to keep me warm in extreme temperatures. While at Cooper Hill, we lived in squad tents heated by potbellied stoves. It was an adventure, and we survived. I'm glad I did it; I wouldn't want to do it again.

My time in the army was brief. I was a draftee; the army wanted people to join the Regular Army. That meant you committed for a definite number of years. I refused to go "regular army." So in 1947, the army began to cycle draftees out. After I had been in one year (March 1947), I was discharged. The army did three things for me.

• It exposed me to people who were raw and rough. When they lusted, they found outlets for their lust. The slightest offense was settled with a fight. I learned to watch my mouth. The eighteen-year-olds ran together. We were different from the older men; sometimes we needed each other.

- It helped me physically. When I went into the army, I barely weighed enough to pass the physical; at my height I had to weigh 147. I barely did. In one year I weighed 172. I was stronger and very healthy.
- It made the GI Bill available to me. My first stay at Baylor was paid for by money I had saved from odd jobs I had during high school. That money was spent in my two quarters at Baylor before the army. The GI Bill was administered by the Veteran's Administration. I got one day of school for each day I was in the army . . . plus 365 days. I had 730 days of school available to me when I was discharged. That was enough to get me a college degree. I will ever be grateful to our government for the GI Bill.

My discharge came just in time for me to enroll in the spring quarter at Baylor. I hurried back to Waco, found a room on the fifth floor of Brooks Hall, and enrolled in school. I was elated to be back, but my enthusiasm was tempered by a letter that appeared in my mailbox just a few days into the new quarter. The letter instructed me to come to the office of the academic dean, Dr. Truett Grant, at 10:00 a.m. on a Thursday morning. I dropped by the office of the dean to tell his secretary that I could not come; I was supposed to be in chapel at 10:00 a.m. on Thursday. She told me my appointment with the dean was more important than chapel. I must keep the appointment. That message gave me pause.

I met the appointment. Dean Truett Grant was a small man. He was dressed like an undertaker—dark suit, dark tie, white shirt, wire-rimmed glasses. When I walked in his office he sprang from his chair as if he were glad to see me. "Mr. Sherman, won't you sit down." His hospitality intimidated me; I wondered what was coming next. He wasted no time on small talk. He pushed a photostat across the desk and said, "Are these your grades from your previous time at Baylor?" And there they were. All those C's and that D in chemistry were right in front of me. I said, "Yes, sir." Then he pushed a laminated piece at me and said, "This is the GI Bill. Read it." I did. Baylor had to admit back into the university any veteran who had an honorable discharge and had been a student before going into the service. But Baylor only had to admit the returning veteran for one quarter. At the end of that quarter, Baylor was free to retain or dismiss the student from the university.

The dean continued, "Mr. Sherman, Baylor is a different place from the school you knew before you went to the army. Now we have nearly 6,000 students . . . most are veterans. We don't have a place for people who do not apply themselves. Your record condemns you. At the end of this quarter, you will be dismissed from the university. You may want to make other arrangements."

I was stunned! I had looked forward to returning to Baylor, and now the dean was telling me I had but one quarter and I was gone. I was shocked. When I gathered my thoughts, I did three things:

- I got a book from the dean's secretary that told me the rules of the university; I'm ashamed to say, I'd never bothered to learn those rules my first stay at Baylor. I learned there was a faculty advisor for each student.
- I found my faculty advisor that afternoon and told him my story. I also told him I did not want to be put out of the university. I was willing to work to change my status. He recommended I drop two courses and enroll in two others. They were easier. I needed to make good grades *now*. I did what he said.
- I decided on a way to study. I sat on the front row in each class. I took notes as fast as I could. After class I went to my room and condensed my notes into one typewritten page. I kept that page in a loose-leaf notebook. Before each test, I committed to memory each of the pages in my notebook. I also faithfully did the outside reading. I resolved I would not go home that quarter. I would not date. I would study.

At the end of the quarter I had an A+, an A, and a B+. I did not wait for the dean to call me. I went to him with my grades and asked if I might enroll for another quarter. He tried to look serious, but I saw a tiny smile at the edges of his mouth as he reviewed my grades. He said, "Mr. Sherman, you may enroll for another quarter." From then on, my grades were A's and B's. I had a way to study, and I began to enjoy learning. I was beginning to grow up. I've told this story in full, because Dean Truett Grant called me to accountability. He made me take hold of myself and do what I came to Baylor to do—prepare for ministry. That was the best thing Baylor did for me.

One other incident at Baylor was especially memorable. A notice was posted on the bulletin board: "The President of Southern Baptist Theological Seminary at Louisville will be in a room in the Student Union at 3 o'clock. Students preparing for seminary are invited." I went. The president's name was Fuller. In the course of his conversation with us he said, "Boys, don't major in Bible or religion. We can teach you New and Old Testament as well as they can here at Baylor. Major in English, history, political science, sociology, psychology. We don't teach those courses at the seminary. Get a broad foundation for your studies in religion while you are at Baylor. We will teach you religion." That made sense to me. I had been planning to major in religion. Dr. Fuller changed my mind. The GI Bill would pay for all the hours I chose to take if I maintained a B average. That was not very difficult, so I double-majored in English and history with minors in Greek, Bible, and speech. I had a good foundation for seminary.

The days at Baylor slipped by. Though I had the GI Bill, I still worked in the girls' dormitory serving food. I was elected to the Student Council, was active in religious affairs, enjoyed intramural sports, and dated several lovely girls. There was but one real romance, and that came before I went into the army. The girl was special. When I went to the army I wrote to her regularly. At first she answered; then her letters came less frequently. Then they stopped altogether. She had found another. It was painful, but it was a learning lesson. The girl had found a good man who had come back from the service. He was more mature and ready to marry. I was neither. When I came back to Baylor, I enjoyed dating, but I was not ready for a serious romance.

Baylor did what it was supposed to do. It got me ready for the next step. At Baylor I learned to write a term paper, how to study for a test, and how to manage my time. Baylor and the army taught me how to choose friends. Some had my values, and I wanted them for friends. The rest I gave a little space. Five years after I went to Baylor, I was graduated (June 1950). I still had a lot to learn, but I was not quite as green as I was when I arrived. I'm grateful for my Baylor experience.

Graduation was on a Sunday night. After the ceremony a fellow graduate and I boarded a train and spent the night making our way to Beaumont, Texas. The two of us were to do Vacation Bible School for junior and senior high school students at the First Baptist Church of Beaumont. In our class was a redheaded fellow. He was the pastor's son; his name was Paige Patterson. Paige was about thirteen or fourteen years old. Years later when the Southern Baptist Convention was torn apart, I remembered the bright young man who knew the answers to most of the questions. In 1950, he was a friend.

Southwestern Baptist Theological Seminary in Fort Worth, Texas, was my seminary choice. I had exhausted my GI Bill at Baylor, so I lived at home with my parents, bought a used car, and drove to and from the seminary. The tuition at Southwestern in fall 1950 was $25.00 a semester for a full load. Southern Baptists subsidized the seminary, making it possible for people like me to get an education. It was a gift.

Southwestern Seminary was suffering growing pains in fall 1950. Two factors caused the growing pains: (1) There was an awakening of religion in the Southwest. More people were answering the call of God to ministry; therefore more people were enrolling in the seminary. (2) The return of veterans was delayed for the seminary. We had to finish college before entering seminary. By 1948, the influx of veterans was in full swing. Southwestern had been a school of 400 before World War II. By 1950, there were 2,200 of us. Everything was crowded. My survey courses routinely had 200 enrolled. Three teachers powerfully influenced the way I've done ministry:

• T. B. Maston taught Christian Ethics. The man had a gift to teach and a passion for his subject. His Yale Ph.D. brought serious scholarship; his Puritan ethic made us work. I minored with him in my doctorate. My way of sorting out right and wrong has been shaped by Dr. Maston.
• G. Earl Guinn taught preaching. Dr. Guinn was tall, a little bit intimidating for a student, and had the gift to teach preaching.

When he criticized a student's sermon in class, he could be tough, but he cared about us and made us handle Scripture responsibly. My sermons and my commentaries for Sunday school teachers are built to standards given me by G. Earl Guinn. I'm in his debt.

• Charles Trentham was a young theology professor just back from studying in Europe. Dr. Trentham was a little flashy in the way he dressed (some at Southwestern were drab). Students liked that. He had been exposed to Karl Barth and Emil Brunner while in Switzerland; he wasn't so much committed to neo-orthodoxy as he was knowledgeable about it. He was a breath of fresh air at Southwestern. I liked him. One day he stopped me in the hall, invited me into his office, and said, "Cecil, I want you to do graduate work here. We've been reworking the standards for our graduate school. Here's what you have to do to get in. When you get your basic degree you will be too young to do a church any good. Stay in school. Take the time to grow up." I was flattered that he had taken notice of me. I was uninformed about standards for admission for graduate school (a 3.5 grade-point average on the three years of undergraduate work). I was working, but Dr. Trentham gave me a target. I set out to get into graduate school.

There were some good teachers at Southwestern. They built on what I learned at Baylor. I was getting ready to be a preacher. Three things happened in those three years that mattered.

• After World War II there was a revival of religion in the Southwest. Among Texas Baptists, one expression of this revival was Youth Revivals. W. F. Howard directed Student Ministries for the Baptist General Convention of Texas. He supervised and gave order to the movement. A church would write Dr. Howard requesting a youth revival team for a week in the summer. Dr. Howard would send that church a preacher and a musician. He was in touch with students in colleges and the seminary. He pulled teams together and sent us out. Making Dr. Howard's team was not easy.

In February or March, Dr. Howard would assemble all of us who were going and give assignments. He gave us rules about the way we were to conduct ourselves as we functioned as evangelists. His rules have been a guide for me in morals and manners from then and until now. Here are some of them.

1. When an assignment was received, we were to write the host pastor and tell him our travel plans. This was to assure him we were taking the assignment seriously.

2. No one was to date or have any romantic connection with anyone while on assignment.

3. When hospitality was given (such as a meal in a home), thank-you notes were to be written.

4. No one was to say anything about money. We took what we were given and said "thank you." I received as much as $200 and as little as $25 for a week's work, and for both I gave thanks.

W. F. Howard helped me. I'm still following his rules and passing them along to my students at Baptist Theological Seminary at Richmond.

• I got my first church. One of my Youth Revival assignments in summer 1950 was at the First Baptist Church of Bonham, Texas. I told the pastor that I was looking for a small church to pastor while studying at seminary. He remembered my comment, and soon Selfs Baptist Church asked that pastor if he knew anyone to recommend to them as a pastor. He recommended me, and near the end of August 1950, I got a penny postcard. Written in pencil were these words: "Come preach for us first Sunday. Rufe Newberry." That's all. I showed the card to my parents, and Dad looked at the postmark and saw Honey Grove, Texas. He said, "Son, go to Honey Grove on Saturday afternoon before the first Sunday in September. Ask one of the farmers around the town square if he knows Rufe Newberry." I did what Daddy said. About 5:30 on the first Saturday in September, I walked up to a cluster of farmers in bib overalls and asked, "Do any of you know Rufe Newberry?" Then I read the card to them to explain why I wanted information. To my relief, all knew Rufe Newberry. They told me how to find his house, and I was on my way to being the pastor of a country church.

I'm not sure I helped the people at Selfs, but they helped me. I was their first student pastor (previous pastors had been farmers). I slept in their guest rooms, ate their food, spent Saturday nights with them. I got to know them. They forgave my immature pastoral skills. They suffered through my sermons. The church prospered, and I learned a little about being a pastor. Most of those people are gone now; I will always be in their debt.

- I met Dot Hair. It was December 1950, near the end of my first semester at Southwestern Seminary. Tom Norfleet, Dick Wentworth, and I entered the office of Dr. J. M. Price to inquire about our grades in Dr. Price's "Introduction to Religious Education." Final examinations were near. Dr. Price's secretary was Dot Hair, and when we walked into Price's office I was surprised. There sat this beautiful young woman with a bright smile and possessed of unusual charm and poise. I nearly forgot why I had come. She gave us our grade averages, and we went on our way. That afternoon I called Dot Hair to ask her to go out with me. She had forgotten who I was. Only when I told her my grade could she identify me. She said she would get me a date with one of the students. I told her I wanted a date with her. Reluctantly, as it seemed against her better judgment, she said she would go out with me for a Coke.

I took what I could get, and that was the beginning. Dot was from Spartanburg, South Carolina, a graduate of Southwestern with a Master's in Religious Education, had been an editor for the Sunday School Board in Nashville, Tennessee, and had returned to Southwestern to work for Dr. Price as his secretary. She was ten years older than I and not at all worried about being single. In three months I knew Dot was the girl I wanted to marry, but she was not of the same mind. She said we must stop dating; "there's too much difference in our ages." I had no choice but to honor her request. From March 1951 until November 1952, we did not date.

Then Dot relented. She was willing to see me again. For a year we dated steadily. I graduated from Southwestern in May 1953. Dot and my parents were there. During summer 1953, I pressed her to marry me. My pressure had an unintended result. Dot slipped into clinical depression and had to return to her home in South Carolina. She was a patient in the psychiatric ward of Greenville General Hospital. I entered graduate school at Southwestern, but my heart was in South Carolina. Dot, with the help of a fine doctor, climbed out of her depression. In November 1953, I journeyed to her home in Spartanburg, asked her to marry me, and to my surprise she set a date—December 23 . . . a month away. We were married in the pastor's office at the First Baptist Church of Greer, South Carolina, by Rev. O. K. Webb. He had been Dot's pastor before she left home. My brother and his wife, Veta, were the only members of my family who made the trip. Bill stood beside me. Dot's sister, Helen, stood beside her, and we made our promises. She kept her promise and I kept mine. Dot's name is Dorothy. The name means "gift of God," and she has been that to me.

Dr. Trentham, the professor who invited me to do graduate work, said, "Cecil, you've grown up in a Baptist hothouse. Now that you have your basic education, get away from Southwestern for a while. Broaden yourself with travel and another point of view on the Christian faith." I looked into going to Europe or Scotland, but Dot and I didn't have enough money to make the trip. We settled for application to Princeton Theological Seminary in Princeton, New Jersey. I was accepted, and in September 1954, we set out for New Jersey. I was nervous on two counts: Would I be able to compete academically at Princeton? Would my conservative, Southern Baptist faith be damaged by study at Princeton Seminary? Those questions were in the back of my mind as we left Texas.

My goal was a Master of Theology degree. I had a letter from the academic dean at Southwestern; they would accept the year at Princeton as credit toward a Doctor of Theology degree when I returned to Southwestern.

There were no interstate highways in 1954. We poked up US 1 through Raleigh to Richmond. We saw Washington, D.C., for the first time; both of us were impressed. We arrived in Princeton a week before school started. Dot needed a job. She found employment with George Gallup in his opinion research business. She walked a mile down Mercer Street to work. I stayed at the seminary, went to class, and studied.

There wasn't much difference in the academic requirements at Princeton and Southwestern. I had been a good student in Texas; the same study habits produced about the same results in New Jersey. One of my questions was answered.

John Mackay, a Scot, was president of Princeton Theological Seminary. He had been a missionary and seminary president in South America and, in a time of tension and division, had come to Princeton. Dr. Mackay was famous for his ecumenicity; he truly wanted divided Christendom to come together. Dr. Mackay took seriously the prayer of Jesus "that they may be one, as we are one . . ." (John 17:11b NRSV). He wasn't liberal at all; he just took a different part of the Bible to heart than the people in Texas did.

I was asked to pastor the Baptist Students of Princeton, for there was no Baptist church in town with a ministry to students. Our group met in Murray-Dodge Hall, a building set aside for religious groups on campus. A rabbi lived on the third floor in the garret. He smoked. During Easter weekend 1955, the rabbi was smoking in bed and set the building on fire. The building burned down; all that remained was a shell. The meeting place for the Baptist Students of Princeton was gone. What could we do?

Miller Chapel on the seminary campus was not used on Sunday morning. I decided to ask Dr. Mackay if the Baptist Students might use the chapel until the end of the school year. I went to see him. Nearly sixty-five years old, he retained his Scottish brogue. He welcomed me and asked my reason for coming. I explained my need, and then he did the gracious thing in a delightful way. He turned his chair toward the window and looked out into the quadrangle. I saw only the silhouette of his face. He was quiet for a time; then he said, "If I let Baptists use Miller Chapel for worship, I will offend some of my trustees, and if I don't, the lassie I met in Charlotte Square Baptist Church in Edinburgh [Scotland] forty years ago . . . the lassie who gives me my breakfast . . . will not be happy with me. You may have it." The man practiced what he preached.

It was while we were at Princeton that we met Paul Pressler. He had been a student at Princeton University and graduated in the spring before Dot and I arrived in September 1954. As a student he had been active in the Baptist Students of Princeton. His ties to the group were strong, so he came back to Princeton for a visit, and we met. He was a first-year law student at the University of Texas. Our interests were connected; we kept in touch. It was Paul's custom to write Christmas letters to friends. Dot and I received his letters for twenty years. When Paul Pressler's name became known in Southern Baptist circles in June 1979, I didn't start from scratch. I had known the man and had read his Christmas letters. I knew he was intelligent and tended to Fundamental views in matters of faith. That acquaintance was useful to me when I had to interpret his intentions in 1980.

Princeton broadened me. I learned God had a lot more going for him than Southern Baptists. There were some liberals at Princeton, but there were also some of the finest Christians I've ever met. Liberals and conservatives lived together. I had to sort out my mind. What constituted liberalism? What made a conservative *conservative?* Where was I in all this? Those questions were sorted out in an environment where I was one of two Baptists in a student body of four hundred. No longer was I in a "Baptist hothouse." I ate every meal around a table for ten students who had all kinds of points of view. Not everybody had Southern good manners; the students were aggressive about what they believed. If you didn't come to some resolution about who you were and what you believed, you could be pushed around. In the privacy of our apartment in 417 Hodge Hall, Dot and I had long conversations about these things. It was a good experience, one that would serve me well when charges of liberalism were thrown about in Southern Baptist wars.

My time at Princeton lasted only a year. In August 1955 we went back to Southwestern to finish my graduate work in preaching. By this time I was eager for student days to end. I wanted to get out and try my skills as a pastor. In one year I did a year's worth of seminars toward my Th.D. at Southwestern, finished my Th.M. thesis at Princeton, and took my orals. It was too much, but it was time to move on.

In November 1955, I asked the Southwestern placement office to begin sending out my name to churches seeking a pastor. They did, but nothing happened. Several churches looking for a pastor interviewed me, but none called. I became discouraged. I was twenty-eight years old, had spent eleven years preparing myself to be a pastor, and now no church would take a chance on me. During this dry season, Dot spoke up. It was the first time she showed the strength of her faith. She braced me and assured me this would "work out" in the providence of God. Sometimes I wondered if God had forgotten my address. Dot had no faith-failure . . . in God or in me. She looked like a lady; inside she was strong.

In summer 1956 the telephone rang twice. Roy McClain at the First Baptist Church Atlanta, Georgia, needed an associate pastor. He wanted me to come for an interview. At exactly the same time, the First Baptist Church of Chamblee, Georgia, wanted a pastor. Chamblee was but twelve miles from First Atlanta. I had no connections in Atlanta; that the two invitations were so close was an accident of Providence. Both interviews led to invitations. From no choice I had two choices. Dot and I talked to each other, we talked to people we trusted at Southwestern, and we talked to God. Out of it all, we decided Chamblee was right for us. First Atlanta offered more money, but Chamblee offered more opportunity for leadership. I've always been grateful to Roy McClain for his confidence in me, but we made the right choice in Chamblee.

Orals were taken in mid-September 1956, and my school days came to an end. Chamblee sent a Mayflower moving van to get us. We had but two wardrobes, eight boxes of books, and a Toro lawnmower Daddy gave us as we parted. I had committed to ministry in July-August 1945. Now it was September 1956. I had spent eleven years in preparation. It was time to put my education to use in the service of a church.

Looking back on those eleven years, I see gaps in my education. There were things I needed to know that they forgot to tell me at college and seminary. But to dwell on the down side does not do justice to those who taught me. In the main they treated me gently, brought me to a fuller understanding of the Bible, taught me how to interpret a text, and forced me to begin writing. Along the way I was put in front of congregations. At first I was afraid, but with the passing of time I became "at home" in front of an audience. All these things helped. I've thanked some of my teachers; others are gone. I wish I could thank them too.

Chapter 4

# CHAMBLEE, COLLEGE STATION, AND THE BAPTIST GENERAL CONVENTION OF TEXAS

The First Baptist Church of Chamblee, Georgia, was my first full-time church. I had some experience. Four years in the country church at Selfs helped, and the year with the Baptist Students of Princeton was a type of experience. Neither of those assignments equipped me for a real, full-time church. I did not know this when I arrived in Chamblee.

Chamblee was a small town on the northeast side of Atlanta. Until 1945 (the end of World War II), the little town was almost rural. But by 1956, Atlanta had become the industrial and commercial engine of the new South. In those years, 60,000 new jobs were created in Atlanta every year. People left small towns and moved to Atlanta; that's where the jobs were. Developers bought the dairy farms that had surrounded Chamblee, and pastures turned into subdivisions. In ten years the little country church became a part of suburbia. It was not easy. For fifteen years a good man had served the church; the younger generation wanted different leadership. The old pastor was pushed out, and I became the new pastor. Some people were not happy with what had been done; that did not enlarge my welcome.

Dot and I were housed in a parsonage. It was a nice home on Chamblee-Dunwoody Road. We came with no furniture at all. A friendly banker looked at my salary ($400 a month plus parsonage) and agreed to loan Dot and me $1,500. We bought a bed, two bachelors' chests, a breakfast table with four captain's chairs, a dining table, a washing machine, and a vacuum. It was a start. The dining and living rooms had no furniture at all except a harvest table. Dot could have been demanding about furnishing the house, but she wasn't. She was understanding; we would make do with what we had. She said, "We will get things in God's good time," and we did.

I look on Chamblee as a four-year cram course in practical theology. I had not realized I was ever going to be the administrator of a church. There was a secretary and three part-time employees: a minister of music, a cook, and a custodian. I was twenty-eight, I had no experience in administration, and I was supposed to give them direction. No one had explained to me the importance of people skills in pastoring a church. I never realized I was going to be responsible for raising a budget each year. There is no way a novice can know just how many committee meetings and parties a pastor is supposed to attend. Sundays and Wednesdays came often. I preached on Sunday and taught on Wednesday. I was asked to speak more often than I had anything to say. All at once it was exciting and exhausting. In the 1950s people were quick to join a church in the South. Chamblee had a good location; middle-class subdivisions were popping up all around. But our growth was more than the accident of location. There were reasons: (1) The members wanted the church to grow. (2) We were on the growing edge of Atlanta. (3) Dot and I poured ourselves into the task. When we went to Atlanta, about 300 attended church each Sunday. By the time we left, First Chamblee was running about 600 a Sunday. Any pastor could have done as well. The pace was fast.

And so was the learning curve. When I look back on those days, I am amazed at the grace of those people and their willingness to follow us. One secretary became two. A new minister was added; he did both music and religious education. I was forced to learn all the parts of church life. As pastor I was the principal of Vacation Bible School, which involved hundreds of children. We took youth to camp in the summer. The minister of music resigned, so I led the choir for a year.

Until we got a minister of education, I enlisted teachers for Sunday school and trained them. It was church work, and I liked it.

Dot and I had been married more than three years, were working hard at Chamblee, and then she made an announcement that took me by surprise: "Honey, we're going to have a baby." Once before, Dot had been pregnant (1956); that ended in a miscarriage. This time we sought out the best doctor we could find and put Dot in his care. The pregnancy went well, and on November 22, 1957, at about 1:00 in the morning Dot wakened me and said it was time to go to the hospital. In the dark of the night I took her to Georgia Baptist Hospital in downtown Atlanta. In those days husbands were second-class citizens at childbirth. I had to leave Dot in the care of a nurse and go to a waiting room reserved for soon-to-be fathers. From 2:00 in the morning until 10:00 there was silence. Then a nurse came through the door from the delivery room announcing, "Mr. Sherman, you are the father of a baby girl!" The doctor had told us to expect a boy. When the baby appeared, the doctor was corrected. We had chosen a name for a boy; we had a girl. I did an impertinent thing: I named the girl for her mother on the spot, and Dorothy Eugenia Sherman came into our house. We called her "Genie." Dot was nearly forty when Genie was born. Genie is our only child. Dot was delighted to be a mother; in earlier days she had wondered if she would ever be one. We have pictures of Dot and baby Genie. Dot's joy at being Genie's mother radiantly beams through in every one of them.

In 1957, it was common for women to stay in the hospital for several days after delivery. Dot remained at Georgia Baptist for nine days. When Dot and Genie came home, our orderly, rather tranquil house turned over. Dot had not yet regained her strength, so it was agreed that I would get up with the baby her first night at home. I was up with that little girl eight or ten times that night. I changed her, fed her, and when she cried, I walked her. Back and forth in that empty living room we walked; I held her close with her head on my shoulder. That night something happened to me. I became invested in that little girl. I became her daddy; she became my girl.

Chamblee did not present any real theological tests. I worked hard; my work was rewarded in the health of the congregation. Good times do not test. Some ideas I took for granted would eventually be tested and require careful examination during harder times. I had little place in Georgia Baptist life, and that was to be expected. I was from Texas, knew almost no one, and was consumed with doing my job. I followed the life of the denomination, but I had little part in it. Our church made contributions to the denomination, but the focus of my work was Chamblee, not the Southern Baptist Convention.

When I came to Chamblee, one last piece of my education was unfinished. I had not written my dissertation for my doctorate in theology at Southwestern Baptist Theological Seminary. That hung over my head all the while I was at Chamblee. In 1958, I went to work on the dissertation in earnest. My subject was "Baptist Preaching in the South Before 1845." My major was preaching; my subject was a combination of Baptist preaching and Baptist history. Most Baptist preaching before 1845 was done by people who did not write their sermons. Finding material was my assignment. So in 1958–1959, I searched Baptist historical societies and the archives of Baptist college libraries. I didn't have much money or time. The Chamblee church was generous with time, and Dot and I spent from our limited resources to make the trips. I stayed in the YMCA on several research trips. I brought home what I found and began writing the dissertation; it took several months.

As I look back on that process, I see the hand of God. What I learned about Baptist preaching was incidental. What I learned about Baptists—who they are, how they emerged from the underclass of the South, how they did church, how they began to piece together a denomination, the limits placed on the denomination (limits that protected the autonomy of the local church) from the start—*mattered.* Years later when I was in a place I never expected to be, the information I gathered in my dissertation research became useful. Moses never dreamed he would lead Hebrews out of Egypt and into the wilderness when he was shepherding his father-in-law's sheep in that same wilderness. In hindsight, we know God was teaching Moses survival skills in the wilderness. That's the way I view my dissertation research. I thought I was gathering information for my dissertation; actually I was getting an education in Baptist polity and history. In June 1960, I was given a Th.D. by Southwestern Baptist Theological Seminary.

In spring 1960, the search committee from the First Baptist Church of College Station, Texas, called. They wanted Dot and me to come back to Texas and pastor their church. The decision was not easy. We had made friends in Chamblee, and the church was prospering. But the appeal of serving a church dedicated to serving a college community was strong. Concluding that the invitation was of God, we accepted and began our ministry in College Station on July 1, 1960.

First College Station was truly unique. The church existed to serve the Texas A&M community. Nearly all the people in the church were tied to the college; most were teachers or administrators. Literally 55 percent of the membership was students from the college. It was a strange way to do church. One Sunday we would have more than five hundred at church; the next Sunday the college was on holiday and we had one hundred and fifty.

The church had little money. When more than half the membership is students, the offering is never large. But the poverty did not touch dedication. I have never worked in a church where the dedication level was so high. If people joined that church, it was understood they would teach, serve, do committee work. And the talent pool was deep. All sorts of teachers were at church every Sunday. Some were in the sciences, in agriculture, in engineering. Somebody in that church knew something about almost everything. They were a great group of people, and they were fun to be around.

All of the staff was part-time except me. I had a secretary a half-day a week. Chamblee was a cram course in practical church work. College Station enlarged my library and improved my preaching. On Sundays I preached; on Wednesday nights I taught the Bible. I had to prepare to preach to those people. They drove me into the study; I had to preach better.

The church had a standard meal that was served every Wednesday—fried chicken, mashed potatoes and gravy, green beans, fresh-made rolls, iced tea, and a dessert—and that drew a crowd of students. After the meal we moved to the sanctuary, and I became a

Bible teacher. To teach two hundred faculty and students from Texas A&M, I had to organize my mind about the Bible. Each Wednesday I would print an outline of my subject, usually two to four pages. This gave the students something to keep if they wanted to organize their minds about the Bible. Years later while traveling for the Cooperative Baptist Fellowship, I met fifty-year-old men who were still using those outlines. It was good to connect with those good people again.

The College Station church also had a parsonage. It was a lovely home a couple of miles from the church where houses give way to fields and pasture. We were almost out in the country. Dot and Genie spent most of their time in that house. We planted trees in the yard. A kind church member helped me plant a rose garden. Genie was two years old when we arrived, and the students treated her like a queen. Aggies (as A&M students are called) carried her around, granted her wishes, slipped her goodies. She loved them. When Genie addressed Aggies, she called them "Agonies." The students said she had it right. All three of us were part of the college scene. We watched the band practice, went to football games, and took in lectures and cultural events. Those were good times, but they were too brief.

While at College Station I had reason to think through a dimension of Baptist polity that impacted that congregation. It is Baptist polity that a church stands on her own financial base. If the First Baptist Church of College Station needed a new building, it was up to the membership of that church to come forward with the money to pay for the building. Normally this is a good principle. A church ought to spend only what the members of that church will provide. But First College Station was different. When 55 percent of the membership is college students, then the income of that part of the congregation is going to be reduced to the giving abilities of college students. Every congregation in Texas, not to mention the extended influence of that vast university, has been and continues to be touched by Texas A&M. Future deacons, Sunday school teachers, and members of the finance committee for hundreds of churches in Texas are present in the College Station church membership; they are just a few years away from being church leaders.

If the College Station church does a poor job because the church is financially strapped, then some of students are lost to the life of the larger Church. I came to the conclusion that Baptists need to subsidize churches that have as their primary mission service to students. We have student ministries, but those ministries do not enable churches. Students need to grow in Christ during their college years, *and* they need to become church men and church women. Too often the college years separate students from participation in the life of a local church. Para-church groups are not a church, and reattaching those people to congregational life after their college years is not easy.

For the first time in my life health became a problem. Always I had been bothered with hay fever, but in College Station hay fever slipped into asthma, and I suffered from it for nearly three months of the year. Saint Augustine grass pollen triggered asthma. My doctor said this seasonal problem would likely become chronic if I stayed in that area. The church was healthy. We paid off a debt. I'm almost ashamed of the brevity of our stay (one year and nine months); we surely did not stay as long as I'd have liked.

While at College Station the larger life of the denomination began to open to me. I was a speaker for Baptist Student Union retreats. Evangelism had not been my strength, but in the college setting I had some success at persuading young men to profess faith. Along the way I met C. Wade Freeman, Director of Evangelism for the Baptist General Convention of Texas. He wanted to employ a person to do campus evangelism. I was asked to move to Dallas (location of the offices of the Baptist General Convention of Texas) and encourage campus evangelism in Texas colleges and universities. It was something I had the heart to do. My asthma was not getting better. We took the job and left College Station, but I've always had a fondness for Texas Aggies.

In Dallas we found an apartment owned by and near Southern Methodist University. We rented it and began a strange sort of life. Most of the time I was traveling; nearly all the time Dot and Genie stayed in Dallas. The Wilshire Baptist Church welcomed us into membership. Bruce McIver was pastor; he and his family became good friends.

The 1960s were not friendly to evangelism. Ten years earlier, evangelism and church growth thrived among Baptists in the South. But the 1960s were the season of civil rights, campus revolts, the discovery of ecology, the peace movement, and the war on poverty. Rather than evangelism, the faddish thing was social service and civil rights. All the time I was in evangelism, students were forcing me to justify it. This was not difficult for me; I argued for evangelism with a good conscience.

Another side of the evangelism job was teaching pastors. I would go to an association by appointment and teach a group of gathered pastors the New Testament doctrine of evangelism. It was stimulating work, and the pastors responded. I remain convinced that tradition has laid a heavy hand on the way Baptists do evangelism. In the present environment, evangelism is a mangled doctrine. Too often it has become a way to advance a career rather than a way to serve the Lord of the Church. Laypeople want results; whatever it takes to get results is what most pastors are willing to do. When "the bottom line" becomes the measure of all things, then the Spirit of God goes out the window. The pastor has to get people "down the aisle," no matter what. These were some of the ideas I discussed with pastors. Not all pastors were pragmatic; some gave me a hearing. They were as concerned about the integrity of evangelism as I was.

Child evangelism was another sticking point. Records in the Dallas office indicated that some churches in Texas were baptizing children as young as four years old. From the basis of the New Testament, I argued against this practice. The youngest convert recorded in the New Testament was Timothy; we don't know how old he was when Paul persuaded him to follow Christ. But straightway he was traveling with Paul; it is unlikely he was younger than fifteen. Baptists in the seventeenth century rarely baptized anyone younger than fifteen. But by the mid-twentieth century, it was the custom in Baptist churches in the South to baptize children who were eight, seven, and younger. I had encountered college students at Texas A&M who came into church membership at six or seven years of age, and most of them did not count that experience life-ordering. My ideas on child evangelism, no matter how biblical they might have been, were not approved by everyone, and that opened "a can of worms."

C. Wade Freeman was my supervisor. The man over Dr. Freeman was T. A. Patterson, executive secretary of the Baptist General Convention of Texas. This was my second time to make an acquaintance of the Patterson family (in 1950 I had met them at the First Baptist Church of Beaumont where Patterson was pastor). By 1962, Dr. Patterson had resigned from the Beaumont church and was chief operating officer of the Baptist Building in Dallas.

Texas Baptists decided to lead a special mission to Japan. Pastors, musicians, and laypeople traveled to Japan and gave witness in Japanese churches. Mrs. T. A. Patterson had an interest in the Japan mission. She set up a desk in the Evangelism Department office next to mine. I saw her often. By now her son, Paige, was a graduate student at New Orleans Baptist Theological Seminary. Sometimes she talked with me about Paige and her dreams and concerns for him. She said he went to Hardin Simmons University so he would avoid the liberalism he might find at Baylor. He had chosen New Orleans seminary instead of Southwestern for the same reason. But I still recall her comment. "But Cecil, do you know what?" she asked. "He found liberalism at New Orleans." Then I said an intemperate thing: "Mrs. Patterson, that took skill."

Those were the days when some Southern Baptists were upset about a book written by a professor at Midwestern Baptist Theological Seminary. The professor was Ralph H. Elliott; the book was titled *The Message of Genesis*. Elliott did not hold to a literal interpretation of the first chapters of Genesis. He raised questions about the sacrifice of Isaac that were new to some Southern Baptists and offensive to others. The book was mildly conservative, but it was not Fundamentalist. Actually, Dr. Elliott's book put in print what Southern Baptist seminaries had been teaching for years, yet when the book appeared, people of a Fundamentalist bent became very upset. Should Dr. Elliott be fired? Should the Sunday School Board have published the book? Where I worked it was assumed all were firm friends of everything conservative. I recall going to a lunch arranged by Dr. Patterson and attended by people from the Baptist Building and important pastors from the Dallas-Fort Worth area. The purpose of the lunch was to shore up support for the conservative side of the fight to suppress Elliott's book. I had mixed feelings. I did not want teachers to remain in our school if they were undermining belief in the reliability of the Bible, but there was a spirit about that lunch that was unsettling to me. Those people were not only out to "save the Bible"; they were out to get anyone who was not of their opinion. The comments of Mrs. Patterson about Paige and the luncheon pulled together by Dr. Patterson informed me fifteen years later. I would not have acted as I did in 1980 without the experiences I've described that took place in 1963–1964. I was becoming uncomfortable; I was not sure I belonged with these people.

Those feelings came to a head at the Texas Baptist Evangelism Conference at the First Baptist Church of Lubbock, Texas, in February 1964. I persuaded my boss, Dr. Freeman, to bring John Newport, a professor at Southwestern Seminary, as one of the speakers for the conference. Dr. Newport's assignment would be to lecture on "What the New Testament Says about the Evangelism of the Child." Newport did what he was asked to do. Methodically and carefully, he outlined the paucity of New Testament material on the evangelism of the child. He exposed Baptist practices in child evangelism as pragmatic rather than biblical. He did a good job, and given the crowd, he did a courageous job.

When he finished his address, I took Dr. Newport back to the Lubbock airport so he could return to his home. I hurried back to First Baptist Church, for there was a dinner sponsored by the Evangelism Division. When I entered the dining hall, Mrs. Patterson was at the microphone. She was very unhappy. "Who brought that seminary professor into this meeting? If I could find who invited him, I would give him a piece of my mind." She went on to say she knew children could become Christians at five and six years old. Her children had, and child evangelism ought to be encouraged, not questioned. I stood against the back wall of the dining room and listened. There might be times when I could argue with my boss; it was hard to oppose Mrs. Patterson. When the dinner ended, I went to Dr. Freeman and volunteered to speak to Mrs. Patterson and own up to my part in Dr. Newport's presence on the program. He said I should do nothing. I followed his counsel, but I was out of sync with the people who were ordering Texas Baptist life. I was not sure I could be forthright about some of my ideas about evangelism and keep my job.

There was another part of my unhappiness with the Texas Baptist job. I was away from home too much. In April 1964, I spent twenty-nine nights in motels and one night at home. Dr. Freeman said I would be away from home "one third of the time" when he offered me the job. It was not working out that way. Often he said in jest, "I'm going to promote evangelism with every drop of blood in your body." When campus ministers called, I was supposed to go. The effect of that expectation was severe. Dot was rearing Genie by herself. I recall that one night I was home in April 1964. Genie dressed up for dinner as if she were going to church. "Daddy is home!" What should have been normal became an affair of state. Genie was four when we moved to Dallas; she was six years and eight months when we left. I know little about that part of her life; most of the time I was away.

I went back to my hotel room that night in Lubbock, sat down, and wrote John Newport a full account of what Mrs. Patterson said. I also told him why I was getting uncomfortable in my job; I didn't fit. At the end of the letter I asked him to help me find a church. He did what I asked. Newport recommended me to River Oaks Church in Houston and to the First Baptist Church of Asheville, North Carolina. Apparently a recommendation from Dr. Newport carried some weight. In short order Dot and I heard from Asheville. On our way home from the 1964 Southern Baptist Convention in Atlantic City, New Jersey, we arranged to preach before the Asheville search committee. An interview followed, and by the time we drove home to Dallas, the committee had come to a decision.

In June 1964, Dot, Genie, and I were in Glorieta, New Mexico. Baptists had a conference center there, and I was scheduled for a part on one of the programs. A friend told me I had a message posted on the bulletin board. I was to call Carter Pressler in Asheville, North Carolina. Mr. Pressler, who chaired the First Baptist Asheville search committee, told me I had been "called" by the congregation to be their pastor. Dot and I had already decided that if called to Asheville, we would accept. Immediately I told Mr. Pressler we would accept their invitation. When I told Dot the news, she said, "Let's eat out tonight; this calls for a celebration," and we did. Genie was six and would start first grade soon. We were scheduled to begin our duties in Asheville on August 1, 1964. We had much to do.

Looking back on the two-and-a-half years in Dallas, there were good times mixed with the conflicts and travel. An illustration of the good times involved Kenneth Chafin. Ken was teaching evangelism at Southwestern Seminary in Fort Worth. Often we met in Arlington for a Tex-Mex lunch. We had known each other in seminary days. We both began as pastors. Now we were encouraging evangelism. Both of us had happy marriages and young children. We had much to talk about. His job had "problems" like mine. It was in those years that Ken and I learned one could support evangelism and still not feel "at home" with most of the people who were doing evangelism. Over enchiladas, Ken and I had our first discussion about the difference between one who is conservative theologically and one who is a Fundamentalist. Both of us saw ourselves as conservative; both of us were discovering Fundamentalism and not liking what we saw. Ken had a gift for sorting things out and making sense of what was happening in Baptist life. I came to trust his judgment.

We left Texas with some sadness. My parents were in Fort Worth, so while I was in Dallas we saw them regularly. My sister, Ruth, and her husband were nearby. My brother, Bill, was married and the father of three; he pastored a church in Stillwater, Oklahoma. While we lived in Dallas, Dot's mother, who lived in Spartanburg, South Carolina, died (March 1963). The move to North Carolina brought Dot closer to her sister, but for the most part we were separating ourselves from our family support system. I grew up with aunts and uncles, cousins and grandparents nearby. Genie would find her uncles and aunts, cousins and grandparents in the church at Asheville. Those people were not blood kin, but they were wonderful. We didn't know it as we packed and moved to North Carolina, but we were beginning a new chapter in our lives.

Chapter 5

# EARLY YEARS AT ASHEVILLE

Though Dot and I had been married for ten years, we had not gathered much furniture. We were still traveling light. What we had was put in a moving van, and the three of us followed in our small car. I remember the day we drove out of Dallas. A large thermometer registered 104. We were leaving the heat of Texas and going to the cool mountains of North Carolina. I was leaving denominational work to be a pastor again. The move was the right thing, and all three of us were excited.

The people in Asheville know how to welcome and entertain. They are old-fashioned Southerners when it comes to small kindnesses and thoughtfulness. They do it right. We were received as if we were royalty. Dot had a hard time unpacking; people kept coming to the door with a small gift for the house or a plate of food for the next meal. Late at night we were unpacking boxes and arranging things in the kitchen. To be interrupted by kindness was a good problem.

First Baptist Church Asheville was old by Texas standards; the congregation was constituted in 1829. The Great Depression hit Asheville hard. A building boom was interrupted, and a lot of projects were built but not paid for when the economy went into a tailspin (October 1929). The deflation that followed left town and people strapped with debt. The church was part of that pattern. A lovely set of buildings was built in 1927; they were to be paid for over a period of fifteen years. The pastor who urged the building project went to a larger church, and the Asheville church was saddled with debt just when the Depression hit.

My predecessor, Dr. Perry Crouch, was pastor of the church for twenty years (1944–1964) and had done an exceptionally good job. In about ten years he got the church out of debt. It freed the church to her real mission. Most churches prospered after World War II, and First Asheville set attendance records in the 1940s and '50s that have not been broken. The church thrived, and Dr. Crouch was the archi tect of its prosperity. As he did this remarkable work as a pastor, he still had time to be active in the North Carolina Baptist Convention. In 1963, the convention asked Dr. Crouch to become executive secretary (CEO of the convention). He took that assignment January 1, 1964, and that led to the vacancy at Asheville.

There was a movement among Southern Baptists in the 1950s to start new churches. Dr. Crouch participated in that movement. First Asheville started a new church on the east side of town; it was named Beverly Hills Baptist Church. Then a couple of years later a second church was started south of town; it was called First Baptist Church, Arden. Both churches are still alive and well.

The effect of these two church starts on First Asheville was not immediately evident. Most of the young adults on the east side of town left First Asheville and became the nucleus of Beverly Hills. "Stack-pole" people are at the center of a community; they are strong, reliable folks who attract others and whom others admire and lean on. Most of the young adults on the south side of town became stack-pole people for First Arden. The French Broad River separated the town. West Asheville was another community, and only a few of our members came from there. The effect of the two church starts left First Asheville with few young adult families. To a casual observer this was a small matter. Attendance was still around nine hundred each Sunday; gifts to the church remained strong. But the exodus of young adults to start the new churches left First Asheville an old membership—a problem that had to be addressed.

August Sundays at First Asheville in 1964 were almost celebrations. The house was full. The spirit of the people was upbeat. I was on a fast learning curve at the church. Dot was furnishing a large parsonage on Charlotte Street. Genie entered first grade at Claxton School. All three of us had work to do, and we threw ourselves into our tasks. And then something happened that changed everything.

I had noticed a cluster of eight or nine young black women in each service those August Sundays. They were fashionably dressed and possessed of elegant manners. The young women were from Allen School, a school operated by North Carolina Methodists. The school catered to wealthy black girls; they came from Texas, Ohio, Illinois, New York. Allen School was only a block from the First Baptist Church. Accompanying the young women was the school's music teacher, Carol Chaney. Miss Chaney was a recent graduate of Johnson C. Smith University in Charlotte, North Carolina. The excellence of our music program attracted her.

The first Sunday in September 1964, my sixth Sunday as pastor, Miss Chaney made a point to go out the door where I was greeting people as they exited the church. She said, "Pastor, may I join your church? The interim pastor told me to wait until a permanent pastor came and then request membership." I said, "Have you professed faith in Christ as your Lord and Savior?" She said, "I have." Then I asked a question the First Baptist Asheville constitution required me to ask, "Have you been baptized by immersion after you professed faith?" She said, "I have." By that time she had told me her name, so I said, "Miss Chaney, we will be happy to receive you into membership. Come forward next Sunday and I will present you to the congregation."

Shadowing this after-church conversation with Miss Chaney was the chair of our board of deacons. He was soft-spoken as he said, "Pastor, when people have greeted you I would like to see you in your office." I agreed to the meeting, and for the next ten minutes spoke to others as they left the church. I had no inkling of what was to follow. Looking back, I marvel at how naive I was.

The chair of deacons and I went to my office. He pulled from his pocket a copy of the constitution of the church. It was called "The Policy" and contained a section on membership. At the bottom of the page was a footnote that said membership would be granted only when there was a unanimous vote of the members present and voting. I had been given a copy of the Policy when the search committee interviewed Dot and me. I had looked at the Policy at the end of a long day, but I had not followed an asterisk to the bottom of the page and read the footnote.

The chair of deacons, in a clear, even voice, said, "I want you to go see Miss Chaney [he knew her name] and tell her not to come forward next Sunday. There is no possibility of her getting a unanimous vote. Her rejection will be the kind of stuff newspapers enjoy printing. You will save the church unwanted publicity." I was stunned at what was in the Policy, but I was more stunned by the way the chair wanted me to resolve "the problem."

Until this day I can still recall the way I answered the man. And looking back on the event from more than forty years, I am amazed at my answer. That time I said the right thing. "I work for you people. Under normal conditions I would do anything you ask me to do. But what you have asked me to do I believe immoral. It would be like asking me to rob a bank. I can't do what you have asked." Both of us had spoken in a moderate, civil tone of voice. There was no anger in the conversation; there was serious disagreement.

I asked the chair, "How do you change the Policy?" He turned to the back page of the Policy and read the conditions for amendment:

- Deacons had to recommend a change by a majority of the deacons present and voting.
- The recommended change had to be printed in the church paper at least thirty days before the congregational meeting called to vote on the change.
- At a congregational meeting called for the purpose of voting on the proposed change, at least three-fourths of the members present and voting had to approve the change. Should that come to pass, the change would be incorporated into the Policy.

My conversation with the chair of deacons ended with me saying, "I will bring my thoughts to the deacons at the October meeting. I hope they will approve them and move them forward to the congregation." The chair said nothing in response. We parted after conducting ourselves decently. That was Labor Day Sunday. I would not be bringing my proposed change to the deacons until the Monday after the first Sunday in October. The chair returned to my office at least once a week throughout September. He never raised his voice; he always asked the same thing. I was to go to Miss Chaney and persuade her to withdraw her request for membership in our church. Each time I politely declined.

Dot and I did go see Miss Chaney. We met her in her apartment, sat with her, and told her what the Policy required for membership. I requested that she postpone her request for membership until I had a chance to see how the congregation would receive my proposed change. She graciously consented to allow time for me to work for change.

Looking back on that month, I wonder how we made it. I had been in the church for six weeks. I had no "pastoral collateral." I had buried no one's mother, married no one's daughter, gotten no one's child into college, nor had I helped anyone through a job loss. I was without the connections pastoral care provides. Pastoring a Baptist church has a political quality to it. You get the job by vote; you can lose it by a second vote. Dot realized the seriousness of this test of wills; she announced, "I'm not going to unpack anymore. I'm going to wait and see how this turns out."

Race was *the* social issue in the 1960s. Martin Luther King, Jr., strode the country making those memorable speeches that are still quoted. George Wallace stood in the schoolhouse door vowing "never." The Supreme Court had declared "separate but equal" schools a violation of the Constitution (May 17, 1954). Schools were being ordered to integrate. Private academies were springing up all over the South to frustrate the courts, and sometimes churches sponsored those schools. It was a tense time, and feelings were high. Everything that was happening in the nation was happening in our little world in Asheville.

Miss Chaney's request for membership was not known to the congregation through September. But at the October deacons' meeting, that changed. I went before the deacons and told them every detail I knew about Miss Chaney, recounted her request for membership, and then proposed a change in the Policy. I requested that the Policy be changed so that a two-thirds vote would admit one to membership. A friendly deacon made a motion to that point, and then discussion began.

There were forty-eight deacons on the board, all male. More than forty were present. Most of them were more than sixty years old; only two were younger than I (I was thirty-six). Of course, those people were reading newspapers and were aware that race was a divisive issue in the larger society. None of them expected the race issue would trouble our church. Their first response to my request was surprise. One question after another was put to me. I tried to answer truthfully and candidly. A lawyer in the group was so pointed in his questioning that his own supporters tried to restrain him. They pled, "This is not a trial. Ease up a little." He did not ease up. In the ways of a lawyer, he shifted the subject from the motion. All of a sudden, I was on trial. He questioned my knowledge of Baptist polity (church governance) and Baptist history. What I am describing did not pass in five minutes; it went on and on. For at least thirty minutes I faced a barrage of questions. I was no longer the new pastor who was being given the benefit of the doubt; I was a newcomer who had injected an unwelcome subject into the meeting.

Finally the question was called on the amendment. I had no idea how the vote would go. To my surprise, the amendment passed by a majority of two. The deacons were split almost down the middle. The meeting closed, and everything changed. What had been a private test of wills between the chair of deacons and me became an open debate. Before sundown the next day everyone in the congregation knew about Miss Chaney's request.

The proposed amendment was printed in the church paper and mailed to the membership. I wrote an article that explained the background for the change. I called Carol Chaney by name and told the congregation as much as I could about her. I listed the questions I asked of her when she made her request: Had she trusted herself in faith to Jesus Christ, and had she been baptized by immersion? All the details were on the table. The date set for a congregational vote on the amendment was Wednesday, December 2, 1964.

What happened between early October and December 2 gave me an education in hardball politics . . . and human nature. To give a window into what it was like, here are some illustrations:

- My status changed in the minds of some of the congregation. I was not the new fellow who was welcomed warmly. I was an interloper from Texas who came to Asheville to integrate First Baptist. They said it was my agenda in coming.
- Other critics said, "He has been sent here by the National Association for the Advancement of Colored People. He will be paid if the church integrates. Black people are going to take over our church."
- One night Dot, Genie, and I were at dinner. The telephone rang. Genie had been trained to answer the phone; she spoke as she was taught: "Shermans' residence. Genie Sherman speaking." Then she was quiet for two or three minutes; a puzzled look came over her face. She held the phone in her hand and said, "Daddy, there is a lady on the phone; she says you want me to marry a . . . . " And there was a pause. I said, "Genie, did she say that word we never say?" Genie softly said, "Yes." I went to the phone and said, "This is Cecil Sherman." From the other end of the line there came a laugh that was more of a witch's cackle; then she hung up. I never knew who made the call.
- During that time, a former sheriff of Buncombe County walked into my office. He was a giant of a man, and he was plainspoken. He made no small talk. "Preacher, I've heard that you want to let a nigger into this church. I don't believe it, and I've come to hear you say it isn't so. What is the straight of this?" I said, "You are referring to Miss Carol Chaney. She teaches at Allen School, and she has asked membership in our church. The rules are rigged to prevent her membership, and I'm trying to change them." The man said, "Well, I'll be damned! It's so." Then he asked, "Why would you do such a thing?" A Bible was on my desk. I read to him from Acts 10 and Galatians 3. He dismissed the Bible reading, saying, "You can prove anything by the Bible." Then he concluded our meeting by saying,

"Well I'll tell you one thing, preacher; we're going to beat you December 2nd." And with that he walked out of the office.

• It became clear to me that the leader of the segregation party in our church was the lawyer who grilled me in the deacons' meeting. He taught a men's Bible class with many members. Their lesson was broadcast on a local radio station; the man was colorful and had a following. I decided to ask him if there were anything we could do to prevent a church split over the race issue. I went to his office and asked to see him. His office was full of people, but he saw me immediately. The man was about seventy years old and was established in Asheville. I said, "It has become apparent that you are the leader of the part of our church who does not want Miss Chaney to be a member. I am becoming the leader of those who do. If we are not careful, we are going to split our church. Is there any way we can prevent that from happening?" There was a long pause. I still remember his breathing during the pause; he had emphysema. He whistled as he breathed. Then his breathing turned to a chuckle as he said, "You're hurting, aren't you, kid?"

It was a slap in the face. I didn't know whether any good could come of my visit, but I was not expecting the answer I got. Then it was my time to be quiet for a while. He sat silently while I collected my thoughts. Then I said, "You've interpreted concern for our church for weakness; I'll see you at church." And I was gone.

• The wife of the lawyer who grilled me came to the back door of the parsonage one afternoon. She had a plate of fresh-baked, warm cookies. I thanked her, took her gift, and invited her in. She declined. Her voice cracked, and a tear fell from her eye. She said in a quiet voice, "He's a good daddy." Then she was gone. The woman disagreed with her husband; she was in an impossible situation. Our church was torn by race; families in our church were torn too. Years later, and after her husband's death, that woman would be one of the first female deacons in First Asheville. She was a wonderful woman.

Finally, December 2 came. About a thousand people were present at the meeting. Those who wanted to defeat the amendment had telephoned the membership, determined who would vote against, and carpooled them to the meeting. I saw people at that meeting I had not seen at church before . . . and never saw at church again. The motion was read, and discussion of the motion followed. In the custom of that church, I presided. A number of short, strong statements were made for the amendment. A dentist spoke for it. A professor of history at the local college made an appeal for the amendment. A housewife asked for fairness and referenced the mission message of our church.

But the other side had their say too. The chief of police had a black man accused of raping an older, white woman in the city jail awaiting trial. He held a picture of the black man before the congregation and said, "I'm voting to defeat this amendment so I can keep people like this out of our church." Then he added, "If the search committee had gotten us someone who was dry behind the ears, we would not be in this mess. Dr. Crouch would have taken care of this, and we would not have this problem."

The vote was 406 in favor of the amendment. There were exactly 250 opposed (several hundred did not vote; they only came to witness the event). But the motion had to pass with a 75 percent vote. We had a majority, but we didn't have enough votes to change the Policy. We had 62 percent. There followed a strange time. A minority of the congregation wanted to fire me. A few carried a petition around town gathering names to force a vote on my removal. They got some names but not enough to matter. The majority of the church wanted to admit Miss Carol Chaney into membership, but they were frustrated by rules that empowered the minority. It was an awkward time for me and the church.

Miss Chaney was still waiting. Again Dot and I walked back up the hill to her apartment. I told her what had happened in detail, and I was ashamed of the message I brought, I was ashamed of our church, and I was ashamed of my inability to effect change. I did not know how Carol Chaney would respond. At the time she did nothing, but about a month later, in mid-January 1965, she came forward on a Sunday morning and asked membership. She forced the church to face themselves. To give the congregation a chance to think about their decision, I postponed the vote on her admission until Wednesday night. That Sunday night I spoke directly to the vote that faced us. The title of my remarks was, "Before You Cast That Negative Vote . . .," and I tried to appeal to the very best in our members. I begged them not to vote her down.

Wednesday night a strange thing happened. Not many who opposed her coming came (it only took one). But about three hundred who were for her admission packed our chapel. The vote was something like 300 for and exactly 41 opposed. Just about all of those who opposed were senior citizens. That night I was not the only one who was ashamed. Then Dot and I made a third trip to see Miss Chaney. She anticipated our message. She was not happy, yet she thanked Dot and me for our attempt to make wrongs right. Miss Chaney did not come back to First Baptist Asheville.

From her first request for membership to her rejection, the process took about five months. This first year of my Asheville ministry was a turbulent time for our family and the congregation. I was not happy with the outcome, and a lot of people in the church were unhappy too. Our unhappiness colored everything. It was hard to "do church." I learned from the experience.

1. I learned that the race issue is  important. Racial inclusiveness is not petty morality; it is at the heart of Bible ideas. Violation of those Bible rules corrupts. Turning away people who have professed faith in Christ is out of step with the spirit of the New Testament.

2. I learned that congregational peace is fragile; once broken it is hard, hard, hard to repair. Our church was not fully together again for several years. A few people didn't get over that division until they died.

3. I learned that "taking a stand" is not something you plan to do. I did not anticipate the division. I did not plan my response. It was on me like a traffic accident; it happens before you know it.

4. The division in our church actually went three ways. One group was for Miss Chaney coming into membership; another group was against. But there was also a third group; they did not want to go public on the issue. They were the swing vote. They were more upset over the unpleasantness in the fellowship than they were over race. They expected the pastor to keep everyone happy. Forcing the congregation to process the issue caused division, and they didn't like that.

5. Dot and I reflected on the whole affair. Was there any way we could have handled things and gotten a different response? Both of us concluded there was probably nothing we could have done that would have moved the opposition. They were set in stone. The problem was not a failure in leadership; the problem was a strong difference of opinion on the issue. I might have had a chance had I been pastor of the church for twenty years.

6. Neither Dot nor I ever considered backing down on the issue. There was never a time when she wanted me to "cut a deal" with the opposition. She and I believed we were right, and we were willing to lose the Asheville job over it. T. B. Maston's ethics classes at Southwestern had convinced both of us that racial inclusiveness is right.

7. Lost in most of this story is the response of the majority. Of course we made enemies in the fight; what came clear to me later was the opposite result. We made fast friends. Years later Mary Dalton said, "Cecil, Eileen Rowe and I watched you in that race fight. You did not back down. That's when we decided we were going to make a success of you." Any success I had at Asheville was in large part due to the support and encouragement of Mary, Eileen, and others. They could "make bricks without straw."

8. I thought what we were doing in Asheville was unreported outside our town; that was not so. Baptist Press picked up our story, and the Asheville *Citizen-Times* had articles on the subject. I came to Asheville from the Evangelism Division of the Texas Convention; that connection had defined me. I was a friend of evangelism. In a few years I was appointed to the Christian Life Commission of the Southern Baptist Convention (the agency of the Convention concerned with ethics and social issues). I remain interested in evangelism, but perception of me changed among my peers in the professional clergy.

9. The fall-out from the fight enlarged my predecessor, Perry Crouch. Those who opposed me (and Miss Chaney) deified Dr. Crouch. They reasoned like this: "If only Dr. Crouch had been here, we would not have had this awful scene." Dr. Crouch had nothing to do with their reasoning, but in their minds the church had fallen into

young, incompetent hands. They wished for the experienced care of their former pastor, and often I was compared to him.

10. The whole process raised a question in my mind about Baptist polity. Baptists believe questions of Bible interpretation are to be put before the congregation so the membership may decide. I did that. I made no attempt to arrange the outcome of the vote. As I saw it, my job was to give the congregation information. I told the congregation about Miss Chaney, what I thought the Bible said on the matter, and where I stood. The vote was in their hands. It was in the open; the congregation made the decision. But when I witnessed members who worked like politicians to get out the vote, I began to question our system of decision-making. Does it make sense to invite people to a congregational meeting who have not been present in five or ten years? I remain committed to the Baptist way, but there is weakness in our system when we do not prune our rolls of people who have not come to church in years.

The fall-out from the Carol Chaney vote hung in the air. The church was divided. I recall a small matter before the finance committee; the committee divided. The lines were exactly as they were on the Chaney vote. Appointments to committees each year tried to take into account those who were on one side or the other. Those appointing tried to be fair and include both sides. It was an awkward way to do church, and for several years the Chaney decision shadowed our fellowship and limited our ability to work together.

People who took Carol Chaney's side found it expensive. The dentist who spoke for her lost patients who had used his services for forty years. He was older; he broke with his generation and they made him pay. A major construction firm moved their bank account from Wachovia Bank to the Bank of Asheville. The president of Wachovia had spoken in favor of amending the Policy; the president of the Bank of Asheville had spoken against. The Supreme Court ruled for black people; that ruling did not change Old South values, especially in the older generation. About forty families left the church, and the fellowship of the church was damaged. A number of those who opposed Miss Chaney did not move their membership; they protested by reducing their gifts, or they stopped giving altogether. On the other side, those who believed in the Chaney issue rallied behind Dot and me. They took us into their homes and tried in every way to tell us they cared and wanted us to become at home in Asheville.

By the end of January 1965, we had been in Asheville six months. By no design of our own, the church had divided. A large minority of older members viewed me with some hostility; I was too "hot" on race and I was not willing to make a deal to protect the fellowship. Another group was delighted with my leadership on race and was happy with the search committee's choice. A third group was quiet; they were waiting to see what would happen next. They weren't sure about me. The "honeymoon" was over.

Chapter 6

# BECOMING A PASTOR

## PART 1: UNFINISHED BUSINESS

The race issue was still unsettled. I had spent the goodwill usually given a new pastor in an attempt to change the constitution of the church and admit Miss Carol Chaney. That effort failed, and the issue was left dangling. I was not in a place to bring the issue before the congregation again; the first attempt caused too much pain. Resolution of the race issue came from events outside our congregation.

On a Thursday night in April 1968, Dr. Martin Luther King, Jr., was shot and killed in Memphis, Tennessee. Riots broke out in some of the major cities in America. Asheville was tense, but there was no violence. On Friday a pastor of a black church nearby called and asked a favor. He wondered if the sanctuary of the First Baptist Church would be available for a service of tribute to Dr. King on Sunday afternoon at 3:00 p.m. Our church was chosen because it was wired for television; the local station planned to carry the service. I still remember the way I felt when the question was asked. If I requested time to go to the chair of deacons, I reasoned that I would probably get a "No"; race was a sensitive issue in the membership since the Carol Chaney vote. If I said "Yes" without consulting him, I would be vulnerable to another outbreak of criticism. I said "Yes" without checking with the chair of deacons.

That Sunday a telegram arrived at our door from President Lyndon B. Johnson; the same telegram was sent to 5,000 pastors across the nation. It was a plea for pastors to use the influence of their pulpits to steady the country . . . and to state both the American and the biblical ideal on race. I had already planned to address the issue. My sermon was titled "A Tribute to Dr. Martin Luther King, Jr." Most of the audience appreciated the sermon; the television audience asked more copies of that sermon than any I preached in the eighteen years we were on television.

Sunday afternoon at 3:00 our sanctuary had standing room only. About two-thirds of those present were black, but important parts of the white community were present as well. All denominations were represented. I had a bit part; I welcomed the audience, stated the purpose of the meeting, and gave the invocation. From that point I was a spectator.

Monday morning there was a march in tribute to Dr. King. About six hundred marched; only thirty-five of us were white. I will never forget the silence as we marched up College Street to Pack Square. Shops were closed and locked. People stood watching at second-floor windows. The only sound was the sound of footsteps. After a block or so, we were in step. You could hear every foot strike the pavement, and that's all you heard. That afternoon Dr. King was buried in Atlanta. All the nation paused, reflected, and was forced to face the message his life had shouted. To this point not one person in my congregation had spoken a negative word about my sermon or the Sunday afternoon service given in tribute to Dr. King. That ended with the deacons' meeting Monday night.

The meeting was held in the chapel; nearly all forty-eight deacons were present. Dr. Jesse P. Chapman, Jr., presented a motion that there be a special committee appointed by the chair of deacons to review our membership policy. His stated reason for the motion was to put our policy in line with our understandings of the New Testament. His remarks were not inflammatory; he was careful to control both the text of his motion and his temper. But the effect of Dr. Chapman's motion was like the lancing of a boil. Those who had disagreed with my sermon, with the community tribute being held in our church, with my stance on race since Carol Chaney . . . all their anger was emptied into the debate. It was so intense that one deacon had a heart attack. An ambulance was called, and he was taken to the hospital. The man stricken was opposed to the admission of black people; two doctors who were for the inclusion of black people rode with the sick man to the hospital. I still remember the calculating thought that crossed my mind: the man is beating me even in his heart attack; he's taking two "for" votes out of the meeting.

But the majority voted for Dr. Chapman's motion. The chair of deacons appointed Fenton Erwin chair of the special committee. The new group began a review of the policy with special attention to the conditions for membership. Fenton came to me soon after his appointment and said, "Cecil, everyone knows where you stand on this issue. You've become a lightning rod. I want you to stay out of our meetings. When I get something you can live with, I will come to you and talk." That was fine with me.

I did not hear from them until August 1969, sixteen months after their appointment. Fenton came to my office and presented their work. He got the committee to recommend unanimously that a vote of two-thirds of members present and voting would admit someone to membership. I was pleased. It had been nearly five years since the tempest over Miss Chaney. Some of the more vocal voices opposed to integrating our church had died. Nearly all of the newer members were for integration. It was not a perfect proposal; it was the best anyone could have done at the time. The recommendation from the deacons was put to the membership in writing. Thirty days passed. At a meeting announced for the express purpose of voting on a policy change, the congregation voted. About twenty voted against the change. Well over two hundred voted for the recommendation. The doors of the church were now opened a little wider.

Clarence Batts was an engineer fresh out of North Carolina State University; he moved to Asheville in late 1969 to work for American Enka. He was single, black, and took church seriously. In January 1970, Clarence Batts asked membership in our church. I don't believe anyone voted against him (even the opposition realized their game was up). For the first time since thirteen black members of First Baptist withdrew to go out and form the First Nazareth Baptist Church in 1867, our membership included at least one black member. What was left dangling in 1965 was resolved in 1970. The constitution of the church moved a little closer to the New Testament. It was a giant step forward in self-definition for our church. One black in more than two thousand members was token integration; in the next ten years black membership rose to sixteen. It was never large, but everyone knew the door was open and a troublesome issue was closed. I was the new pastor, and I did not have the good opinion of enough people to effect change, but what I couldn't do was generously covered by the convictions and influence of men like Jess Chapman and Fenton Erwin. They got the job done.

The Clarence Batts story is beautiful. Clarence immediately began working with youth, and for several years his primary place at church was with teenagers. But Clarence was so faithful and effective in what he did that he was asked to be Sunday school superintendent for the entire church, and he served in that capacity for several years. One year Clarence's name appeared as a candidate for the board of deacons. He was elected. An older member of the church was asked if he voted for "that black man." He answered, "You mean Clarence? Sure I voted for him. I forgot he was black." Because of Clarence's work in the church and the relationships he forged there, what many people first saw in him was the "content of his character"—not the color of his skin. Clarence Batts was exactly the right person to be the first black member of our church.

## PART 2: BECOMING CREDIBLE

After five difficult years, one thing became clear: the new pastor was willing to risk the unity of his congregation and even his job for a cause. Most people agreed I had a moral backbone. What was not clear was whether or not I had good judgment. Part of the membership believed that the highest good was maintaining the unity of the church. Unity was more important than taking a right stand on race; I suspect they thought the search committee had made a mistake. Others admired my courage, but aside from the race issue, what would I do, what could I do, for the health of the congregation?

Most members were of my parents' generation. In December 1964, there was social life at the church. Sunday school groups had parties. The eldest Sunday school department was large. They rented the ballroom of the Vanderbilt Hotel, sold tickets to a dinner, and employed professional entertainment. More than four hundred attended; most guests were seventy years or older. Those people had a question about the judgment of the young pastor. Would he bless and enlarge the health of the congregation?

My appearance did not help. At Christmas I took a poinsettia to each "shut-in" in the membership. On a cold December afternoon I knocked on the door of a modest house. The woman was confined to her bed; her husband was her caregiver, and he was nearly deaf. I saw the couple through the door, but I could not get the husband's attention. I knocked louder. Eventually he heard me, came to the door, opened it as if I were not there, and took the flower. The door slammed shut behind him. I knocked again. He came to the door a second time and said in a rough voice, "What do you want?" I said, "I'm your new pastor; may I come in?" He warmed a bit and said, "I thought you were the delivery boy."

I was learning a raw truth about being a pastor. You may be called to a church, and they may paint your name on the sign outside, but that does not mean you will be allowed to do pastoral things for the membership. With some pain, I learned that a pastor is not the pastor until the members allow him to do pastoral things, and that takes time. My apprenticeship at First Baptist Church Asheville lasted at least five years; sometimes I was impatient as I waited.

## PART 3: DOING CHURCH

The great need of First Baptist Church Asheville was an infusion of new, young members. My assignment was to design a strategy that would gather new members. We were downtown; a prospective member was going to have to drive a few miles to get to us. Most of our members were senior adults, and that meant I was trying to get young adults to come into a church where there were few other young adults. I wanted my church to grow, but I didn't want growth to crowd out the other things a church is supposed to do. With the wisdom of some thoughtful lay-people, we came up with a strategy for doing the gospel and gathering a new generation to First Baptist. Here's what we did . . .

1. My predecessor had worked hard to pay off debt, and he accomplished what he set out to do. In one of the opening interviews with the search committee I learned that Dr. Crouch and lay leadership of the church dreamed of a day when they could build new buildings and renovate old ones. The last year the church had built was 1927. In the interim there had been little money to maintain the property; parts of the church were run down. The search committee laid the plan before me; it was a good plan. I bought into it without reservation.

In the 1950s the church bought a fine house for the parsonage; it was about a mile from the church. The old parsonage beside the church was made into Sunday school space for children. Bedrooms became classrooms, but the house was not meant to be a school. It was inferior space for religious education, and we needed to build a new building to educate our children.

As I began to advance the idea of constructing a children's building, I encountered questions. In a discussion at a deacons' meeting, a man said, "Pastor, why do we need a children's building? It's like Abraham and Sarah adding a nursery onto their house. They're too old to have children, and so are we." Mr. Buckner was right. Most of the church was gray. They weren't parents; they were grandparents. My response was, "If we don't make our properties attractive, young people will choose other churches. We say we want new families; this is part of the price to attract our target audience."

Questions were answered to the satisfaction of most, an architect was employed, and the project moved forward. Bids were received in spring 1969, and the congregation voted on a Sunday night in May. About two hundred people were present; 180 voted to build, and 20 voted against. Lucille Fitzgerald, one of our older members, voted against building.

When the meeting was over I greeted people as they left the church, and Lucille Fitzgerald went out my door. I wondered why she voted against the children's building; so as she went out I said, "Lucille, I noticed you voted against the building. You know we need new facilities for our children. Why did you do that?" Her answer took me to school.

Lucille said, "Cecil Sherman, you follow me, and I'll tell you exactly why I voted against a new children's building." With that she briskly walked outdoors and over to the side of the sanctuary. "He stood right here; it was 1929."

"Who was 'he'?" I interrupted.

She answered, "Robert Bateman. [He was pastor of the church from 1921–1929.] He waved his hand to the new sanctuary [built in 1927] as if to say, 'Look what we've built since I've been here.' Then he was off to pastor the First Baptist Church of Memphis, Tennessee. He left in late summer; the Great Depression began in October. I had bought bonds in 1926 to finance the building; they were to be repaid on a five-, ten-, and fifteen-year schedule. I got my money back in the 1950s. Some of my friends died before they recovered the money they loaned the church."

I said, "Lucille, I will be here when the debt on the children's building is paid."

My words had no impact. Disgust and frustration were written all over her face, and she said, "That's what you *all* say." With that she turned on her heels and walked away.

I was left standing in the parking lot pondering what Lucille had said. Everything she said was true. Dot and I had a long talk that night. We knew Lucille was a mirror into the collective mind of the older members of the congregation. They didn't trust me. I said the agenda was a children's building; they were wondering if the real agenda was my career. I still had a long way to go to become pastor.

The new children's building opened in August 1970. Becky Pace was children's minister, and she had as much credibility as any minister on the staff. Becky put a day care program in the new building. Young adults from all over town put their children in our program, and soon 160 children were at the church from 7:30 in the morning until 5:45 in the evening five days a week. The weekday program was an instant success; getting those same people to come back on Sunday was not so easy. Two years after the building was finished, I walked through the Sunday school area, peered in a little window in each door, and saw three teachers and two students in spacious, lovely rooms. We still were not attracting young families.

In summer 1976, the chair of deacons came forward after church on a Sunday morning and showed the congregation a canceled note from Northwest Bank. The children's building debt was paid in full. The congregation broke into applause. I looked over the house, and there was a white-haired lady wearing a wide-brimmed hat . . . Lucille Fitzgerald. I said, "Lucille, I'm still here." She smiled broadly; in spite of her tart remarks in 1969, we were friends. Older members were beginning to trust.

2. WLOS-TV, the ABC outlet for the Greenville, Spartanburg, and Asheville market, was located in Asheville. The station was willing to broadcast our 11:00 worship service if we were willing to bear the cost. The congregation decided it was the right thing to do, and we went on the air. We changed nothing in our worship for television; we gave people a church service, not a show. We did not attract millions of viewers; we gathered a substantial audience of thousands. Many older people who could not get to their church tuned in to worship with us. We made friends for the faith and for our church. Between 1970 and 1980, 41 percent of our new members were introduced to First Baptist by means of television.

3. Our church was almost downtown. Alongside us was an impoverished neighborhood called Valley Street. Medical services for poor people were spotty. Our church had doctors in the membership, and we were near Valley Street. Why not open a clinic and provide primary medical services to the poor? It was one of those things that could happen if the right people were brought together. I began meeting with doctors over breakfast on Sunday mornings. We talked about the need for medical services for the poor. We talked about problems in providing it. We talked about the resources we possessed to make a medical clinic happen. We decided we could do it. The plan was to open a clinic in the church basement on Monday nights. To open the clinic, we needed basic medical supplies and personnel. The supplies were easy enough. We begged and borrowed. Lining up help was the

next step. We had to have a doctor, a nurse, and a medical secretary. It all fell into place, and the clinic opened.

At the outset the response to our clinic was modest. But that changed. By word of mouth those in need learned of the service; they came. Then we needed two doctors and two nurses and two medical secretaries each Monday night. A few dramatic stories came out of the clinic, but most of the need was routine. Hypertension was the most common ailment of the poor.

Buncombe County noticed the efficiency of our clinic and approached the church asking if they could help us. They believed it was more efficient to treat the poor in our clinic than to send them to hospital emergency rooms. They found a doctor to work daytime hours, and the clinic opened five days a week.

Alongside the clinic came the Clothes Closet. What had been a careless operation was organized and enlarged. Norma Kibler became director of the Clothes Closet. Sixty people volunteered, and a ragged little pile of clothes became an efficient distribution center. No longer could we get enough used clothes from the membership; we begged from the big mills that made jeans, shirts, jackets, underwear, socks, etc. Vans brought children from Asheville public schools. Volunteers fitted the children. I had a small part in begging seconds from the large mills that dotted North and South Carolina. Most of the mills were generous, and the poor children of Asheville had clothes in the winter. The Clothes Closet served more than three thousand people a year.

Dot worked in the Clothes Closet with Olive Murphy. Olive was older, a widow, and capable of speaking her mind. One day I dropped by the Clothes Closet to thank the volunteers; Olive and Dot were at work. Olive surprised me by saying, "Cecil, if you should leave here I would be sad." That was as generous as Olive had ever been with a compliment to me. I said, "Thank you, Olive; that's kind of you." Then she added, "If Dot left, I think I should die." Olive's remark pointed to the quiet, steady presence of Dot in everything we did. She didn't call attention to herself, yet she blessed everyone she encountered.

4. Dot was thirty-five years old when we married. She knew what it was like to be single in a church designed for married adults. Her first volunteer assignment at the church was teaching a group of young married women. The class flourished, but with the passing of time it came clear to Dot that our church had no Sunday school for single adults. She talked with the minister of education, and they set a date and a place. The class would meet in the church kitchen; there was no other location. A few singles gathered in the kitchen; Dot tried to teach them, but the place was not right. Dot thought about her options and decided to invite the singles to our home for class. It was about a mile from the church; the living room was large, and compared to the church kitchen our living room looked regal.

For nine years single adults gathered at our house each Sunday morning. It became a routine: Each Saturday Genie vacuumed the living and dining rooms. Preparations were made for coffee and pastries. Orange juice was always available. The trickle of singles became forty, sometimes fifty. One class enlarged to three, and singles became a presence in the life of the church. Dot had good people to help her. She was a pastor to those people, and they pastored each other. When someone lost a job, all pitched in and helped. With the passing years, weddings resulted from that group. The church turned to them for leadership. Dot's quiet presence blessed again.

5. Large churches have several pastors; no one can do everything for two thousand people. In Asheville, for the first time in my life, I was the administrator of more than two or three people. Alden Angline was the religious educator; he had been on the job fourteen years when I arrived. Alden was a native of Asheville and had grown up in the church. His experience gave me a window into the mind of the congregation. Charles Crocker was minister of music. He was a South Carolina native, possessed of unusual talent, and could sing as well as direct. For seventeen years we worked together, and our church had the best music in town. I did not go to the hospitals every day, but Gordon Hux did. Gordon was a veteran of twenty-five years in the army. He retired from the army, got some education for ministry, and began serving on our staff. He was the minister who was with the sick every day. Often Gordon would come in my office to tell me one of

our members was dangerously ill. Immediately the two of us went to the hospital. Children were well served by Becky Pace. When Becky retired, Billie Placey stepped into her role. Always children were a high priority at First Asheville. Two secretaries truly invested themselves in the job. Henrietta Emerson Walker and Betty Rusk smoothed my way.

When I took the Asheville job, I was young and inexperienced at the work of administration. I wanted staff to like me more than I wanted to supervise them; therefore, I gave them little direction. The effect of my withholding supervision was fragmentation. Each staff member went his or her own way. There was little coordination of the parts. Much good work was done, but there was no overall purpose or direction. That was my fault. I did not know how to coordinate the parts. I had a low opinion of administration and was reluctant to be an administrator.

I began to function as the administrator of the church when I decided to take on the issue of church growth. I did not do it gracefully at first, but in a fumbling way, I began to give direction to all the departments of the church. Staff began to work together toward agreed-upon goals. Numerical measurement was used to evaluate our work. I set goals for myself; I set goals for staff. The result was surprising. It did not sour my relationship with most of the staff. They seemed to appreciate knowing what they were expected to do. The church began to grow. More people came to church. More ministry was getting done. Laypeople noticed and were pleased. We had a sense of purpose, and we had the pleasure of seeing goals met. Becoming the administrator was part of my growing into the job of being a pastor. In some ways I was a slow learner.

6. Raising money tests a preacher. When I came to Asheville, I had little experience raising money and preferred to avoid the subject. I had enough trouble with the race issue. Why irritate people further by asking for money? So I handled money lightly. The effect of my easy approach was a struggling budget and needs that went unmet.

In February 1971, the finance committee met and heard a final tally on pledges for the 1971 budget; we had pledged 80 percent of the budget . . . nothing to get excited about. A judge said, "Why bother with pledging? It irritates some of our members. I wouldn't give a penny less if there were no pledge campaign. Let's quit doing it." Others on the committee spoke in support of the judge's opinion. It looked like the committee was about to take a vote to discontinue pledging as a means to fund the church.

Bill Shackelton was a member of the committee, a skilled accountant and an employee of the Internal Revenue Service. As the judge's idea gathered steam, Bill became concerned. He stepped into the conversation and said, "Don't you think we ought to examine how much pledging means to the finances of our church before you discontinue the practice?" Bill's question made such good sense that the committee decided to take a serious look at pledging. A committee of four was formed. They were to study the previous year's gifts and how much of those gifts came from pledged money. Naturally, Bill became chair of the special study group.

Four men met regularly from February until August. They studied the pledges for the year 1970. Then they studied the gifts that came in during 1970. How much of the money collected came from people who had pledged? One warm August day, Bill called. His committee's report was complete; they wanted to review it with me before they took it to the finance committee.

All four men met with me; their report was a ledger book of their own making. Actually, the study committee learned more about our church than they did about pledging. For years, records of giving had been super-secret. Only the finance secretary knew who gave what, and she was committed to silence. A member could hold high office, but no check was made of his or her giving. The study revealed that 88 percent of all gifts to the church came from people who pledged. It made no sense to abandon a system that was so essential to the financial health of the church. As Bill prepared to leave my house that August night, he said, "Cecil, you need to look at that ledger book." I replied, "Bill, I don't want to; if I do it will mess up my mind." Bill said, "What would you think of a doctor who prescribed medicine for his patients but refused to examine them?" He walked into the darkness, and I was left with his question . . . and the ledger book.

The ledger book sat on our coffee table for eleven days. Then on a Tuesday morning I sat down and began to turn through the book a page at a time. More than a third of our members gave nothing to the church in 1971; five serving deacons gave nothing. Some adult Sunday school teachers gave nothing. People who chaired committees gave so little it was embarrassing. Our church struggled with money, and there was a reason. The pastor had not provided leadership. I was the problem; the money was there.

The next Sunday I put the ledger book on the altar table just below the pulpit. I began my sermon by saying, "Most Sundays I speak to you from this book [I held up my Bible]. This Sunday I'm going to speak to you from *this* book [I pointed to the ledger book]." I gave the background, listed the results of the study, and proceeded to name some steps that could help our church. A real change took place in me. I never backed off asking for money again. From 1971, most years First Asheville pledged 100 percent of her budget. When I gave leadership, the church responded. First Asheville didn't have many people of means, but the church had plenty of generous people.

7. The hardest task at Asheville was enlarging the membership. First Asheville was not an evangelistic church by Baptist standards. The worship pattern was mildly liturgical, more formal than most Baptist churches. We worked at good music; I studied to prepare thoughtful sermons; but for all our efforts, membership declined. After I had been at Asheville ten years (from 1964 until 1974), the attendance on a Sunday morning had declined about 200 (from 900 to 700). The older generation was dying off; new people were not being added. I could not blame our condition on my predecessor or circumstance. After ten years the pastor is responsible, and I was the pastor. Something had to be done.

With the help of staff, I began a concentrated effort to enlist young couples. The staff made exploratory visits. They came back and reported on their visits and made suggestions to me about further contacts. I set up appointments with the best prospects with a point of view to their joining our church. The results were slow but gratifying. In 1976, for the first time in years, average Sunday school attendance went up. By experience, I learned that what attracts young couples to church is not my preaching; it is the quality of children's programs. Alongside my visitation was a drive for excellence in our ministry to children. In 1980, Sunday school attendance went up by fifty-nine for that year alone. Young adults were coming back to church. Children were all over the place; it was a great problem. My best service to First Asheville was the gathering of a next generation of lay leadership.

8. Because First Asheville had had such unpleasant experience with debt, the church was unwilling to attempt more than one project at a time. We built a children's building in 1969–1970; we paid it off in 1976. We built parking lots and landscaped them in 1977–1978; we paid for them as we went. Always there was the intention to build a gymnasium with multiple athletic facilities. Not all members were excited about the project. One good deacon said, "I'm not ready to build a million-dollar playroom." But most were. In spring 1978, we brought in a fundraising consultant; this was a first for our church. Our goal was to pledge at least $800,000 above budget over three years.

I still remember an early visit of that consultant. He called ahead and said he wanted to meet with Dot and me for lunch. We met him at the Asheville airport on a snowy day. At lunch he was direct to the point of being blunt. He said, "If the two of you make a sacrificial pledge, there is nothing I can do to make this pledge campaign fail. If the two of you try to 'low-ball' this pledge, there is nothing I can do to make it succeed." He insisted that the two of us had to stand in front of the church and make our pledge public on a Sunday morning. It was a bit like being asked to take off your financial clothes in public . . . very uncomfortable. We intended to make a generous gift for our means; we had not intended to tell God and everybody about it.

On a Sunday morning in 1978, Dot and I did as the consultant insisted. We stood and "witnessed" our pledge. It was not a lot of money ($7,200 over the three years), but the effect of our statement was amazing. Several people said, "We are going to have to reconsider our gift. If you and Dot are going to give that much, we will have to do more." And they did. We pledged $810,000 over three years . . . over and above our budget. The campaign was a success, and we built the building.

I know some people don't have a high opinion of building buildings for a church. They want the money directed to other good causes. But there is a kind of money that can be raised for a tangible, visible church building that cannot be raised for any other good cause. Two good things came from the 1978 capital campaign:

- New ministries were offered. Bobby Butler became minister of activities. He supervised athletic activities like aerobics, volleyball, basketball, etc. I called Bobby "the resident Christian on the church staff." Every staff needs at least one. It was one more way our church could serve and become attractive to some people.
- The Capital Campaign involved a new generation of leadership. Thirty-year-olds took responsibility for the campaign. They gave serious money. Every generation needs to "buy the church." When they get involved, they become members of the church. Jesus had it right; "Where your treasure is, there your heart will be also" (Matt 6:21 NRSV). Asking people for money is religious work of the highest order.

## PART 4: DENOMINATIONAL SERVICE

From birth I was involved with the Southern Baptist Convention. There were preachers on both sides of my family. I was reared in a church that took the denomination seriously; Southwestern seminary professors preached in my home church regularly. I was a member of the Royal Ambassadors (called R.A.'s), a boys' mission education group sponsored by the Woman's Missionary Union. That program taught me the location of the mission boards, about mission offerings, about missionaries. All was part of the Southern Baptist Convention.

During seminary days, my education was subsidized by the Convention. Tuition was $25.00 per semester when I was a student at Southwestern Baptist Theological Seminary. The real cost was much more; every theology student of my generation was helped by the gift. I had run out of the GI Bill getting through Baylor. The Convention gave me a theological education. Quietly, the convention created a sense of obligation in my generation. They had given me something of value; I wanted to give something back.

My first churches were small, sometimes struggling financially. They were not in a position to give much to the SBC. First Baptist Asheville was different. They had the means, and they had the tradition. Dr. Perry Crouch had "denominationalized" First Asheville. When I arrived in 1964, 20 percent of the budget went to the Cooperative Program (the umbrella funding system of the SBC). In fact, giving to the denomination was just about the only form of missions the church knew.

The pastor of First Asheville was given a place in North Carolina Baptist life by virtue of his office. I inherited that. Slowly invitations came. I was put on committees of the North Carolina Baptist Convention. I was asked to preach the convention sermon. Pastors opened their pulpits to me, and over a period of time I was accepted into North Carolina Baptist life. In 1979, Nane Starnes, an Asheville pastor, put my name forward to be president of the NCBC and I was elected. For two turbulent years (1979–1981), I presided over North Carolina Baptist life. During that time, Wake Forest University broke free of the North Carolina Baptist Convention; this was divisive. Wake's roots were deep in North Carolina Baptist life. Some Baptists were glad to see her go; others were grieved at the separation. It was in June 1979 that political Fundamentalism emerged as a controlling presence in the Southern Baptist Convention. This pleased some Baptists in North Carolina, and others were at first confused and then dismayed. I served North Carolina Baptists in a troubled time.

In spite of the conflicts, there were good times. Cecil Ray was the CEO of the North Carolina convention. He was a man of exceptional good sense. Always he was under control; always he knew the subject at hand. Always he was trying to pull people together and toward a mission that would honor Christ. Dewey Hobbs (pastor of the First Baptist Church of Marion, North Carolina) was chair of the Executive Committee of the NCBC. The three of us met often. My appreciation for the two men grew with each meeting. I never saw them as devious or careless. I never saw them afraid to tackle a difficult subject. Experience with the North Carolina Baptist Convention did not sour me on denomination; it made me more enthusiastic about it.

Officially I had a small part in the Southern Baptist Convention. After the race issue upon my arrival to Asheville, I was identified as one who had a sense of social justice. I was appointed as the North Carolina representative to the Christian Life Commission of the SBC. That appointment came in 1968, and I served two terms. During the second term I chaired the CLC. Since the SBC is a conservative people, it is not surprising that parts of the Christian Life Commission's agenda offended some in the SBC. In 1968, race bothered people in Mississippi and Alabama. They did not want to be lectured on the subject. The CLC prodded the Convention toward an open policy regarding blacks. As the SBC tilted to the right on national issues, the CLC became more of an irritant. Actually, the CLC was not very liberal, but compared to the rank and file in the SBC, we were on the left side of a conservative company. In the larger body politic, most of us who set the agenda for the Christian Life Commission would not be counted liberal at all. The label you wear depends on the company you keep.

The SBC has a conference center at Ridgecrest, just seventeen miles from First Asheville. Sometimes I was invited to have a part on the programs of those conferences. In little ways and over an extended period of time, I was invited to speak and teach. Trust was extended and friendships were formed. Those associations would be useful to me when I tried to influence the direction of the SBC in years of controversy. Voluntary work for the SBC was not my job. I was pastor of the First Baptist Church of Asheville, but taking part in the denomination was an outlet. First Asheville was generous with me. They allowed me to do denominational work; I hope I did not take advantage of their kindness. I am not cynical about denomination. Before Fundamentalists possessed her and excluded everyone who would not sign on to their agenda, the SBC did a lot of good. And along the way I made many friends.

# PART 5: A PRIVATE LIFE

Serving a large church in the South is a public job. Life is lived in a fish bowl. Most of the time, my family and I did not find this oppressive.

We were housed in a large, two-story parsonage; we had to furnish it. With the help of a friend, Dot assembled pictures, furniture, and bric-a-brac. An attractive house was not a vanity; often church business was done in our home.

Genie was six when we moved to Asheville. It was time for her to go to school. Claxton School was a half-mile from our house. Her first teacher was Katherine Burgess; Genie was a fortunate girl. Miss Burgess introduced Genie to group learning (actually it was at Dot's knee that her education began). Dot presided over the homeroom mothers. School was all at once fun and serious business, and Genie did well. She rode her bicycle to Claxton for several years, and when I was out calling for the church I made it a point to show up on her route home at the time when she was coming out of school. Those happy "accidents" were good times. By the time Genie was in middle and high school, I was the appointed driver. Her friends would gather at our house, pile in the car, and we were off to school.

Genie's friends were frequently at our home. When snowstorms shut down schools in January 1966, neighborhood kids gathered at the Sherman residence. Dot became the director, and the kids became actors. *The Sound of Music* was the rage, so during the more than three weeks that the kids were out of school, they learned the lines and memorized the songs. The neighborhood production of *The Sound of Music* required everyone's attendance. For that play, the girls had their hair cut to look like Julie Andrews . . . that was a first for Genie.

Dot seemed to know that we were in Asheville to stay. She put flowers on the breakfast table. Meals were not thrown together; the food was good and presentation was important to her. We usually ate breakfast together, and when Genie was small we took the evening meal together too.

Dot loved cats, and somewhere, somehow, Elsa the cat came into our lives. Elsa was with us nineteen of the twenty years we lived in Asheville. Genie read propped in bed with Elsa at her feet. She studied, and Elsa was within reach. Not surprisingly, Genie has chosen to live her adult life with the companionship of cats.

The rhythm of the church and school year influenced the way we lived at home. At Christmas we decorated the house, put up a tree, and invited the staff to dinner. That was a major production for between forty and fifty people (spouses swelled the number). I remember how Dot worked on that party. I remember how late both of us stayed up cleaning the house afterward. Nostalgia makes the memory good, but at the time we were pretty worn out. Christmas was heavy duty at church; all sorts of parties required our presence. When the Christmas Eve service ended, Christmas duty was over. We took the next week off.

The best rest and relaxation came in the summer. Weeks at Peaks of Otter on the Blue Ridge Parkway were a favorite. The food was good, the scenery displayed the Appalachians at their best, and there was plenty to do. Park rangers challenged and educated us, and long winding trails up Sharp Top Mountain tested our stamina. Other years we went to Glorieta, New Mexico, for Baptist conferences. I had speaking assignments, but that did not crowd family time. Always we made time for a trip to Santa Fe and some Mexican food. Dot shopped. Genie and I strolled the streets and enjoyed another culture.

The longer we were in Asheville, the more demanding the job became. No one at the church willed it so; it was the nature of the job. The more people knew us, the more they came forward with their real problems. Dot and I had become their pastors. That was good, but it had at least one bad side effect; Dot and I saw less and less of each other. I was home less at night. As the health of the church improved, Dot and I had to make sure the health of our marriage didn't deteriorate. We devised a plan: we took Genie to school, and then we went out to breakfast. We tried to find good food and a quiet place, and then we simply enjoyed each other's company. She said what mattered to her in the moment; I spoke my thoughts. We had a date, and we did it two or three times a week. I had no pain of conscience going in at 10:15 in the morning after being at a church meeting until 9:30 the previous night. And Dot and I stayed in touch with each other. I found a way to use this idea in my preaching. So many young professionals were facing the same problem; their careers were taking off at some risk to their marriages. When I spoke of the problem from the pulpit, it was obvious that I addressed a subject others were wrestling with too. If Dot and I could find a way to make time for each other, they could also find a way.

In summertime, Dot set up a card table out in the backyard under an apple tree. There she served vegetable lunches; best of all was her cornbread. A little honey on cornbread will make the idea of dessert go away.

And in this wonder world, when both of us had health, when Genie was still at home, when church was going strong, the years slipped away. Dot had illnesses, but each was treatable. Genie moved through public schools. She skipped her senior year in high school and went straight into Baylor University. It was the right move for her. Dot said, "I thought I had one more year to be the perfect mother, and now that chance is taken from me." When Genie left home, I had my first brush with grief. It was time for us to let her go, but it hurt. In 1979, we had been in Asheville fifteen years. We bought the parsonage; Asheville had become home. A set of friends had gathered; it seemed we would be there until we retired.

Looking back, I am amazed at our good fortune. In retrospect, I see the hand of Providence leading us "beside still waters." It was not what we deserved; it was a good life from the hand of a gracious God. We were in Asheville for twenty years and five months . . . half of my professional life.

Chapter 7

# A New Start in a Familiar Place

When Dot and I completed twenty years in Asheville, the church gave us a wonderful gift: six weeks in England with all expenses paid. It was a dream come true for us; we had spent most of our lives tied to our work. We rented a "flat" (a student apartment) at Regent's Park College in Oxford. We bought a rail pass that allowed us to ride anywhere in England, Scotland, and Wales. We were in and out of London several times. We visited Princeton friends at Paisley, Scotland, and took in the August Edinburgh Festival. Barrie White, principal of Regent's Park College, hosted us several times. It was a "once-in-a-lifetime" vacation, and it was all a gift from the Asheville people.

We returned to Asheville on a Tuesday. On Thursday I received a telephone call from Roland Johnson, chair of the search committee at Broadway Baptist Church in Fort Worth, Texas. He asked if four members of the committee could come to Asheville for a visit with Dot and me. Their committee had decided Dot and I were their choice. We didn't even know they were considering us. Later we learned that the search committee had visited First Asheville, listened to some of my sermons, and inquired about my work. There were nine people on the search committee. I knew but one, Dr. Franklin Segler; he taught my Pastoral Ministries class at Southwestern Baptist Theological Seminary during the time I was a student. I recognized him in the audience at First Asheville on a July Sunday; the thought that he represented a search committee never entered my mind.

I did not give an immediate reply to Roland Johnson's request for a visit. I remember the strange feeling I had as I got out of the car and walked into the house for lunch that Thursday. Was this the beginning of the end for Dot and me in Asheville? When I told Dot of the Broadway committee's request, she was as surprised as I was. We had bought the parsonage; we planned to stay in Asheville until we retired. We had made long-term friendships. I was fifty-six years old, and Baptist pastors rarely move at that age.

But the invitation from Fort Worth did not fall on deaf ears. Several little things in my work at First Asheville hinted at something I didn't want to acknowledge. I had preached Easter sermons twenty times. I had asked people to pledge the budget twenty times. I had gone through the Christmas story twenty times. I had buried several hundred people. There was no real opposition to my ministry; the church was quietly, steadily growing. But there was a nagging feeling that even my friends would like to hear the gospel stories from a different voice. Years later Chevis Horne, pastor at First Baptist Church Martinsville, Virginia, for thirty-five years, said, "After twenty years in Martinsville, I never quite seemed to please them." I understood what Chevis was saying. I was at the edge of that time in Asheville. This restless feeling influenced my answer to Roland Johnson. After Dot and I talked, we agreed that we would open a conversation with the people from Broadway.

Four of them came. They were given the assignment of persuading Dot and me to consider a call to Broadway. Dr. Franklin Segler, the retired professor from Southwestern Seminary, was one of them. They came on a Thursday and stayed until Sunday afternoon. By the time they arrived, Dot and I had become curious—and a little bit excited. They came to our home in mid-afternoon. We had just returned from England, and Dot had gotten a recipe for scones. She baked some, put out orange marmalade and butter, and all ate more than they intended. After the scones, they knew they wanted her, and I could come along as baggage!

At one point in the conversation, the Broadway people asked, "Do you have questions?" Immediately Dot spoke up. "Do you know how old we are?" That evoked a laugh; they did know I was fifty-six and

Dot was sixty-six, and they wanted us to come anyway. One piece in that long conversation was the difference. Dr. Segler said, "Cecil, we want you to come to Broadway and do what you've done here in Asheville." I replied, "Dr. Segler, it has taken twenty years to do what we've done in Asheville; I'm fifty-six and I don't have twenty years left." He said, "You're older and smarter; you can work faster. Our church needs you; the Asheville church is in good shape."

That part of the conversation went round and round in my mind. "You're older and smarter; you can work faster. Our church needs you . . . ." I could not get Dr. Segler's words out of my mind. Most of Friday and Saturday we entertained them, talked with them, and pondered what a move at this stage of our lives would mean. We did not give them an answer, but their visit had quickened our interest. We visited Fort Worth. Both of us earnestly tried to discern God's leadership, and after much soul-searching we told the committee we would accept their invitation if the Broadway congregation called. On the third Sunday in November 1984, Broadway Baptist Church extended a call to Dot and me. We were on our way to Fort Worth.

That Sunday night I told the Asheville congregation. It was hard. Our love for those people was real. We had put down roots, reared our child in their company, wrestled with substantial problems, buried dear friends, married kids we helped to rear. It seemed strange, but it was time to go. I believe Dot and I did what we were called to do at Asheville. In 1964, that church needed to gather a new generation of young adults. It took me ten years longer than I expected, but the job was done.

For six weeks we said "goodbye" in Asheville. There was pain in parting, but we were on our way to a church that needed us. I was going back to the town where I was reared, and still in Fort Worth were John and Annie Mae Sherman, my parents. They had never left the area. Dad was eighty-four; Mother was seventy-nine. Both were able to live independently. We did not return to Fort Worth to be near my parents, but it was nice to be close to them. They were slowing down.

Duty began at Broadway on January 2, 1985. Broadway had a sparkling past; there had been a time when she was the leading Baptist church in the city. Years and the shifting tides of the neighborhood reduced her. A magnificent sanctuary was built in 1950. Stained-glass windows were installed that would have been the envy of a European cathedral. A lovely chapel was also part of the 1950 building. The rest of the property was merely sufficient. Slowly a favored neighborhood declined. After World War II, the Presbyterian church that was nearby relocated. Lovely homes were cut up into apartment buildings and then torn down. Drifters wandered back and forth across the property. A block away were seedy bars. It was not safe to be around the church after dark. Attendance declined from an average of 1,300 in Sunday school in the 1950s to 700 in 1985. The membership became gray. Young adults were few; seniors were the backbone of the church. On a Wednesday night soon after I arrived, I was making the point that we had to gather young adults. I asked, "How many of you can expect to have an active part in the life of Broadway in twenty years?" Of 200 present, about 20 raised their hands.

From the profile I've just given, one could conclude that I thought little of the stewardship of my predecessors. The church had declined; therefore my predecessors were to blame, but that is not true. Some extraordinarily good preachers came before me at Broadway. The neighborhood went away, and businesses moved away. Safety was compromised. What was a fashionable part of Fort Worth in 1900 had become a slum by 1970. It was not a matter of blame; the question was, "Can a church live in this place?"

We had two things going for us:

1. We had an older membership who had some money. To get that money, I had to convince them there was a future for the church.
2. We had some dedicated people. They loved Broadway and wanted her to live. If I could come up with a plan that made sense, they were willing to support me.

There were two things I had to do:

1. I had to convince the membership that the church had a future. When asked to give to a capital campaign to improve properties, one dear lady said, "I'm not going to give anymore until I see a prospect for Broadway." She was not willing to invest in what appeared to her a dying cause.

2. I had to strengthen the staff. As the church declined in membership, the staff had become more and more a collection of part-time
workers. Several of the most capable people we had were faculty
from Southwestern Seminary. Their full-time job was at the seminary; their weekend job was at Broadway. It's hard to do serious
church with staff who give fragments of their time and energy.

Two part-time people were offered full-time jobs; both declined.
They wanted to continue to be teachers. When they declined the invitation to come full-time at Broadway, I was free to pursue people who
would be full-time. Slowly, as the finances of the church would allow,
we added staff. Tom Stoker in music, Al Travis at the organ, Terry
Hamrick doing adult religious education, Jan Hill with children,
Karen Gilbert leading our ministry to the poor, and Bob Hammond
(another I inherited) presiding over activities; they were a great team.
We learned to live with each other, help each other, and do church.

Sometimes doing church work is not especially exciting. It's work.
True, it is the Lord's work, but it's still work. Day in and day out you
try to make little things better. You try to replace a careless Sunday
school teacher with a careful one. You try to stock committees with
intelligent, dedicated people. You try to lift the sights of discouraged
people by giving them a vision of what we could do if only we were
committed enough to do it.

Slowly the culture of the church shifted. Old staff members either
stepped aside or "got on board." I was blessed with chairs of deacons
who were exceptional people. Each was gifted. Each wanted the good
for Broadway. Each was willing to give time to imagine what our
church could be. Twice at Asheville I had allowed myself to get in an
adversarial relationship with the chair of deacons; it was as much my
fault as theirs. At Broadway I resolved not to let that happen. I developed the pattern of going to lunch once each week with the chair of
deacons. I told the chair everything I was thinking. Those chairs gave
sound advice, offered real encouragement, and smoothed my way.

On the Friday after Thanksgiving 1985, after I had been at
Broadway eleven months, I invited three church leaders to lunch: the
chair and vice chair of deacons and the chair of finance. I proposed a
broad plan to improve the properties. The church was more than 100

years old, and there was not one parking space off the street. We had the property; we simply needed to improve it. An educational building built in the 1920s had been condemned by the Fort Worth Fire Department. The third and fourth floors were declared unsafe; we were forbidden to use them. I proposed we either completely remodel the building or tear it down and replace it with a new one. Children's space had to be renovated. And if there were enough money, we would replace the organ; the old one was falling apart.

The leaders listened to what I had to say. The chair of deacons said it was in his power to create a study group. He did, and for three months fourteen people looked at our properties with a view to their improvement. Out of that study group came a proposal. In March 1986, the deacons heard the proposal. It was tabled. Argument was made that this was not the right time for a capital campaign; the Fort Worth-Dallas area was in a financial mess. Oil and gas, cattle and banking were in depression. In April and May, the proposal was tabled again. When motion was made to table the proposal in June, I asked for an exception to Robert's Rules of Order. A motion to table is not debatable; an exception was granted. I spoke with feeling. I had come to Broadway to do what Dr. Segler asked me to do: gather a new generation of young adults to the church. I could not do my assignment with the properties I was given. It was in the power of the membership to improve those properties *if* they were willing to tax themselves for the future of the church.

At the end of my speech to the deacons, no vote was taken. It was agreed that there would be a Saturday meeting of all deacons, those serving and those who had served in the past. In July, that meeting came to pass. It began at 8:30 in the morning and did not conclude until after 2:00 in the afternoon. By a vote of 70-30, the proposal to improve the properties passed. That was far from unanimous.

Broadway was and is a church that puts high store on fellowship. Protecting the fellowship was the duty of the pastor. By pressing a controversial capital improvement, I was threatening congregational unity. The wife of a seminary professor said, "Cecil, you have divided our church," and she was right. But I had no "feel-good" options. If I did nothing, the church would continue to decline. If I pressed improvements, I divided the house. Two previous "studies" had been proposed to Broadway. In the 1960s and again in the 1970s, proposals had been offered to the membership. Fellowship trumped progress in each. Since they could not get unanimity, they did nothing. I was not willing to do nothing, and I was willing to risk the ire of some of the membership to give the church a future. The capital improvements proposal was the most important decision made during my seven years at Broadway.

When I was younger, I doubt I would have pushed as I did at Broadway, but in Asheville I had learned that capital improvements often do more than build buildings; they build godly people. It had been thirty years since Broadway had asked her membership to sacrifice for the sake of the church. A generation had grown up who had never "bought into the church." When the issue came before the congregation, Bob Cargill recognized the divided state of the house and argued this way: "I know some of you are not willing to give to this campaign, but I ask you not to vote against it. I'm not asking you to give. I'm asking you to allow me to give." And so the campaign inched forward.

A few people gave nothing; others made token gifts. But enough stepped up to get us started. We pledged $3,400,000. The new organ had to be postponed until a later date, but all the rest of the improvements came to pass. By 1990, the church had some of the best facilities in town. We had the property. We had the personnel. It was not long before we had the programs that allowed a church to do what a church is supposed to do.

My part in making Broadway grow was simple but not easy. My job was "closing the sale." Most people will not join a church until they have a "sit-down visit" with the pastor. Since that is true, I decided it was my assignment to be the primary salesman for Broadway. I know some take offense when I call myself a "salesman." I'm supposed to use religious language. But my thinking about evangelism has changed over the years. I don't know when people become Christians. Maybe they are converted when they walk down the aisle, but it seemed to me a lot of people walked down the aisle, went through the formalities of joining the church, and then at a later time had a life-reordering experience that brought them nearer to God and congregation. When those mystical, wonderful moments happen is not in my control. That is God's doing, and I can't schedule God. So, I worked as a salesman and left the rest to God. To do this good work I had to organize myself.

1. I set a goal of inviting one Fort Worth couple a week to join our church. I did not ask laity or staff to do this work. It was mine. I wanted to be the one to describe our church to a prospect, and I wanted to be the one to say what we expected of new members.
2. I became systematic in gathering the names of visitors. Once a year I registered everyone in the congregation for four Sundays. I did this because only one in four visitors will sign a guest register. The best prospect is one who has already visited my church. Jan Hill, minister to children, was a source for visitors. When couples checked their baby into the nursery, they gave their name and address.
3. Each week my secretary typed out a list of visitors. I called those visitors, got acquainted, and tried to schedule an appointment for a visit. Sometimes I took them to lunch; other times we met in my office on Sunday morning during Sunday school. Not everyone who consented to an appointment joined Broadway; about half of my conversations resulted in new members. The work never stopped.
4. When visitors would not schedule an appointment, I dated my call, and in six weeks I called again. Persistence and gentle persuasion often got results. I never gave up on a prospect.

Slowly results came of my work. In 1986, sixteen new couples joined Broadway; I had not met my goal of one couple a week. By 1991, thirty-one new couples came into the church. What I had learned in Asheville was adapted to Broadway. I don't think "the system" I've described is simply an accident of my personality; it is a formula that will work for any pastor in any place. Broadway was in a tough location; if that church can grow, any church can grow.

We did not change our worship from traditional to contemporary. In fact, Broadway is as liturgical as any traditional Baptist church. What we did was basic church work. We did children's work well. We did youth work well. We did music well. We did activities well. We did ministry well (Broadway had a full-time minister to homeless people, Karen Gilbert). And I tried to preach sermons that were faithful to Scripture each Sunday. Intensity of focus and excellence in ministry made Broadway go. There were no shortcuts. It was daily . . . it was work . . . it required consistent effort.

I gave away my golf clubs when I moved to Fort Worth. The church consumed me. It took me a while to establish credibility, but it came faster than it did in Asheville. I don't know whether trust came faster at Broadway because I was older or because of the difference in nature between western North Carolina and Texas. Whatever the reason, I was allowed to give leadership at Broadway much faster than at Asheville. There was a satisfaction in the work at Broadway that exceeded anything I had ever done. Work was fun. Seeing the church thrive fueled us. Our progress invited more progress. The staff learned to enjoy each other; we became friends. We all knew we were a part of something that was sacred and exciting.

Seven years passed too quickly. Dot did her quiet magic. She had a gift for putting people at ease. Mother and Dad grew old, became infirm, and slipped away. Dad's doctor said he had dementia. He never lost touch with his family; always he could call us by name. But the gregarious, fun-loving, hard-working man he had always been slowly bent to age. Dad grew old and slow, and God took him gently. He died of a stroke in November 1988. With Mother it was different. She had asthma as a child, and it went away. But when she carried her children, it returned seasonally. Occasional asthma became chronic. Chronic asthma developed into emphysema. Though she had never smoked, she slowly lost the ability to process oxygen from the air she breathed.

My sister and Dot found a nursing home for her. As she checked into the nursing home, Mother said, "I don't like this; I'm going to make the best of it." She was there for a year and a half. She grew frail. On Thanksgiving 1991, we took her out to eat. We spoke of getting together on Christmas. Mother said, "If I continue the way I'm going now, I won't be here Christmas day." She died on Christmas day. My sister and I were by her side. My brother was in Nashville and stayed in touch. I'm glad I was near. They needed me, and I needed them. Broadway people were magnificent during those days. Roles were reversed; they pastored me. If we have length of life, all of us become orphans, but there is no way to give up your Mother and Daddy without pain.

When we buried Mother, I didn't know it, but my time at Broadway was nearing an end. In November and December 1991, the search committee of the Coordinating Council of the fledgling Cooperative Baptist Fellowship (CBF) was seeking a full-time coordinator. CBF was young, new, and fragile. I had had a part in Moderate politics in the SBC travail. The CBF search committee was chaired by my friend, Jim Slatton, of Richmond, Virginia. The question was put to Dot and me: Would we leave Broadway and help CBF grow into a haven and later a home for Moderate Baptist churches in the South? The decision was difficult. My work at Broadway was thriving but not finished. Leaving would be an interruption of a ministry in progress. I was sixty-four years old; that is not the time for taking on "start-up" assignments.

On the other hand, I was suited to the job. I had grown up in Texas, and most of my education had been in Texas. I had done most of my ministry in Georgia and North Carolina. I had connections on "both sides of the river." My part in creating a Moderate political network had given me a set of friends who would be useful in the growth of the CBF. I had heart for CBF because convictional Moderates had no place to stand in the SBC; we had been put out. There had to be another way for those of our mindset to gather and do missions. The story of the growth of CBF will be told in a later chapter; the question for us was more personal. Would and should Dot and I leave Broadway and move to Atlanta to head CBF?

The disparity between Broadway and CBF was glaring. Here are some of the thoughts that were going through my mind as Dot and I wrestled with our decision:

- If I went to CBF, I would no longer be a pastor. I had played the pastor's part for so long until I had become one. It was my life, and I loved it. I didn't want to leave my church.
- My vision for Broadway had not been fully realized. We had made real progress, but we had a ways to go. We had been fully staffed for only two years. Average Sunday school attendance was up to 922 the last quarter I was at Broadway. I wanted us to go further. Deacons had approached me about continuing as pastor beyond my sixty-fifth birthday. That was flattering, and I planned to do it.
- CBF had an income of $700,000 in 1991. Broadway had a budget of $1,900,000. Broadway was strong and getting stronger. CBF was an infant organization; it might or might not "make it." Would I, could I persuade enough churches to shift their monies from SBC to CBF? If I went to CBF, it would be a leap of faith. I liked to talk about faith in the pulpit; living by faith was a different matter.
- There would be a contentious element in the CBF job. I had to "take on" the colossus that is the SBC. The SBC was led by people who saw CBF as the enemy and felt that we were trying to take churches from them. And that was true. If CBF were to grow, it had to grow at the expense of the SBC. I had struggled with Fundamentalism; I did not look forward to that part of the job.

Dot and I talked and prayed, prayed and talked. What to do? I sought the counsel of three friends. I talked with my brother, Bill; I knew he cared about me and wanted the good for me. I talked to Tom Graves, who had recently become president of the new Baptist Theological Seminary at Richmond. He knew what it was like to stop being the pastor of a strong Baptist church and trust yourself to a new institution. When I told Tom the reason for my call, his response was, "So they've asked you to jump off that cliff too." And then on a Saturday morning in January 1992, I traveled to Hillsboro, Texas, and met Herbert Reynolds, president of Baylor University. I had watched him work and listened to him speak. He had unusual good sense, and I wanted his thoughts. None of the three told me what to do; all three graciously gave their best thoughts.

Near the end of January, I called Jim Slatton and told him we would accept the CBF invitation, effective April 1. Dot was in complete agreement on the CBF decision. It meant a move to Atlanta and a new life. I wept when I left Broadway. I was going into the unknown, and I was ending my life as a pastor. I came to the conclusion that I was doing the right thing, but I was leaving a life I knew and loved. Going to CBF was a step into the dark.

Cecil as a baby, c. 1928

Cecil (at about age 8), Bill, and Ruth, 1935

Cecil (at about age 8), Ruth, and Bill with their father, 1935

Dot in high school (Spartanburg, South Carolina), 1935

Dot when she was a student at Winthrop College
in Rock Hill, South Carolina, 1938

Dot with her long-time friend Josephine Pile Broaddus,
dressed for church in Nashville, Tennessee, 1944

Cecil, high school graduation picture, 1945

John and Annie Mae Sherman, Cecil's parents, c. 1950

Cecil and Dot leaving on their wedding trip,
Greer, South Carolina, December 1953

Wedding picture, with Dot's sister, Helen (matron of honor),
and Cecil's brother, Bill (best man), 1953

Dot and Cecil on their wedding day, Greer,
South Carolina, December 23, 1953

Dot and Cecil on the quad at Princeton Seminary, 1954

Dot and Cecil at Cecil's graduation from Princeton Seminary, 1956

Cecil, Dot, and Genie at First Baptist Church, Chamblee, Georgia, 1960

John Newport at Cecil's Th.D graduation at Southwestern Seminary, 1960

Cecil on a Sunday afternoon, College Station, Texas, 1961

Cecil and Genie, Dallas, Texas, on a snow day, 1963

Dot, Cecil, and Genie in Asheville, North Carolina, at about the time they began their ministry there, 1964

Genie and Dot on the boardwalk in Atlantic City, New Jersey,
site of SBC Convention, 1964

Cecil and Dot in the backyard of the parsonage,
Asheville, North Carolina, 1965

Cecil reading from the New Testament at a sacred site in Jerusalem,
with Glenn Wilcox, the travel agent who sponsored the trip, 1973

Cecil, Dorothy, Genie, a Christmas card, c. 1976

Cecil, c. 1979

Cecil and his father, John F. Sherman, Asheville, North Carolina, c. 1980

Dorothy and Cecil in the backyard of their home,
Asheville, North Carolina, c. 1982

Dr. Douglas Brown, our daughter's husband, and Eugenia, 1985

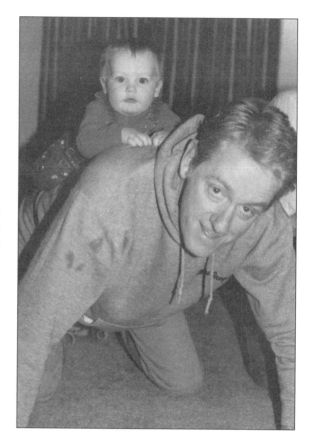

Cecil playing with
his grandson,
Nathaniel, c. 1988

Cecil and
Nathaniel,
c. 1989

Cecil, Nathaniel, and Dorothy, c. 1989

Dorothy Sherman, c. 1990

Preaching at Broadway Baptist Church, Fort Worth, Texas, 1990

Cecil in his study, Broadway Baptist Church, 1990

Cecil in his study, Broadway Baptist Church, 1990

Eugenia Sherman Brown, 1995

Dot and Cecil at Cecil's retirement from CBF,
Richmond, Virginia, June 1996

Dot, Caroline Massey, and T. E. Boland at Cecil's retirement from CBF,
Richmond, Virginia, June 1996

Dot at a luncheon given in her honor at Cecil's retirement from CBF,
Richmond, Virginia, June 1996

Cecil and his grandson, Nathaniel Brown, at Cecil's retirement from CBF,
Richmond, Virginia, June 1996

Cecil at CBF General Assembly, Richmond, Virginia, 1996

Dot and Cecil, Atlanta, Georgia, 1996

Cecil, Dot, and Pastor Malcolm Bane, at the 75th anniversary of
First Baptist Church, College Station, Texas, 1998

Cecil in the pulpit at the University Baptist Church,
Charlottesville, Virginia, 2001

Cecil with his brother, Bill, and his sister, Ruth Hamm,
First Baptist Church, Asheville, North Carolina, 2006

Cecil and Dot, Westminster-Canterbury,
Richmond, Virginia, January 2006

Back row: Eugenia Sherman Brown, Veta and Bill Sherman, Ruth and
Roger Hamm; Front row: Nathaniel, Cecil, Dorothy, and Doug, 2008

# Chapter 8
# AN INTRODUCTION TO THE SBC CONTROVERSY
## (from a Moderate Point of View)

The title to this chapter has a subscript, "from a Moderate Point of View."

That is the only truthful way to introduce the subject. No one who is informed on the subject of the SBC controversy is objective. Some don't care, but they are unlikely to be writing about it. Everyone else has a "point of view," and that means a slant, a bias. I have a point of view. That does not give me license to twist truth or bend facts, but from the beginning I opposed Fundamentalism. I thought it was wrong. This chapter is not a recitation of what happened so much as it is an explanation of *why* Moderates did what they did. Knowing what we did is one thing; knowing why we did it is another. The "why we did" drove the "what we did."

It has been twenty-eight years since controversy came to the SBC. Most people are content to leave the subject alone. If I am to tell the story of my life, I can't do that. There were years when "the controversy" rivaled my church in the division of my time. This chapter gives the reasoning of Moderates who turned aside from preaching and missions, ministry and administration to save a denomination from Fundamentalism. We failed, and that failure was a grief to us. Those who come after need to know what we were thinking as we worked to turn a major denomination from Fundamentalism. Here's the way we saw the controversy.

## The Nature of the SBC before 1979

The Southern Baptist Convention was and is a very large Protestant body. It has never been uniform in theology or practice. The Convention was born out of division over slavery in 1845. Southern Baptists went with Southern culture, defended slavery, and paid dearly for it. Not until after World War II did the South (and Southern Baptists) come to a broad prosperity. For 100 years Southern Baptists were scattered, poor, and mostly uneducated.

Again, that changed after World War II. The GI Bill educated our sons and daughters. A rising tide of prosperity moved South. Churches grew large in the 1950s. Southern Baptists created a way to fund their institutions and missions; it was called "the Cooperative Program." All institutions received a percentage of the money sent to a central counting house in Nashville, Tennessee. More missionaries were sent. More students enrolled in seminaries (five of the six largest seminaries in the US were Southern Baptist in 1960). Baptists passed Methodists and became the largest Protestant denomination in the United States.

So large a denomination had to develop a bureaucracy and a policy. Pastors who persuaded their churches to invest in the Cooperative Program usually were given appointments in the governance of the institutions of the SBC. There was cronyism in it, but it was pretty straightforward. The people who cared surfaced, were given positions, and ran the denomination. Not all pastors or laity cared. They were not excluded, but they rarely were leaders. The system made sense. It's the same system used in a church. The people who care become chairs of committees; the people who don't care don't chair.

It is not a redundancy to say that the Southern Baptist Convention was Baptist. The business of the denomination was missions, the production of literature for churches, and the education of young ministers. Those three assignments consumed 90 percent of the money of the Convention. The Convention was "a missions delivery system." Churches were not given specific instruction about theology. Each Baptist church was free to interpret the New Testament as that church thought best. There was diversity. Churches in Virginia did not have "closed Communion." Churches in Oklahoma did. Churches in the east often had female deacons; churches west of the Mississippi rarely did. Churches in the east were more into ministry than churches in the west. Churches in the west were more likely to be evangelistic than those in the east. The differences were tolerated; little mention was made of them. The focus of the convention was missions, not theology. Churches were supposed to do their own theology. All was not "sweetness and light," but we were at peace with each other and planning new and larger ways to reach out with the gospel of Jesus Christ.

## WHEN POLITICAL FUNDAMENTALISM INVADED THE SBC

Then the 1979 annual meeting of the Southern Baptist Convention in Houston, Texas, changed everything. For years, a small group had been watching Southern Baptist institutions. This group was bound together by one opinion: they were convinced the SBC was "drifting into liberalism" (a phrase they often used but rarely defined; it was assumed that liberalism was dreadful and awful). Leaders in the group were Paul Pressler (the young man I had met at Princeton University in 1955, now an appeals court judge in Houston) and Paige Patterson (the pastor's son I had met in 1950 at First Baptist Church Beaumont, Texas, now president of Criswell College in Dallas, Texas). The code word for their theology was "inerrancy." These people were advertising that they believed the Bible more than people who would not say "inerrant." My introduction to these men has already been stated. The two of them (and others) designed a strategy to change the SBC and make it serve their theology. Here's what they did:

1. They harnessed the power vested in the president's office to their purposes. The president of the SBC was elected at the annual meeting. The president has the power to appoint whomever he chooses to the Committee on Committees; he need not consult with

anyone. They would appoint people who subscribed to an inerrantist theology and were committed to their political agenda. That would allow them to become a majority and then control the boards that govern the institutions of the SBC.

2. They gathered people to the annual meeting of the SBC who shared their theological point of view and were willing to be part of the policy to implement the theology. A system was created to get people to the annual meeting. Buses were used to bring people who had never come to a convention before. They came to vote; then they left.

3. They were careful about appointments. Theology was the concern. Were those being appointed committed to the inerrancy of the Bible, *and* were they committed to the political agenda of the inerrancy party? It did not matter how much a person was giving to the denomination. It did not matter if the person was uneducated about the mission boards or seminaries. What mattered was their theology.

4. They stayed on message. They did not waver from their stated purpose. To make the inerrancy strategy work, they had to elect a president several years in sequence. One year would do little good. The plan took time, a lot of effort, and persistence.

5. They marginalized anyone who opposed them or publicly refused to embrace their inerrantist language. Such people were defined as second-class Southern Baptists; they "did not believe the Bible." None who opposed them was appointed to the boards that govern the institutions of the SBC. The effect of the inerrancy movement was division. But the people running the inerrancy party were not troubled that they were dividing the house. It appears they intended to do so.

## FIGURING OUT THE FUNDAMENTALISTS' STRATEGY

The strategy I've outlined was not clear in Houston in 1979. The first candidate of the inerrancy party was Adrian Rogers, pastor of Bellevue Baptist Church in Memphis, Tennessee. Other people who were known and prominent in the SBC were nominated too—people like Bill Self (a pastor from Wieuca Road Baptist Church in Atlanta, Georgia), Robert Naylor (past president of Southwestern Seminary), and Porter Routh (highest-ranking administrator in the SBC). Rogers won on the first ballot, getting just a little more than 50 percent of the vote. In 1979, we were witnessing something very new to the SBC. One group was organized and militant. The other was working out of a "good ole boy" system.

I did not attend that Houston convention. My church was in a building program, and I saw no need for my presence. I read about Rogers's election. Paul Pressler orchestrated runners on the floor of the convention from a skybox. All of this was new to Southern Baptists. Previous elections were little more than popularity contests. This was different.

In 1980 the convention was in St. Louis, Missouri. Dot and I went. Adrian Rogers did not run for reelection. Bailey Smith, an Oklahoma pastor, was the nominee of the inerrancy party. Three other strong candidates were put before the house: Richard Jackson, James Pleitz, and Frank Pollard. All were from churches that supported the SBC generously. Bailey Smith's church was different; the total receipts of his church in 1980 were $3,745,900. Only $41,334, or 1.10 percent, was given to the Cooperative Program. Why would the SBC elect a pastor whose church cared so little for the life of the Convention? Missions support was no longer the measuring stick; theology was. Smith would say inerrancy; the others might not.

Dot and I sat with a cluster of friends in St. Louis. We tried to sort out what we were hearing. Angry people exercised a drumbeat of code words and suggested that anyone who did not agree with them "did not believe the Bible." My wife listened, was confused, and finally said, "Did we come the wrong week? This sounds more like a political convention than a religious gathering." Moderates did not know how to interpret what was happening. We did not know the strategy of the inerrancy party in June 1980, but soon it came to light. Paul Pressler, one of the creators of the inerrancy strategy, came to Virginia. It was September 1980. At Old Forrest Road Baptist Church in Lynchburg, Pressler made clear the intentions of the Fundamentalist party (which

I outlined above). Tom Miller from the *Religious Herald* (the Baptist state paper in Virginia) was in attendance when Pressler made his speech. Miller's digest of that speech became my window into the intentions of Pressler and his helpers. He said the trustees appointed by the inerrancy party would not "rubberstamp" recommendations from denominational bureaucrats, and his inerrancy party was "going for the jugular." That meant they were in the fight to win, and they would persist until they did.

News of Pressler's speech was carried in Baptist papers from Virginia to California. The reaction was immediate and negative. Pressler and his friends were considered wicked for bringing hardball politics into the convention, and editors agreed that the inerrancy strategy would never work. Southern Baptists would surely reject it. For all the ink used in response to Pressler, the only thing that really changed was that a few of us saw clearly what the inerrancy party was doing. Until that point we had been guessing; now we saw their design.

In the next chapter I will describe the Moderate political response to Fundamentalist politics. Looking back on 1980, we were a fairly innocent people. We didn't think anything as stable as the Southern Baptist Convention was vulnerable to "takeover." Events proved us dead wrong. Before Pressler and his friends could impose their will on the SBC, they had to deal with some dedicated people who were willing to resist them. For a Southern Baptist pastor to resist Fundamentalism, you had to be willing to put your career on the line. Baptists are a conservative people. Moderates and Fundamentalists (among Southern Baptists) are conservative. Ask any Methodist or Presbyterian if a Moderate Baptist is conservative; from outside the SBC, all Baptist pastors look conservative. But when you push conservatism far enough, you slip into Fundamentalism. Distinguishing between degrees of conservatism is delicate business; most Baptists have a hard time telling the difference between a conservative and a Fundamentalist. Should a pastor be charged with "not believing the Bible," that pastor could bring division to his congregation and possibly be removed from office. Why put yourself in a fight that would be hard to win and could endanger your career? But a lot of good people did, and here's why:

1. Moderates loved the SBC. I am a child of the SBC, a product of a Baptist church, a Baptist university, and a Baptist seminary. I was reared in a Southern Baptist hothouse. I was proud to be a member of the body.

2. The Southern Baptist Convention was doing much good. There was a breadth and a scope to SBC ministries in 1979 that deserved to live. Our seminaries were more conservative than most, but their scholarship was good and getting better. Our missionaries worked on a broad front. Education, medicine, agriculture, evangelism, church planting, feeding the hungry: all were part of the missionary effort of a dedicated, diverse people. Only Roman Catholics and Mormons could rival the dollars invested in missions by the SBC. Fundamentalists wanted to lay hands on this system. It was the target of their strategy. To stand down and let them have their way with the denomination was not a moral option.

3. Mainly Moderates administered the institutions of the SBC—people like Keith Parks (president of the Foreign Mission Board), Russell Dilday (president of Southwestern Seminary), Roy Honeycutt (president of Southern Seminary), Randall Lolley (president of Southeastern Seminary), Milton Ferguson (president of Midwestern Seminary), and the teachers in our seminaries; all were able, good people. The reason I didn't use the term "inerrancy" to describe the Bible was because of the honest, reverent teachers who taught me better. To stand down and let a group "take over" the SBC would put all these people in harm's way. (Some of our teachers did not see any need for defense. They refused to believe Fundamentalists could possess the SBC; they refused to believe harm would come to them if Fundamentalists did take over. Events proved those people wrong).

4. I didn't think "inerrancy" was an honest word to describe the Bible. It is a slippery word. The less you know about the Bible, the easier it is to say the Bible is inerrant; the more you know about the Bible,

the harder it is to use the word. It was not that we were "soft on the Bible." It was a case of care, academic precision, and honesty.

A gentle word: I believe Fundamentalists (a broader group than Southern Baptist Fundamentalists) intend to defend the Bible. In fact, they have become modern Pharisees. In their desire to stand up for the Bible, they have made the Christian religion unbelievable to moderns. Fundamentalism misdirects the energies of the Church, divides the Church, and makes for poor public relations for the Church.

## What's the Difference between Moderates and Fundamentalists?

After I went to work for the Cooperative Baptist Fellowship, I was often asked to explain the differences between Moderates and Fundamentalists. I finally had to work out an answer to this question. My answer does not include all that is different about the two groups, but it is a start.

1. We use different words to describe the Bible. Fundamentalists say the Bible is inerrant. Moderates say the Bible is trustworthy and reliable. Underlying the different approach we take to the Bible is the different approach we take to biblical criticism. The Chicago Statement on Biblical Inerrancy lists sixteen "exceptions." An "exception" refers to "the human element in scripture," "figures of speech," "imprecise speech," or numbers cited in parallel accounts (such as Samuel-Kings and Chronicles). The Bible has all of the above; an inerrantist must be concerned about explaining away these variations in the text.

Jimmy Draper, Jr. (a Baptist pastor who labored in the Fundamentalist camp and later became president of Lifeway) wrote a book titled *Authority: The Critical Issue for Southern Baptists*. Draper set out to explain how a thoughtful person could hold to an inerrant view of Scripture. Writing about "imprecise speech," Draper reasoned, "Inspiration does not eliminate approximations and loose quotations. We do this in common speech. Why should we not recognize that the biblical writers do the same? . . . It is acceptable in our vernacular today. It was also acceptable in the day of the biblical writers, and does not mislead or deceive the reader" (Old Tappan NJ: Fleming H. Revell Co., 1984, p. 87).

Draper reasoned like a Moderate while holding to inerrancy. He can't have it both ways. If "approximations" are acceptable, does it not follow that the Bible is "approximately inerrant"? And what of the variations in numbers in the Samuel-Kings history when compared to the Chronicles history? If such variations were not in Scripture, I would call the Bible inerrant too. There are limits to how far you can stretch the meaning of words before they lose touch with reality. "Inerrancy" is a technical word that does not admit elasticity. It means no errors. I did not choose the word; Fundamentalists did. By the time you get through listing the "exceptions," you can describe the Bible as inerrant, but by then inerrant does not mean "without error." Suppose I said I was faithful to my wife . . . with sixteen "exceptions." My "exceptions" redefine the meaning of "faithful." If such were the case, I would not be "faithful" at all. "Inerrant" is a slippery word, and even those who insist upon it cannot agree on its definition.

Moderate Baptists have a high view of the Bible. It is our authority. We are accused of using Bible criticism, and we do. We were taught to use Bible criticism in Southern Baptist seminaries. Those seminaries have been teaching young preachers to use Bible criticism for years. The Southern Baptist Theological Seminary catalog for 1929–1930 described a Bible introduction course this way: "This course covers the entire field of Old Testament Criticism from the earliest days down to the present . . . . The work is chiefly concerned with Higher or Historical Criticism of the Old Testament." Lower criticism sets out to find a reliable text; higher criticism includes everything scholars do to determine the meaning of the text. Some nineteenth-century European scholars used Bible criticism in a destructive way; European liberals gave Bible criticism a bad name. Suspicion still lingers about Bible criticism until this day. It is a tool that helps us get at the meaning of the text. The Bible doesn't mean what *I* say it means; it means what it means. By use of reverent Bible criticism, I can approach the intended meaning of the original authors. I believe the Bible is God-inspired. In all things related to the first purpose of the Bible (to bring wayward humankind back to God), the Bible is without error. But when the Bible speaks of science and historical detail, the Bible has some errors.

Moderates do not believe the Bible is full of errors, but there are errors. Inerrantists do not admit this; Moderates do because it is the truth. In an earlier contentious time, William Chillingsworth said, "I am assured that God does not and therefore that men ought not to require any more of any man than this: To believe Scripture to be God's Word, to endeavor to find the true sense of it, and to live according to it" (*Great Voices of the Reformation*, ed. Harry Emerson Fosdick, [New York: Random House, Inc., 1952], 334). Chillingsworth spoke carefully and made room for a thoughtful person to be a modern *and* believe the Bible. Fundamentalists ask too much when they demand us to say the Bible is inerrant.

2. Moderates and Fundamentalists differ in our opinion of women in church leadership. The point of issue for the Fundamentalist party was inerrancy regarding the Bible. But as time passed, it became obvious that there was more to their agenda. In 1984, at the annual meeting of the SBC, a second issue surfaced. A resolution was brought to the Convention about the ordination of women. Its title was "On Ordination and the Role of Women in Ministry." Randall Lolley, president of Southeastern Seminary, studied the resolution and said

> The resolution consists of 86 lines; it has 542 words. Four times it mentions "ordination." Four times it mentions "ministry." Fifteen times it mentions "women." Thus the real agenda in the resolution was neither ministry nor ordination, but *women*. Women themselves—all the women in all the churches of this convention. And in that hotly controverted resolution, the most debated concept is the 10th *whereas*—the woman was last in the creation and "first in the Edenic fall." (President's opening convocation address, fall semester, Southeastern Seminary, Wake Forest NC, 28 August 1984)

A Bible student can construct an argument for or against women in ministry. The proof-texts are there for both points of view. Genesis makes women "last in creation and first in the fall." Paul cites the same text in 1 Timothy 2:13-14. Text could be piled on top of text, making the point that no woman should speak in church (and that could also mean sing a solo), teach a Sunday school class of men and women, or serve as a missionary (presuming missionaries preach the gospel).

But the same Bible tells of Deborah leading several tribes of Israel in war and giving judgments in disputes. Ruth and Hannah are held high as examples. Women traveled with Jesus and funded his ministry (Luke 8:1-3). Phoebe was "commended" and called "a deacon" by Paul (Rom 16:16). Women played a prominent part in the ministries of both Peter (Acts 9:36-42) and Paul (Acts 16:11-15). So when Paul was describing the long progression of events that moved from law to grace, he said,

> *Now that faith has come, we are no longer subject to a discipli-narian, for in Christ Jesus you are all children of God through faith. As many of you as were baptized in Christ have clothed yourselves with Christ. There is no longer Jew or Greek, there is no longer slave or free, there is no longer male and female; for all of you are one in Christ Jesus. (Gal 3:25-28)*

Fundamentalists have taken the Bible and made a case against women in ministry. Moderates have taken the same Bible and made a case for women in ministry. Both sides use the Bible. How can this be? Two ideas help me make sense of this.

• The Bible was written over a very long period of time. The way women were viewed then is not they way they are viewed now. Women were little more than property in the earliest eras of the Old Testament. But as time passed, and as God revealed more of himself, we came to a larger understanding of the dignity and worth of women.

• The Bible is "culturally conditioned." When Paul urged women to have a low profile in the infant churches, he was working in a Roman world. Paul's aim was not the liberation of women; it was the spread of the gospel. He was willing to downplay any social agenda to help the church get a start. But Paul planted seeds that grew into a place for women in the church.

Moderates believe that if a woman testifies that God has called her to ministry, who are we to deny her? We believe her and rejoice in her calling. Women in ministry leadership roles among Baptists are a small but growing group. Fundamentalists are working against the tide of God's history, and events will prove them wrong. Once the same sort of people defended slavery from the Bible; God and time passed them by.

3. Moderates believe pastors are servants of the church; Fundamentalists believe the pastor should be "the ruler of the church" (1 Tim 5:17). That some pastors are authoritarian, sometimes dictatorial, is no secret. But in Baptist life such conduct is a matter of personality rather than a polity that vests the pastor with authority by virtue of his office. That changed in 1988 at the San Antonio meeting of the SBC. The Pressler-Patterson political party pushed a resolution through the Convention titled "On the Priesthood of the Believer." The sense of the resolution downplays the place of the traditional Baptist doctrine known as the Priesthood of the Believer, but the real target is the role of the pastor in the life of a congregation. The doctrine of the Priesthood of the Believer is considered suspect and "subject to both misunderstanding and abuse" and "can be used to justify the undermining of pastoral authority in a local church." Then the resolution gets to the point:

> Be it further RESOLVED, That the doctrine of the Priesthood of the Believer in no way contradicts the biblical understanding of the role, responsibility, and authority of the pastor which is seen in the command to the local church in Hebrews 13:17, "Obey your leaders, and submit to them; for they keep watch over your souls, as those who will give an account"; and Be it finally RESOLVED, That we affirm the truth that elders, or pastors, are called of God to lead the local church. (Acts 20:28)

Several parts of this resolution were a red flag to traditional Baptists. We opposed it for several reasons.

1. It is out of step with Baptist history. Our Baptist heritage was a rebellion against the abuse of ecclesiastical authority. Bishops tried to make our forbears in the faith worship in a set way, bow and scrape before pastors who were assigned them, and believe doctrines that did not have biblical support. They resisted and were hounded by authorities, imprisoned, and sometimes put to death. Baptists came from the womb shouting *freedom*. The resolution creates pastors who can dominate and control; it does not leave us free. We believe the Holy Spirit speaks to us all: clergy and laypeople.

2. It undermines Baptist polity. The highest authority in a Baptist church is the congregation. Does the congregation have the right to decide what the Bible means? Or is that authority being transferred to the pastor? If that happens, then we have regressed, gone back to the authoritarian clergy from which we rebelled 400 years ago. Moderates believe a pastor advises the congregation about Scripture; the congregation is free to decide if the pastor is right or wrong. That is the Protestant way.

3. Further, there is an example in the Gospels that is foreign to all the texts cited in the resolution:

> *A dispute also arose among them as to which one of them was to be regarded as the greatest. But he said to them, "The kings of the Gentiles lord it over them; and those in authority over them are called benefactors. But not so with you; rather the greatest among you must become like the youngest, and the leader like one who serves. For who is greater, the one who is at the table or the one who serves? Is it not the one at the table? I am among you as one who serves. (Luke 22:24-27)*

Jesus set a servant standard. By the time the late epistles were written (and that is where the supporting texts are found in the resolution), the Church had adopted the power models of the Roman government. Working from the later model, the Catholic Church developed a power pyramid. Pope ruled bishops; bishops ruled priests; priests ruled laity.

Baptists have always had confidence in laity to interpret the Bible and order the life of the congregation (that's why Baptists get to think, to teach a Sunday school class, to choose a pastor, to vote in congregational meetings). The resolution is a step back toward a system the first Baptists rejected. A pastor may offer leadership; he does not get to do it by right of his office. He has to earn the trust to lead.

4. Moderates are different from Fundamentalists in the way we do missions. The old Southern Baptist Convention did missions on a broad front. Some missionaries were evangelists and church starters. Others were teachers. A smaller group did medical missions as nurses and doctors who worked in hospitals. Since World War II, agricultural missionaries were sent to teach people how to farm in a scientific way. Each year an offering was taken from Southern Baptists for the purpose of relieving world hunger. The offering was growing each year, and missionaries distributed food in places where famine threatened life. This missions delivery system was professional and efficient.

Fundamentalists did not want to do missions on a broad front. They wanted missionaries to be evangelists and church starters; other missionaries they brought home or retired. Some of the best mission work Southern Baptists were doing has been dismantled. Their missionaries are evangelists rather than servants.

Evangelism is one of God's high callings, but there are other models for missions in the New Testament. Jesus healed people, fed people, taught people (he was called "teacher" more often than any other title). If we are going to do the work of Jesus, are we not beholden to use the model of Jesus? Our missions programs need the same breadth and diversity found in the ministry of Jesus.

5. Moderates and Fundamentalists differ on the issue of separation of church and state. Since Thomas Helwys (one of the original Baptists), Baptists have worked for separation of church and state. Helwys sent King James I a copy of his book, *A Short Declaration of the Mystery of Iniquity.* On the flyleaf he wrote,

> The king is a mortall man and not God and therefore hath
> no power over the immortall soules of his subjects, to make
> lawes and ordinances for them, and to set spirituall Lords
> over them. If the king have authority to make spiritual

> Lords and lawes over them he is an immortall God, and not
> a mortall man. O king, be not seduced by deceivers to sin
> so against God . . . . (Helwys, *A Short Declaration of the
> Mystery of Iniquity*, ed. and introduced by Richard Groves
> [Mercer University Press: Macon GA, 1998], vi)

Helwys's bold delivery of his book to King James in 1612 resulted in his imprisonment; he died in jail. He was a martyr for the cause of religious liberty and separation of church and state. This is who Baptists were in the beginning.

Roger Williams, founder of Rhode Island, picked up the cause Helwys championed. In the eighteenth century, Isaac Backus and John Leland worked to get religious liberty protected by the new constitution. The First Amendment reads, "Congress shall make no law respecting the establishment of religion or prohibiting the free exercise thereof." Those words were the Baptist position on religious liberty and separation of church and state until lately, but times have changed. Once Baptists were a minority harassed by an established Church; now in the South, Baptists are usually the largest denomination and politically secure. For 200 years a subtle, unwritten rule ordered public schools and government ceremonies. The Christian religion was given favored place, and no mention was made of minorities who might be pinched by our religious understandings. Minorities have gone to court and gotten relief. Now public prayers and overt Protestant ceremony in government life are fading.

Today an aggressive paganism competes with Christian values in the media. Sometimes the paganism is offensive. Aggressive paganism plus court decisions proscribing Christian piety in public places have combined to alarm the Christian Right. Southern Baptist Fundamentalists are part of the Religious Right. These people have reverted to Puritan rather than Baptist patterns. Reasoning as Puritans, they conclude that if the nation is turning away from Christian values, then it is the duty of Christian citizens to use the power of government to reestablish Christian values. Puritans never had a problem using government to enforce their theology. Fundamentalists don't either. W. A. Criswell said the doctrine of the separation of church and state came from "the imagination of an infidel." Criswell didn't know Baptist church history. Southern Baptist Fundamentalists have become one part of the Religious Right, the Moral Majority, and the Republican Party.

Moderate Baptists are as interested in the values of this nation as Fundamentalists. But traditional Baptists are as interested in the religious rights of religious minorities as we are in our own. We have the right to evangelize; we do not have the right to press our religion on anyone. Moderate Baptists are holding to the original Baptist position on church and state. It was right then and it is right now.

6. Moderates and Fundamentalists differ in the way we use the power of the "denomination." The stated purpose of the Southern Baptist Convention is to "elicit, combine, and direct" the energies of the churches in the evangelizing of the world. There is no mention in the constitution of the Southern Baptist Convention about straightening or correcting theology. From 1609 until 1814, there was no Baptist body larger than an association. In 1814, a small body of Baptists came together to form a mission-sending convention. For years it was poor and powerless. But after World War I, that changed. The SBC became strong and centralized. In 1979, the Pressler-Patterson political party decided to use the denomination to define and spread their version of "correct theology."

In another (and more innocent) day, Southern Baptists were a more diverse people. We were conservative by any reasonable standard of measurement, but we were not cookie-cutter identical. Our seminaries took on the flavor of the regions they served. Southeastern (in Wake Forest, North Carolina) was much like North Carolina Baptists: more given to social action than to evangelism. Southwestern (in Fort Worth, Texas) was like Texas Baptists: more active in evangelism than social ministries.

These differences were tolerated. New Orleans Baptist Theological Seminary was probably the most conservative SBC seminary. If a church wanted a conservative pastor, they could go to New Orleans.

Not all teachers interpreted the Bible the same way. Dale Moody at Southern (Louisville, Kentucky) raised questions about the security of the believer; others took issue with him.

If theologians are free to interpret the Bible, is it not inevitable that there is going to be difference of opinion? Room for difference was built into the Baptist system. Before the onset of Fundamentalism, Baptists were becoming more informed and more diverse. This diversity offended the Pressler-Patterson party. They began to draw lines, set fences, and pass resolutions that were used as theological checkpoints. Now anyone (or any church) that seeks to have influence in the SBC must toe the theological party line.

Moderates disagree. We believe a denomination ought to serve churches, not instruct them. Our churches don't need to be herded like sheep. Our pastors and laity are able to chart their way through a puzzling culture. Pastors and laity are able to read their Bibles and determine what the Spirit of God would have them do to meet their culture. Because the SBC has become a theology-standardizing agency, Moderates struggle about remaining in it. We need more freedom than the SBC allows. Contrary to accusations from Fundamentalists, our insistence on freedom is not veiled liberalism. Freedom is the birthright of all the children of God.

The six differences I've cited are important. Of course there are others, and with the passing years the Fundamentalist agenda has grown larger. Homosexuality is now the hot topic. The SBC will pass resolutions on these contentious subjects; CBF will not. Sometimes I agree with the SBC positions, but I don't think it is the business of the SBC to meddle in decisions that Baptists should leave to local churches. The decisions of local churches do not always please me, but that is their business. And that is the Baptist way.

Are these differences important enough for me to break with the denomination that reared me? That's a call each person has to make. Eventually I decided my answer was yes.

This chapter is different from all that has gone before. I've left the story of my life and given an interpretation of a troublesome period in Southern Baptist life. Now I will return to my story, but keep this chapter in mind. It explains why I did what I did. Others will give different reasons for why I did what I did, but you need to know how I was reasoning as I charted my way.

# Chapter 9

# "We Can Handle These People . . ."

The inerrancy controversy that divided the SBC (and continues to splinter churches away from the SBC) lasted for more than ten years. The reason it lasted as long as it did is because both sides created a political organization.

The political organizations were small by secular standards, but they were tenacious. Neither wanted to lose. Since Fundamentalists won, the story of the controversy has been told to Southern Baptists from their point of view, or it has been left untold. This chapter is one-sided. I know little about the strategy Fundamentalists created to possess the SBC. I know a good bit about the Moderate force that resisted them and delayed their possession of the SBC.

To date, *Struggle for the Soul of the SBC* (Walter Shurden [Macon GA: Mercer University Press, 1994]) has been the best window into the Moderate camp. I hope this chapter will be an additional insight into the efforts of Moderates, who in a most public way resisted Fundamentalism.

Paul Pressler's speech in Lynchburg, Virginia, gave me a road map. Paul stated clearly what he (and his friends) intended to do in the Southern Baptist Convention. They intended to possess the SBC by electing a president who was empowered to stack committees and boards with their kind and radically change the nature of the organization. It would not only have a Fundamentalist theology; it would also intentionally perpetuate that theology through the institutions of the SBC.

I had watched the Pressler-Patterson political party do their work in St. Louis (1980). There were two kinds of politics in the room in St. Louis. The Fundamentalists had a strategy; the Moderates didn't. The Fundamentalist group had one candidate; the Moderates put forward three. Fundamentalists had a long-term agenda for the Convention; Moderates had not given it a thought. Sitting in my study in Asheville, a parable came to mind:

Turn back the clock to 1900. The University of North Carolina and Duke are playing their annual football game. Both sides are true amateurs. An English teacher "coaches" the Carolina team. He uses Walter Camp's playbook. A physics teacher "coaches" Duke. The players are all volunteers, and the contest is little more than an intramural game between students. But interest in football is growing. The people from Carolina decide they will have a better chance to beat Duke if they hire a "real" coach and give scholarships to big, athletic fellows. And so they do. Duke decides they cannot and will not hire a coach and give scholarships. They are not going to stoop to professionalism; they are purists. So each school follows its chosen course of preparation for the annual game. Which team do you think is likely to win?

I created that parable to make the point to Southern Baptists that if they didn't organize to resist the Pressler-Patterson group, they were going to lose and lose and lose. And finally they would lose any influence they had in the SBC. But organizing required more than making up a parable.

## GATLINBURG, 1980

After I digested Pressler's speech in Lynchburg (September 1980), I wrote letters to twenty-five pastors. Geography was taken into account. Did the pastor have a following in his locale? Was the pastor likely to be receptive to my invitation? My letter invited them to a meeting in Gatlinburg, Tennessee, on September 25, 1980.

It was an early fall day. Color was just appearing in the trees as Dot and I drove to Gatlinburg. The sun was bright; it was pleasant and warm. We were in casual conversation. Suddenly Dot changed the subject to the meeting in Gatlinburg. She said, "You know this meeting is likely to become public property, and when it becomes known, it is going to change the way Baptists see you. Are you sure you are right?" I didn't give a quick answer; I pondered what she had said for a time. Then I said, "I believe I'm right about those people [Fundamentalists] and what they intend to do. Fundamentalism misrepresents my understanding of the spirit of Jesus. Somebody has got to oppose them or they are going to accomplish what they have set out to do." Dot's question lingered in my mind. She was not worried about my "public image." She was worried about whether or not I was right. Often Dot was my moral compass.

Dot by nature was and is conservative. Making the distinction between a Fundamentalist and conservative was hard for her. Both use the same language. They have the same agenda. I am a conservative. Dot knew that; she had been through the Princeton experience. She knew a real liberal when she met one. She wanted to be sure I was sure in my reading of the people who were leading the charge for Southern Baptist Fundamentalism. Dot had reason to ask the question. What happened in the next ten years did change my life . . . and hers.

I was not certain how many of the twenty-five I invited to Gatlinburg would come. My fears were misplaced. Not all the people who would resist Fundamentalism were at that first meeting, but enough were there to get started. Listed alphabetically are the people who came to Gatlinburg:

- Carl Bates, pastor of First Baptist Church of Charlotte, North Carolina, past president of the SBC and state conventions, a popular speaker.
- Lavonne Brown, pastor of First Baptist Church of Norman, Oklahoma, president of the Oklahoma Baptist Convention, widely sought as a speaker and writer.
- Frank Campbell, pastor of First Baptist Church of Statesville, North Carolina, president of the North Carolina Baptist Convention, influential in both North Carolina and Virginia.
- Kenneth Chafin, pastor of South Main Baptist Church in Houston, Texas, former teacher at both Southwestern and Southern seminaries, led the Home Mission Board's evangelism department, a

lightning-rod personality. Ken had intellectual reflexes as quick as any I've known. Before coming to Gatlinburg, Ken saw through the designs of Pressler and Patterson.

- Henry Crouch, pastor of Providence Baptist Church, Charlotte, North Carolina. No one was and is more mainline Southern Baptist than Henry. He and his father had enormous credibility in North Carolina.

- Earl Davis, pastor of First Baptist Church of Memphis, Tennessee. Earl had distinguished himself while a pastor in Georgia. He came to bring life to an old and distinguished church in Memphis. He was and is an effective speaker.

- Vernon Davis, pastor of First Baptist Church of Alexandria, Virginia. He was a leader in Virginia Baptist life and would soon be president of the General Association. He was quiet, thoughtful, and an effective organizer.

- Clyde Fant, pastor of First Baptist Church of Richardson, Texas, previously professor of preaching at Southwestern Seminary, knowledgeable author and speaker.

- Welton Gaddy, pastor of the Broadway Baptist Church, Fort Worth, Texas, member of the executive committee of the SBC, formerly on staff of the Christian Life Commission of the SBC.

- T. L. McSwain, pastor of a church in Louisville, Kentucky. Until he moved to Georgia, he was active in gathering support for our cause.

- Bill O'Conner, pastor from Eastman, Georgia. Bill was invited by Ches Smith. He did not want to do politics and did not attend another meeting.

- Ed Perry, pastor of Broadway Baptist Church in Louisville, Kentucky. He had been active in Kentucky Baptist and SBC work for years. He proved to be one of the most insightful and effective politicians in the group.

- Carmen Sharp, pastor of Deer Park Baptist Church in Louisville, Kentucky. Carmen had already gathered Baptists to the cause of peace. He had a gentle spirit, but he had heart to resist those who did not.

- Bill Sherman, pastor of Woodmont Baptist Church in Nashville, Tennessee, and my brother. He had been president of the Tennessee

Baptist Convention, was much sought as an evangelist and Bible teacher, and was connected to the several parts of Tennessee Baptist life. Bill quickly recognized political Fundamentalism for the threat that it was. He was quick to support a Moderate viewpoint.

- Jim Slatton, pastor of River Road Church, Baptist, Richmond, Virginia. Jim had a grasp of what was required to do what he called "networking." He could pull together little groups who would "work" a region or association. When I stepped down as chair of the group, Jim was the right man to take my place.
- Ches Smith, pastor of First Baptist Church, Tifton, Georgia. He came to the meeting because I asked him to come. He did not know what would come of our meeting, and he had misgivings about politics. He did not work in the emerging Moderate movement, but he was quick to support CBF in 1990.

There were seventeen of us. Janet Campbell, Myra Bates, and Dot Sherman were present and attended some of our meetings. Dot took notes, and I am using those notes as I write.

Earl Davis opened the meeting with prayer, and then I told them why I had asked them to gather. I gave my background with Paul Pressler and Paige Patterson. I said these men should be taken seriously. I went further and made what sounds even now like a rash statement: "We are going to divide. The important thing is how we divide." Then I told the group we did not have long to do what we had to do. The Fundamentalists had a three-year head start. We had about five years to "turn the Convention around" if it were to be done.

It is difficult to preside over so many strong personalities. Nearly everyone made speeches. Two ideas surfaced again and again: (1) We have a great love for the Southern Baptist Convention, and (2) We are going to be marginalized in the SBC unless we do something.

The people in the room had been selfless in their service to Southern Baptists. Growing up as we did, the Southern Baptist Convention was the stage on which we chose to perform our service to Christ. If that Convention stage were changed, if Fundamentalism became the theology and the spirit of the SBC, we would be dispossessed of a place we knew as our home. The conversation was earnest and intense. The consequences of resisting biblical inerrancy were not lost on anyone. We lived in a conservative family of the Christian faith; we would be described as liberal. If we had the liberal label pinned on us, we knew our chances of resisting Pressler, Patterson, and Fundamentalism were not good. In spite of the slim odds for victory, the group was unanimous. We would organize and choose a candidate to oppose Bailey Smith in Los Angeles.

Then we talked of ways to alert mainline Baptists to the danger before them. We listed groups who might be allies in our effort. Woman's Missionary Union could be our friend. Student workers were likely to support us. Baptist college teachers were another group who could help. A strategy was planned to enlist and mobilize these people.

Finally we turned to politics. We took note of how many votes Bailey Smith had received on the first ballot in St. Louis. We reasoned that we could elect if we could get 6,000 votes for a Moderate candidate in Los Angeles. We divided the states, set goals, and began to think of people in each state who might be willing to help us. This was the beginning of "networking," the backbone of our movement. All talk comes to nothing unless the state leader goes home and does his "networking."

Late in the meeting we asked ourselves the question, "What do we say about this meeting? Who are we?" We decided we would not volunteer anything about our meeting, but if asked, we would tell the truth. We considered names for our group, including "Denominational Loyalists" and "Friends of Missions." None of these was destined to stick. Eventually we were called Moderates. The names we were giving to ourselves give insight into who we thought we were. Fundamentalists were unhappy with SBC institutions. We were happy with them, supported them, and did not want them changed. Naively we thought the denominational leaders would see us as their supporters and rally to us. That turned out to be an illusion. Most did not recognize us as friends. Ken Chafin said of them, "They could not tell the arsonists from the firemen." There were of course exceptions; some agency heads did see the storm clouds. I received letters of encouragement from them. Our group set another meeting for Fort Worth,

Texas, in February 1981 and adjourned. We enjoyed each other, did our work, and went home to harder work. We had committed ourselves to do Baptist politics.

None of the people who came to Gatlinburg knew exactly what would happen at or because of the meeting. Some came out of courtesy to me; they had no stomach for politics and dropped out. Others stayed for a couple of years and faded away. About half the group gave strong leadership, and they did not go away.

They received nothing for their service; they paid their own way to meetings. Often they were criticized for "doing politics." Some were marked for their participation and cut out of denominational life. Their extra income was reduced. They were described as "not believing the Bible." Because we eventually lost our war, some have described Moderates as "bumblers," inept and not very bright. I have a better opinion of them. We took on a most difficult assignment. They didn't have to do it. They labored harder than anyone knows. They received criticism . . . and they stayed.

In this chapter I've tried to describe the Gatlinburg meeting and the state of mind of those who attended. We were not planning another denomination; that thought was not on our minds. We were committed to saving the one we had from a people who were essentially foreign to the Baptist spirit. Fundamentalists insist on uniformity of thought; real Baptists give people and churches some space. It's called freedom.

## Los Angeles, 1981

The Gatlinburg group had agreed to meet again in February 1981. The meeting was at Broadway Baptist Church in Fort Worth. Welton Gaddy hosted us. The first item on the agenda was a question: Should we challenge the reelection of Bailey Smith as president of the SBC? It was a tradition that the president of the SBC would automatically be given a second term. If we ran a candidate against Smith, we would be running against both Smith and tradition. The pros and cons were listed for all to consider. Then we voted. The unanimous decision was that we run a candidate.

Next we had to find the right candidate. We needed someone who was known, someone who had a constituency, someone who was clearly conservative in both theology and lifestyle. Several names were suggested; then Abner McCall's name was proposed. He was president of Baylor University; a large number of people from Texas would follow him and vote for him. He was aware of the threat to serious education the Fundamentalist faction presented, meaning he had a stake in the effort. McCall was trained to be a lawyer, had been a judge on the Texas Supreme Court, was past dean of the Baylor Law School, and was known to possess good judgment. Further, he knew Baptist history and polity.

We called President McCall and asked him if he would be our first candidate. He had no illusions about what we were asking him to do. He knew he was not likely to win. But the man had the courage of his convictions. Winning was not as important to him as making a statement. He agreed to run. I remember his request to me when he took the assignment: "Cecil, I don't expect we can win this election, but we need to try. Can you get me 4,500 votes? I don't want to be embarrassed." I relayed McCall's request to the group, and we set out to gather votes.

Jim Slatton became the captain of the Virginia workers. Henry Crouch gave leadership in North Carolina. Bill Bruster came on board and helped in East Tennessee; Bill Sherman worked Middle Tennessee, while Earl Davis gathered the few votes we had in West Tennessee. Don Harbuck tallied Arkansas. Lavonn Brown and Gene Garrison teamed up to count the Moderate vote in Oklahoma. Several people worked Texas. Kentucky was well served by T. L. McSwain, Ed Perry, and Carmen Sharp. Not all states had a Moderate pyramid to count votes. Georgia, Alabama, South Carolina, and Florida would not organize until later. These people told the Moderate story to their friends, answered their questions, and counted people who said they would go to Los Angeles and vote for McCall.

I prepared a "Fact Sheet" for messengers to the convention. I told my audience I would vote for McCall, and noted when the election would be—3:00 p.m. on Tuesday afternoon of the annual meeting. My justification for voting for McCall and against Bailey Smith was this: "Dr. Smith has repeatedly said that he thought only Baptists who hold his view of inspiration should be on Southern Baptist committees and boards. This is a different and divisive view. His doctrinal measurement for denominational service is new and exclusive." Ralph Langley, pastor of First Baptist Church of Huntsville, Alabama, was chosen to nominate McCall.

We gathered in Los Angeles. Our efforts to gather votes had become public. The Fundamentalists were not happy about McCall running. They marshaled their forces; that was expected. What we did not expect was the response of the denominational bureaucracy. In the lobby of the Hilton Hotel, I chanced to meet Dr. Porter Routh, executive secretary of the SBC Executive Committee, the top administrative post in the denomination. He went out of his way to correct me. "Cecil, you people need to stand down. We have one troublesome group stirring the water [Fundamentalists], and now you people have formed another. We can take care of these people [Pressler, Patterson, and company]. We don't need your help. I want you to disband your group and leave this to us." Dr. Routh was a generation older than I am. I was reluctant to confront him. Cautiously I said, "Dr. Routh, you underestimate these people; they have an agenda for the Convention that will drastically reorder the institutions and replace most of the leadership." I said my peace in good humor, but I wanted to put him on alert that he was dealing with a different kind of people. He did not believe me.

A member of the Executive Committee of the SBC sought me out and said, "You people [Moderates] need to stop. Don't nominate McCall. He won't get 10 percent of the vote. You are going to look foolish." I told the man we had more than 4,000 votes; he did not believe me.

When election time came, Richard Jackson from Arizona nominated Bailey Smith for a second term. Ralph Langley nominated McCall. When the votes were counted, Smith had 6,934 (60.24 percent). McCall had 4,524 (39.30 percent). We lost the election; we kept our promise to Dr. McCall to get 4,500 votes. We made a statement to the SBC that we were a presence they had to take into account. I was exhausted from three months of intense effort to get Moderates to Los Angeles. I felt pretty good about our first effort.

Sometimes Baptist blarney covers what people are really thinking. One part of the Los Angeles meeting was the "sweet talk." From Bailey Smith and others, there were soft words, good intentions about being inclusive, and, of course, the usual line, "I love you, all of you." Baptists are by nature pietists and given to "the language of Zion." Such language may be well intentioned, but Baptist blarney confuses. If you take that kind of talk literally, then we had no controversy. It was just a few people with a bad attitude. Most of the company wanted to "get the controversy behind them and get on with the work of the Convention." It all sounded so great that only a person of warped mind would not believe it. Such talk merrily lathered the unsuspecting before it shaved them . . . close.

The reaction to our Moderate movement was mixed. Two letters from professors are a window into the wishful thinking that was common in 1981.

My ethics teacher, Dr. T. B. Maston, wrote to me on August 6, 1981,

> Thanks for your letter. I really have the feeling that the LA Convention turned out pretty well. I personally think that there was considerable evidence there that the Convention is not going to let a minority group take over. . . .
>
> Since the Convention I have exchanged a couple of letters with Abner McCall, have also written to Bailey Smith, to Jimmy Draper, and to Daniel Vestal. In writing to the last three I did a thing that I have never done before. I wrote a joint letter addressed to all three of them. . . .
>
> I still have more hopes for Jimmy Draper than most folks that I know. I have been rather close to him. . . . If Bailey Smith is halfway serious about some of the things that he has said, and I think some of the things that he did, in Los Angeles, he is not going to be dictated to by the extreme group.
>
> In other words, my viewpoint is that although the battle is not over, I do not believe that the judge [Pressler],

Paige, and few others that have sought clearly to win control of the Convention are going to succeed. . . .

Dr. Wayne Ward taught theology at Southern Baptist Theological Seminary for decades. Ward wrote to me on August 13, 1981,

> Before we head to Jerusalem on a one-semester sabbatical, I had to record the deep gratitude which I tried to express to you on the convention floor. Most of us here [at Southern Seminary] believe that we owe a debt to you and your helpers that we could never repay in a lifetime. It is probably no exaggeration to say that you guys may have saved the Southern Baptist Convention and its agencies.
>
> Much has been written about the "love-in" at Los Angeles. Those who have their heads on straight know that we couldn't have had the luxury of that kind of meeting if some of you had not paid the price to send a very unmistakable signal to Bailey, as well as the whole Pressler-Patterson coalition. I am sanguine enough about such Baptist fights to know that we are not home free, but I believe the corner was turned in L. A. . . .

Another letter from the outgoing chair of the SBC Executive Committee (J. Howard Cobble) is revealing. I had had a conversation with Nelson Duke, a member of the committee, in which I told him I thought the Executive Committee helped Bailey Smith get reelected. Duke passed my opinion along to Cobble, and Cobble responded by writing to me on September 23, 1981,

> Though Nelson did not read the letter in its entirety nor totally restructure the conversation, I gathered that you expressed dissatisfaction with me and perhaps other officers of the Executive Committee for our support of the reelection of Bailey Smith. Evidently you interpreted our expressing personal positions as resulting in a leadership of the Executive Committee to positionize itself.
>
> My support of Bailey was a personal choice and was no attempt to influence the committee. His reelection was in

the best interest of the SBC. He is not anti-denomination
nor in the pocket of any particular group.

I surprised myself by supporting him. Those to whom
I am closest personally and theologically were in support of
your position.

All of these letters were from friends. All were from intelligent
people who knew the SBC from a lifetime of service within the
Convention's systems. All believed our efforts had forced Pressler and
Patterson to change course. All were optimistic, hopeful that the worst
was past. None was naive or normally in want of good judgment. But
all missed the nature of the Pressler-Patterson party. Fundamentalists
were not in a fight to get a piece of the pie; they wanted all of it.
Maston and Ward were stating "conventional wisdom" in the higher
circles of the SBC. Cobble described the state of mind of those who
frequented the Executive Committee. The bureaucracy believed the
message had been sent and received. Now things would get better.

In February 1982, I received an invitation to be the inspirational
speaker at Southwestern Seminary in Fort Worth. Most of my career
had been in Georgia and North Carolina, but Dot and I still had a
soft place in our hearts for Southwestern. We met and courted there.
Friends were on faculty. We were glad to accept the invitation. The
School of Music sponsored the occasion. Ministers of music gathered
for a week to have workshops, fellowship, and study. I was the devotional leader for the group. One part of the assignment was the
opportunity to speak in seminary chapel Tuesday, Wednesday, and
Thursday. At chapel I addressed the larger seminary community. Dean
James McKinney had told me I could speak on any topic I chose at
chapel.

Most Baptists were having a hard time comprehending the issues
in the contest between Moderates and Fundamentalists. Why not take
the chapel time to inform a generation of students of my understanding of the contest? So I did. On Tuesday I named my speech "Must
We All Get in Step?" I spoke of the drive for theological uniformity
being pressed by the Fundamentalists.

The chapel was quiet as a morgue during my speech. One member of the theological faculty spoke to me afterward, only one. It was as if there were an unwritten rule—"Don't talk about that subject in public"—and I had violated it. The music faculty was different; they were glad I had addressed the subject. Dr. Jack Coldiron made a witty remark: "Cecil, I can tell when the speaker is saying something. When the students are 'amen-ing' and carrying on, nothing of consequence is being said. When it is quiet, the speaker must be dealing with substantive material. It was very quiet in there today."

The next day I carried forward my thoughts on what was at stake in the Convention controversy and suggested ways to blunt political Fundamentalism. After my speech, John Newport, dean of the School of Theology faculty, asked me join him in the president's office. Russell Dilday, president of Southwestern, and Newport told me they did not want me to talk about the Convention controversy anymore. "We can handle these people," was their position. Dilday said he visited each new trustee, went to their homes, and informed them of the work of the seminary. "They are not going to do harm to us, and we want you to speak on other matters."

Thursday there was sleet and ice; chapel was canceled. I went back to North Carolina frustrated. Moderates had organized to save seminaries from rank Fundamentalism; the people who guided our seminaries were of the opinion that they did not need our help. They thought they could charm and "wine and dine" and the Fundamentalists would become gentle. Other seminary presidents were of the same mind. They underestimated the nature of Fundamentalists, and they overestimated their ability to influence.

A postscript: At the end of the Los Angeles convention, the Moderate leadership group decided we should rotate leadership. I was replaced by Don Harbuck, pastor of First Baptist Church of Eldorado, Arkansas. That arrangement did not last. Harbuck came to hold the opinion that Moderates could not win the next election. He wanted us to throw our support to John Basaigno, pastor of First Baptist Church of Houston. Don believed that if we supported Basaigno, he would be beholden to us and use his presidential powers to appoint people with our point of view. That idea did not survive. Most of us believed Don was blinded by wishful thinking and that we ought to field a candidate for New Orleans in 1982. I was asked to chair the group again. Our group was not always of the same opinion.

# NEW ORLEANS, 1982

It is difficult to recreate the state of mind of Southern Baptists twenty-five years ago. There had been arguing, charges, counter-charges, and unkind remarks for three years. Most Southern Baptists did not know the intent of the Fundamentalist party, and they were closed-minded to anyone who tried to inform them. What they wanted was peace.

Dan Martin was news editor for Baptist Press. After an interview with Bailey Smith, Martin wrote, "Bailey E. Smith believes the 'new peace' in the Southern Baptist Convention is the greatest contribution he has made during his two years as president which end June 17, at . . . New Orleans. . . . 'I was not offended that somebody was nominated against me in Los Angeles,' he says. 'I had bathed my life in prayer and knew God had put me in this position for the sake of the denomination'" (*Baptist Standard*, 12 May 1982).

But not everyone was asleep in May 1982. C. R. Daley was editor of the *Western Recorder*, state paper of Kentucky Baptists. He watched what Smith did, not what Smith said. Then he wrote,

> It was sincerely hoped president Smith would climax his service as president by making certain the two very important committees he appoints were truly representative of all Southern Baptists. Regretfully this does not appear to be so. Rather president Smith appears to be using his power to advance one viewpoint and thus to foster a partisan spirit and to encourage controversy. . . . His concept of unity is to convince all Southern Baptists that they believe what he does instead of accepting others with their differences at some points. . . . He has lapsed back to the approach of former president Adrian Rogers who put Kentuckians on this committee he didn't know but who were recommended to him because of their particular doctrinal stance.

Thus, chances for a sweet spirited convention this year are not as bright as they appeared earlier. (*Western Recorder*, 12 May 1982)

So thick was the air with talk of harmony that it was hard to foster agreement that Moderates should run a candidate. After Don Harbuck stepped down to support "a centrist" candidate, Jim Slatton wrote to him,

> I came back from Memphis feeling about as discouraged and depressed as I have ever felt about the future of our denomination, and even more discouraged then I have ever been about our effort to do anything about it. In short, I am about to the place that I would not consider it worth while to lift a finger this year. I spent over a thousand dollars of my own money last year, and I know I can't do that again this year. Moreover, I see no reason whatever to expend personal effort to help elect John Bisaigno as president of the convention. . . . The more I've thought of this, the less I think of it. . . . (Slatton to Harbuck, 1 October 1981)

I called the Gatlinburg group together again. We made a list of potential candidates. Russell Dilday, Jess Fletcher, Bill Self, Baker James Cauthen, James Sullivan, Warren Hultgren, Kenneth Chafin . . . all were asked to take the job. All declined. Lavonn Brown agreed to go to Tulsa and ask Warren Hultgren to carry our banner. The conversation took place in Warren's home. Upon being asked to lead us, Hultgren called to his wife in the kitchen and said, "Honey, this man wants me to be nominated in New Orleans and get beat."

One after another, the invitations to lead us were rejected. I had the assignment to talk to Baker James Cauthen, retired president of the Foreign Mission Board. At the time Cauthen was adjunct professor of missions at Golden Gate Seminary. He had been my pastor when I was a boy. Dr. Cauthen said if he ran, it might hurt the missionaries; so he declined.

Finally Walter Shurden, dean of the School of Theology faculty at Southern Seminary, went to breakfast with Duke McCall, retiring president of Southern, and asked him to take the job. McCall saw the real stakes in the contest. He knew the Pressler-Patterson group was targeting seminaries like his for a makeover. He knew his chances for victory were slim. But he took the assignment anyway. I admired his insight and courage and always will. When McCall accepted our invitation to be nominated, we only had four weeks to inform and gather our people. State captains did their "networking." Reservations were made for flights and hotels. I spent most of my time on the telephone encouraging, prodding, and sometimes begging people to go to New Orleans and vote for Duke McCall. Interestingly, Duke McCall made a request much like the one Abner McCall (the two McCalls were not related) made a year earlier. When I thanked him for taking our banner, he said, "Cecil, I don't expect to win. There are too many uninformed people in the Southern Baptist Convention. But I do have a request: Would you get me at least 6,000 votes? I don't want to be embarrassed." So 6,000 became my target. I had no idea how many votes it would take to win.

Pressler and Patterson read the mood of Southern Baptists. They knew most people wanted peace. They put forward Jimmy Draper, pastor of First Baptist Church of Euless, Texas. I knew Jimmy when he was a boy; his father had invited me to his church three times to lead youth revivals. For reasons of his own, he had decided to throw in his lot with Pressler and Patterson. Jimmy was and is a charming man. He is outgoing and gives the impression that he is without agenda. That was exactly the kind of candidate the average Southern Baptist wanted.

On June 15, 1982, the SBC gathered in the Louisiana Superdome. Four candidates were nominated for president. Jimmy Draper represented the Pressler-Patterson party. Duke McCall was our candidate. Two native sons from Louisiana were nominated: Perry Sanders of Lafayette and John Sullivan of Shreveport. When the votes were counted, this was the tally:

Draper: 8,081
McCall: 6,124
Sanders: 1,725
Sullivan: 1,625

Draper had received 46 percent of the votes on the first ballot, so there had to be a runoff. In the runoff Draper won with 8,331 (56.97 percent), and McCall got 6,292 (43.02 percent). We had lost again. Abner McCall had gotten 39.3 percent in Los Angeles; Duke McCall moved up to 43 percent. We were moving in the right direction, and then our leadership group nearly fell apart.

## PITTSBURGH, 1983

Don Harbuck's flirtation with a "centrist" candidate was a preview of 1983. President Jimmy Draper did all he could to complicate our lives. He called an "SBC Leadership Discussion Meeting" for November 12, 1982, at a hotel near the Dallas-Fort Worth airport. The stated purpose was to pull together leaders who represented all the parts of Southern Baptist life. The group expressed the rationale that if everyone could sit down and talk, perhaps they could work their way through some of the disagreements. My name was included on a sizeable invitation list. Agency heads were present too. There was much talk; nothing changed. But many Southern Baptists saw Jimmy Draper as a peacemaker. He was getting the two sides together and trying to settle the controversy.

In one interview after another, Draper said things that any fair person could not reject. Before the Pittsburgh convention, he said, "Conservatives desire to destroy nothing. They simply want to be heard" (from an interview with James R. Ward, *Times-Union* staff writer). About this time, Fundamentalists began using the line, "All we want is parity." They pointed out that few biblical inerrantists were teaching in the six seminaries of the SBC. They wanted "parity." I take it they meant they wanted to have as many teachers who held to their theology as there were teachers who held to ours. It sounded good, and it presented well to the press and Baptist rank and file. The signal they sent was, "We are just ordinary Southern Baptists who have been marginalized; all we want is a place at the table." Jimmy Draper fed Southern Baptists a year of that diet.

Two troubling things happened inside our group in 1982. Their long-term effect was to take us out of political action for two years.

1. Some of the agency heads of the SBC came to the conclusion that we (the Moderate leadership) were not effective. We had lost twice, and they decided a different approach needed to be made.

These people wanted to raise $100,000, hire a political person to give leadership, and use that political guru to organize Moderate people for Pittsburgh.

I had misgivings about the plan. I knew whatever the agency heads did would come to light, and our plan would look like a Baptist Watergate. I could see the headline: "Agency Heads Create Slush Fund, Hire Politico to Influence SBC." It would give Pressler and Patterson the fuel to beat us. That plan would not be acceptable to Baptists. Ken Chafin and Jim Slatton were opposed to the idea too. Our Gatlinburg group did not take part in the plan.

2. Jimmy Draper was so effective at being a peacemaker that it was impossible to mount a campaign to defeat him in Pittsburgh. Our leadership group met, talked about our options, and voted 19 to 6 not to field a candidate to unseat Jimmy Draper after one term. Only Virginia and North Carolina representatives thought we had a chance against him. Everyone else said they could not gather people to vote against so nice a fellow as Jimmy Draper. He was perceived as fair, decent, even-handed. Most thought we shouldn't even try. Better not to fight than to fight and be beaten so badly that we could never fight again. And so Moderates did not field a candidate in Pittsburgh. Jimmy Draper was unopposed.

Several years later I was on the Peace Committee. John Sullivan was a member of that committee too; he had been first vice president of the SBC the two years Draper served as president. In a discussion about the fairness of appointments, Sullivan volunteered this bit of information: He said often he suggested Moderate names for appointment. Uniformly Draper rejected them and appointed only people from the Fundamentalist party. He was perceived to be fair; actually he was doctrinaire in his commitment to the Pressler-Patterson agenda. It is unkind to say, but it is part of the story—deception was a tool in the contest. Draper was reelected without opposition. Another year of appointments was given the Pressler-Patterson party. The SBC was already beginning to take on the language, theology, and manners of those people.

On the last day of the convention in Pittsburgh, Foy Valentine spoke to me about the decision of our group not to field a candidate. He was unhappy with us, and was of the opinion that we had missed a chance to win. He said there would be no need of our gearing up for Kansas City (the 1984 annual meeting). He and some friends were going to use a different approach; our efforts would not be needed. I passed that along to the group, and we did not attempt to field a candidate. We would support whatever plan was advanced by Foy Valentine and his friends.

## Kansas City, 1984

The SBC was due to elect a new president; Jimmy Draper had served his two terms. Grady Cothen, president of the Sunday School Board (the SBC publishing house), was the candidate Foy Valentine and his friends had chosen; our group had no part in the choice but we supported him willingly. The Pressler-Patterson party chose Charles Stanley, pastor of First Baptist Church of Atlanta. John Sullivan was a third candidate; he had been first vice president for two years alongside Draper. Some viewed his nomination as an attempt to find a middle-of-the-road candidate. Our political group had no assignment in the election.

The election results were devastating: Charles Stanley received 7,692 votes (52.18 percent) on the first ballot; Grady Cothen got only 3,874 votes (26.28 percent); and John Sullivan had 3,174 votes (21.53 percent).

There was no need for a runoff. Stanley was president; it was only his second time to attend an SBC meeting. He was not chosen because he knew Southern Baptists or supported the Convention. He was chosen because he held an approved theology. The new plan of Foy Valentine and his friends did not work.

Our side had work to do. We had observed that the pre-convention Pastor's Conference had become the place where Fundamentalists showcased their candidates. The Pastor's Conference traditionally begins on Sunday night and runs through Monday night before the convention begins on Tuesday. Eight to ten thousand people attend. The people who control the speakers can send a signal to a large audience on the eve of the election of president.

Twice I wrote to presidents of the Pastor's Conference (Ed Young and Charles Stanley) asking for a Moderate presence on the program. Both were polite, said they would pray about the people they asked to speak, and thanked me for my letter. Both appointed people who were solidly in their political camp. This one-sided approach led some of us to think about a way to offer messengers to the convention an option.

We created a meeting we called the SBC Forum. Our intention was to address a subject of interest to the convention. Our first was "women in ministry." One side is opposed; the other is for. Why not have an effective advocate of each position make their case? It seemed to make sense, and it could be helpful. We asked Adrian Rogers to present the reasons he opposed women in ministry. Adrian said he would not be on our program, and then he added, "I'm not going to help you people get a crowd." I then turned to Paige Patterson; he said no. Finally, I asked Mark Corts, and he declined. None would take the assignment, and our original idea collapsed.

In 1984 we decided to go forward anyway. Gene Garrison from Oklahoma City presided. David Matthews, Kirby Godsey, Sara Ann Hobbs, Duke McCall, and Ken Chafin were our featured speakers. Two were pastors, one was female, one was president of a Baptist university (Mercer in Macon, Georgia), and one was president of Southern Seminary. All were affirmed by being featured, and about 2,000 people came. The meeting was funded on faith. We took up an offering that more than covered our expenses. The forum continued through 1990, presenting Baptists with an option to the monolithic Pastor's Conference.

One action of the Kansas City convention has had long-term consequences. A resolution was presented about women in ministry titled "On Ordination and the Role of Women in Ministry." The sense of the resolution is contained in these lines:

> WHEREAS, The Scriptures attest to God's delegated order of authority (God the head of Christ, Christ the head of man, man the head of woman, man and woman dependent one upon the other to the glory of God) distinguishing the roles of men and women in public prayer and prophecy (I Cor. 11:2-5); and
>
> WHEREAS, The Scriptures teach that women are not in public worship to assume a role of authority over men lest confusion reign in the local church (I Cor. 14:33-36); and
>
> WHEREAS, While Paul commends women and men alike in other roles of ministry and service (Titus 2:1-10), he excludes women from pastoral leadership (I Tim. 2:12) to preserve a submission God requires because the man was first in creation and the woman was first in the Edenic fall (I Tim. 2:13ff); and . . .
>
> Therefore be it RESOLVED, That we not decide concerns of Christian doctrine and practice by modern cultural, sociological and ecclesiastical trends or by emotional factors; that we remind ourselves of the dearly bought Baptist principle of the final authority of Scripture in matters of faith and conduct; and that we encourage the service of women in all aspects of church life and work other than pastoral functions and leadership roles entailing ordination. (*SBC Bulletin*, vol. 61 [Kansas City MO: Southern Baptist Convention, 14 June 1984], 5-6)

Argument about inerrancy did not interest the secular press; a resolution limiting the role of women did. I have clippings from the *New York Times*, *Newsweek*, and numerous southern newspapers on the subject. The agenda of the Fundamentalist party was attracting the attention of a larger audience, and a vocal minority in the SBC was shocked. For decades, SBC churches in Virginia and the Carolinas had been ordaining women to serve as deacons. Here and there a Baptist church had a woman pastor. These churches paid no attention to the resolution, but it got their attention. The Pressler-Patterson theology was pinching them. Peter Rhea Jones at First Decatur, Georgia; James Flamming at First Richmond; and many others preached sermons rebutting the resolution.

The target of the resolution was the institutions of the SBC, especially the seminaries. All six seminaries had been accepting women for theological study for thirty years. The number of women studying theology was increasing. Seminary teachers were offended by the resolution and voiced their displeasure.

After the Kansas City convention, the seminary presidents, long a target of the Pressler-Patterson group, opened their eyes and found their voice. Russell Dilday, president of Southwestern Seminary, preached the convention sermon he titled "On Higher Ground." He gently rapped the knuckles of Fundamentalists and Moderates when he said, "Let's turn from the muddy swamps of political coercion to the higher ground of spiritual persuasion." Russell was begging for a return to a simpler, kinder day in Baptist life. The real reaction to Kansas City and the women in ministry resolution came in the months that followed:

- Randall Lolley, president of Southeastern Seminary, focused his address at the school's opening convocation on the resolution (August 28, 1984). He was forthright and strong against it.
- Roy Honeycutt, president of Southern Seminary, used his opening convocation address to issue a call to battle against militant Fundamentalism. His message was not veiled; it was bold: "That I should be so bold or so presumptuous as to suggest 'holy war' as an analogy for our current struggle grows out of my conviction that 'unholy forces' are now at work—which if left unchecked, will destroy essential qualities of both our convention and this seminary" (published by Southern Baptist Theological Seminary, Louisville KY, 28 August 1984, p. 3).

I wrote to Russell Dilday complimenting him on his convention sermon. He replied to my letter graciously, and then began to organize a strategy, which indicated a change from his stance in February 1982 when he said he did not need help handling Fundamentalist trustees. He wrote,

> Cecil, I think the best form this response [resistance to organized Fundamentalism] can take would be an informal coalition of . . . networks, each of us working among his own constituency and correlating only to the point of communication and calculations of strength. That kind of an approach, it appears to me, does not require a great deal of national leadership.
>
> I am excited about what I hear coming from Georgia, Louisiana, New Mexico, and from the various seminary constituencies, most of them for the first time now geared up to apply the persuasive power of the seminary constituencies to the decision in Dallas. It appears Winfred Moore [pastor of First Baptist Church in Amarillo, Texas, and president of the Baptist General Convention of Texas] is the best person to consider for nomination there. . . . (Dilday to me, 10 July 1984)

The seminary presidents had joined the Moderate struggle. They had enormous credibility among Southern Baptists. I was glad. They knew we were for them, but they had held back from overtly endorsing the Moderate movement. What changed their minds? At this point I am guessing, but

- they were surprised and offended by the resolution on women.
- they could count. The election of Charles Stanley meant more trustees of the Fundamentalist persuasion serving on their boards. By now they could see that "sweet-talking" the Fundamentalists was not working. Seminaries were a target and at risk.
- the theology of Fundamentalism was different from what was being taught in our seminaries. The nature of Fundamentalist theology was coming to light. I have letters from faculty members at Southern,

Southwestern, and Southeastern. All were grateful for what Moderates were attempting to do.

A new breadth was appearing in Moderate politics. It was possible that our Gatlinburg group would no longer be the face of the group; that did not matter. We needed to win, elect, and redirect the SBC. Fundamentalist trustees were a larger and increasingly threatening presence in all the agencies of the SBC. We were running out of time.

# DALLAS, 1985

In late August 1984, I received a telephone call from Roy Honeycutt, president of Southern Seminary. He and his wife were taking one of their children to Furman University in September. They wanted to arrange a lunch meeting with Dot and me for a Saturday in September. A date was set, and we met Roy and June at the Hilton Hotel in Asheville.

In the course of that lunch, Roy Honeycutt asked that I call our political leadership group together. Speaking for other seminary presidents, he said he wanted us to become active again and help them elect Winfred Moore, pastor of First Baptist Church of Amarillo, Texas, as president of the SBC. That jogged my memory: Russell Dilday had suggested Winfred Moore as a candidate for Dallas in a letter he had written me on July 10. This meant the seminary presidents were talking and taking an active part in a campaign to derail the Fundamentalists at the next convention. I responded, "I will call the group together and let you tell them what you have told me. I believe they will support you, but I do not presume on them." I told him Winfred Moore was unknown in Georgia, the Carolinas, and Virginia; he would have to persuade people in the east to go to Dallas and vote for a man most of them did not know.

Immediately I began notifying the Moderate political network. Since New Orleans (the last time we had fielded a candidate), our group had quietly found regional leadership. We were stronger. The group gathered at the Crown Room of Atlanta Hartsfield Airport in October 1984. There were thirty-seven present, including two seminary presidents (Roy Honeycutt and Randall Lolley). The presidents asked the group to become active again with a view to electing Winfred Moore president of the SBC in Dallas. Questions were asked about Moore. Did he represent us? Was he a closet Fundamentalist? He was from West Texas; could we trust him to serve Moderates if we elected him? These questions were asked and answered to the satisfaction of the group. Unanimously we voted to support the presidents and do politics again. The group appreciated being asked and went to their task with heart.

Larry McSwain taught at Southern Seminary. He had a gift for politics, and he became a friend in the months leading up to Dallas. We were the designated counters for Moderates. The "conventional wisdom" was that 16,000 would elect, for no one could imagine a convention larger than 30,000. We worked and we counted. I made hundreds of calls. State captains were as active as I; some were so meticulous they would report an exact number rather than an approximation. Their work was amazingly accurate. When the totals were compiled on Friday before we left for Dallas, Larry and I had counted more than 16,000 votes for Winfred Moore. I went to Dallas with hope that we would elect a president.

Fundamentalists were at work too. Evangelists trumpeted Dallas: "You've got to go to Dallas to save the Bible. You've got to reelect Charles Stanley; he believes the Bible and those liberals don't." Such was their war cry. W. A. Criswell, pastor of First Baptist Church of Dallas, was doing all he could to stir the pot. Perhaps most damaging to our cause was a telegram from Billy Graham to Charles Stanley on the eve of the election. The telegram was given maximum exposure in the *Dallas Morning News* on election day. Until the telegram, Billy Graham had stayed out of the SBC controversy. His support for Stanley tipped the scales for anyone who was undecided, for Graham is held in high regard in the Southwest.

To our astonishment, registration at the time of the presidential election was 45,049. The meeting hall would not contain the messengers, and overflow halls were packed too. People were standing because there was no place to sit. Only two names were put in nomination.

The results were Charles Stanley with 24,453 votes (55.3 percent) and Winfred Moore with 19,795 votes (44.7 percent).

Stanley was elected. The Pressler-Patterson agenda was on track for another year. In a show of broad-mindedness, our candidate Winfred Moore was elected first vice president. It made the simple feel good. The office was powerless, as the president could make appointments without consulting the vice president. Moore was given a chair when officers met; he could do little more than observe.

It was in Dallas that I first allowed myself to think of losing the SBC to political Fundamentalism. The thought was unwelcome; I had invested myself in prodigal fashion to prevent it. Slowly the realization that there was a bottomless number of people who bought into the "bumper-sticker" theology of inerrancy took hold. Most Moderates did not enjoy doing denominational politics; they thought it either immoral or distasteful. When they did get involved, they did it with one hand while holding their nose with the other. But Fundamentalists were of a different mind. They went into battle against the forces of unbelief, against liberalism, against "people who don't believe the Bible." Doing their brand of politics was supposedly doing the Lord's work. They did it with heart. The idea that the people they opposed might be Christians too seemed never to occur to them. Again and again they said things about us that were not true, such as, "You don't believe the Bible." Convinced that they were serving the Lord when they voted the Fundamentalist ticket,  they sent busloads of people to conventions. They followed their leadership (Pressler and Patterson) as if they were Moses and Aaron.

I was asked to speak to the SBC Forum in Dallas. I took my text from Jeremiah 32. The setting of the text seemed to me to resemble the situation of Moderates in the SBC. Jerusalem was surrounded by the Babylonian army; defeat was staring them in the face. At that point, Jeremiah bought a field outside the walls of Jerusalem, ground that was in the hands of the Babylonians. But Jeremiah believed God's people would possess that land again in God's good time. That was our situation. We were losing. If historic Baptists were to survive the siege of Fundamentalism, we were going to have to reinvent ourselves.

The sermon was a prediction of our future. At the time it received no special acclaim.

Looking back on those days, I marvel at our own political progress. Measured in votes cast, we had done a pretty good job. Three times Moderates had pulled together to elect, with the following results: 4,524 votes for Abner McCall in 1981; 6,292 votes for Duke McCall (runoff count) in 1982; and 19,995 votes for Winfred Moore in 1985.

But for all our work, nothing could hide that we were still losing. Fundamentalists did not reason, "We've got a sizeable minority in the house who are unhappy with the way we are running things. We need to fold them into our plans and give them a place at the table." Their view was quite the opposite. When they won by as little as 51 percent, they took all of the appointive places. It seemed their attitude was that we could leave if we were unhappy.

Since 1981, reports from the Committee on Boards (the group that chooses who will sit on the boards that govern SBC agencies) drew fire. When Fundamentalists took control of that committee, they occasionally decided to hurry their agenda by refusing a second term to people who were not of their party. Sometimes they would "bump" these people and appoint one of their own. They wanted to control SBC agencies (especially the six seminaries). The process of "takeover" was long; bumping hurried their process.

Sometimes we challenged their reports by renominating someone who was being "bumped." Sometimes we won; sometimes we lost. But in 1985, we came forward with a new approach. We would try to change the membership of the Committee on Boards by offering the Committee on Committees (which appoints the Committee on Boards) our own slate of nominees. Jim Slatton of Virginia, an especially articulate and hardworking member of the Moderate group and one who could perform well on stage, offered our nominees. In place of the "theologically correct" appointments of the Committee on Committees, Jim nominated presidents of each state convention and presidents of the Woman's Missionary Union in each state. If this new slate were adopted by the Convention, the strategy of the Fundamentalists to use the appointive powers of the president to gain

control of the institutions of the SBC would be undercut. Charles
Stanley, the Fundamentalist-selected president of SBC at the time,
could not control the election of presidents of state conventions. None
of us could control which women would be chosen to be presidents of
the Woman's Missionary Union in the several states. The system
Slatton proposed would make the Committee on Boards reflect the
make-up of the several states. Neither Fundamentalists nor Moderates
would control. The people elected in the several states would choose
who would be on SBC boards.

Slatton was allowed to speak from the platform. He made his
motion, and President Stanley ruled that he would have to offer one
name at a time. Since there were fifty-two names on his list, that
meant those assembled at the meeting would have to hear and vote
fifty-two times. An appeal was made to the house to overturn the president's ruling. A vote was taken, and that vote overturned Stanley's
ruling (12,576 to overturn and 11,801 to sustain). The meeting
adjourned for a Wednesday afternoon break. Realizing their strategy
was at risk, the officers and parliamentarians met and rejected the vote
of the house. The uproar that came of that ruling was near riot. Jim
Slatton, Bill Sherman (my brother), and I held an impromptu press
conference.

At that conference, Slatton said of Stanley's ruling, "They'll say we
were disturbing the peace. I say a guarantee of peace is due process and
a structure that makes peace possible. Regrettably, we don't have due
process" (reported in "1985 News" from Baptist Press, 12 June 1985,
p. 1).

The result of Stanley's ruling was a lawsuit. Mr. and Mrs. Ray
Crowder and Allen McCartney went to court to challenge. The case
was taken to the Georgia Supreme Court, and the ruling of the courts
was that the internal affairs of a religious body are not in the public
domain. The officers could rule as they pleased; it was not a concern
of the state. Moderates had no prospect of relief from a system that
gave them no place in the decision-making process of the institutions.
We could attend meetings as an unwelcome minority, and there would
be no justice.

So intense had the contest for control of the SBC become that the presidents of the several state conventions feared the rancor would infect their meetings too. They called for the creation of a committee to address the problem. "Affirming that 'peace cannot come by war,' the Southern Baptist Convention appointed a 22-member 'peace committee' to study the causes of controversy within the convention and recommend possible solutions" (Jim Newton, staff writer for *The Baptist Standard*, 13 June 1985, p. 1). At first twenty men were chosen; then in a "tip of the hat" to fairness, two women were added. I was among those chosen to serve on what came to be called the "Peace Committee." Roy Honeycutt, president of Southern Seminary, was one of those who suggested my name, saying, "Cecil will not give away the key to the store." I took that to be a compliment, and I did not forget what Roy expected me to do.

When I joined the Peace Committee, I was asked to give up leadership in Convention politics. Jim Slatton became the chair of our Moderate group, and I did not hold leadership in the group again. Moderates had been gaining in the annual vote. Moore got 44.7 percent of the Dallas vote. Slatton led us to our very best effort in San Antonio in 1988, when the Moderate candidate (Richard Jackson) received more than 48 percent of the vote.

I had the pleasure of convening the Gatlinburg group; they were an insightful and courageous group. Never did I imagine the trail of consequences that would come of doing politics. It marked my path for the rest of my career.

# Chapter 10
# THE PEACE COMMITTEE: A STUDY IN FRUSTRATION

Most Southern Baptists thought the Peace Committee was working toward reconciliation; in fact, we were buying time for the Fundamentalist takeover to get past a point of no return. I had no idea our mission (to make peace) was impossible from the start. Two sides are reconciled when both sides are willing to negotiate and make some compromises. Only one side was willing to do the things that make for peace. The Southern Baptist Convention has gotten past the conflict of the 1980s, but they did not make peace. The winners drove the losers out.

In the past twenty years I've been asked many times to record my experiences on the Peace Committee. I did not want to revisit that painful time. But one reason I consented to write this autobiography was the near dearth of written material about what happened behind those closed doors. Everybody knows the results of the Peace Committee; the report is out for all to see. I am not aware that anyone has written of the way it happened, the pressures that were brought to bear, and the players who acted their parts. Tom Graves, Jim Slatton, and my daughter persuaded me to put to paper what happened. Some of the people on that committee are dead now; all of us are aging. So I agreed to write. Of course I write from a personal point of view. This is not an impartial account of a spectator at the Peace Committee, but it is accurate. I interpret those events from the point of view of an involved Moderate.

Parts of this chapter will put some people in a bad light. It's been more than twenty years since I resigned from the Peace Committee. I'm no longer a Southern Baptist. I haven't the power to hurt anyone within the SBC, nor do I desire to do so. I've read the material I saved from those days. I've tried to get my mind back into that time. My first concern as I became a member of the Peace Committee was theological education among Southern Baptists. Roy Honeycutt, president of Southern Seminary at the time, urged my presence on the committee. As I recalled earlier, he said, "Put Cecil Sherman on the Peace Committee; he won't give away the key to the store." Here is my interpretation of those sad days.

The Southern Baptist Convention met in Dallas on June 11–13, 1985. That convention was mammoth in size; more than 45,000 messengers attended. Moderate denominational leaders who had previously argued, "We can handle these people," were now alarmed. They feared real damage to the SBC if the political fight continued to escalate. With the blessing of the denominational establishment, Bill Hickem of Florida and H. Franklin Paschall of Tennessee (a past president of the SBC) made a motion to form a committee. A condensed quotation of that motion reads as follows:

> That a Special Committee be authorized by this Convention, in session, in Dallas, June, 1985; and

> That this committee seek to determine the sources of the controversies in our Convention, and make findings and recommendations regarding these controversies, so that Southern Baptists might effect reconciliation and effectively discharge their responsibilities to God by cooperating together to accomplish evangelism, missions, Christian education and other causes authorized by our Constitution, all to the Glory of God . . .

> That this Committee follow the 1963 Baptist Faith and Message Statement in regard to theological issues . . .

That to accomplish its work, this Committee shall recognize the role of trustees and shall work with and through appropriate Boards, Commissions and Agencies of the Southern Baptist Convention . . .

That the Committee may make its final report and recommendations to the 1986 Southern Baptist Convention and request that it be discharged, or the Committee may make a preliminary report to the 1986 Convention and may recommend that the Special Committee be continued in existence for an additional year . . .

That all Southern Baptists be urged to exercise restraint, to refrain from divisive action and comments, and to reflect Christian love, while this Committee is doing its work; and

That the following persons be designated to serve on the Special Committee . . . . (from a memo from Harold Bennett, executive secretary of the SBC Executive Committee, June 1985)

I will list the members of the committee with a short comment about each. My comment is not meant to pass judgment; the point is to identify each individual for the reader. We were in a contest. You need to know where each person stood.

1. Charles G. Fuller, Chair. Pastor of the First Baptist Church of Roanoke, Virginia. He was a fair chair; his heart was with the Fundamentalists.
2. Harmon M. Born. A layman from Georgia; he was president of a large Ford dealership in Atlanta. He was concerned about what the controversy was doing to the SBC, but theoretically neutral.
3. Doyle E. Carlton, Jr. A fruit grower from Florida. He was a man of gentle spirit. Once in our discussions, Carlton said, "Can't we talk about the things on which we agree?" He was neutral.

4. Jody Chapman. At the time she was a pastor's wife (FBC Wichita Falls, Texas). She was trained as a nurse; her husband was a rising star in the Fundamentalist camp. She voted Fundamentalist.

5. William Crews. Pastor of Riverside Baptist Church in Riverside, California. He longed to be president of Golden Gate Seminary, and his wish was granted while on the Peace Committee. He voted Fundamentalist.

6. Robert E. Cuttino. Pastor of Beaufort Baptist Church, Beaufort, South Carolina. He was a Moderate by education (Yale), but had at first a hard time recognizing the intransigence of "the other side."

7. Christine Gregory. Past president of the SBC Woman's Missionary Union from Danville, Virginia. By nature she was seeking consensus, and it was difficult to find in our meetings. Christine Gregory was put on the committee as a Moderate balance to Jody Chapman.

8. Jim Henry. Pastor of First Baptist Church, Orlando, Florida. He was what I call "a sweet Fundamentalist." I detected not a mean bone in his body, but he voted Fundamentalist.

9. William E. Hull. Pastor of First Baptist Church, Shreveport, Louisiana. He had been professor of New Testament at Southern Seminary. Hull was the scholar on the committee and voted Moderate.

10. Herschel H. Hobbs. Retired pastor of First Baptist Church, Oklahoma City, Oklahoma. Had been past president of the SBC and chaired the committee that created the 1963 Baptist Faith and Message statement. He was supposed to be a Moderate, but often his interpretations of the Faith and Message Statement favored Fundamentalists.

11. Albert McClellan. For years he had been the number-two man on the SBC Executive Committee. He was, in the best sense of the word, a denominationalist. Sometimes he voted Moderate, and sometimes he didn't.

12. Charles Pickering. A lawyer from Mississippi. At the time of the formation of the committee, Pickering was president of the Mississippi Baptist Convention. He began neutral, but when it became clear who the winners were, he sided with them. In a tele-

phone call on July 8, 1986, he said, "Now our job is to try and minimize the damage."

13. William Poe. Another lawyer from Charlotte, North Carolina. Poe was more perceptive than most. He saw through the Fundamentalist spokespersons on the Peace Committee. He was Moderate.

14. Ray Roberts. Past leader of Ohio Southern Baptists who grew up in Asheville, North Carolina. When he retired, he came back to Asheville and joined my church. He was solidly in the Fundamentalist camp.

15. Adrian P. Rogers. Pastor of Bellevue Baptist Church, Memphis, Tennessee. He was the leader and chief spokesman for the Fundamentalist side of the committee. In a sense, he was the quarterback of their team. He was smooth, street smart, and unyielding.

16. Cecil E. Sherman. I recently had become pastor of Broadway Baptist Church in Fort Worth, Texas. Until I went on the Peace Committee, I had been active in Moderate politics.

17. John Sullivan. At the time he was pastor of a church in Shreveport, Louisiana. For two years he had been vice president of the SBC while Jimmy Draper was president (1982–1984). He declared himself a neutral and probably was. But when Fundamentalists won, John was content to remain a Southern Baptist.

18. Daniel G. Vestal. At the time he was pastor of First Baptist Church, Midland, Texas. He was neutral when he came to the Peace Committee. The experience moved him toward Moderates; now he heads the Cooperative Baptist Fellowship.

19. Jerry Vines. Had been pastor in Georgia; became co-pastor of First Baptist Church of Jacksonville, Florida. He was firmly in the Fundamentalist camp and not at all shy about saying so.

20. Edwin H. Young. Pastor of Second Baptist Church in Houston, Texas. He was offended by teachers at Southeastern Seminary as a student; the experience made him sympathetic to Fundamentalists.

21. Charles F. Stanley. Pastor of First Baptist Church, Atlanta, Georgia and president of the SBC (1984–1986). He was the single member of the committee who was casual in attendance. When he was there, he voted Fundamentalist.

22. W. Winfred Moore. Pastor of First Baptist Church, Amarillo, Texas, and vice president of the SBC. By background he should have been in the Fundamentalist camp, but there was a native intelligence in the man that saw through Fundamentalism. He was the one person on the committee who never cancelled my vote. Winfred and I became friends from service together on the Peace Committee.

Three other people attended most meetings. They were Harold Bennett from the Executive Committee; Martha Gaddis, secretary to the Executive Committee; and Dan Martin, a representative from Baptist Press who taped our conversations. At the first meeting it was agreed that any communication from the Peace Committee would be from the chairman, Charles Fuller. Our meetings would be closed to the public. Tapes were made, and those tapes could be opened in ten years. Those decisions were more important than I realized at the time.

When the first meeting opened (August 5, 1985), most of us did not know each other. I counted Bill Hull a friend, and had him teach a Bible study at First Asheville while I was pastor there. I knew Ray Roberts, for he was a member of my church in Asheville. I had met Albert McClellan, Daniel Vestal, Ed Young, and Winfred Moore. Once in a pastor's meeting I had been in the company of Adrian Rogers. For the rest, it was a first meeting. We had to get acquainted.

## GETTING ACQUAINTED WITH THE FUNDAMENTALIST MIND

Anyone involved with Southern Baptists had to be in the company of Fundamentalists. But when I had been in face-to-face contact with people of a Fundamentalist mind, I was usually on a committee where all sides were committed to a common task. When I had chaired a

North Carolina Baptist committee studying Sunday school growth, all sorts of people took part, but all of us were focused to the task of enlarging Sunday schools. The Peace Committee was different. Conflict called the Peace Committee into existence. Both sides had turf to defend. The committee was made up of people who were invested in one side or the other. I was looking for a way to live with Fundamentalists; I was ready to make concessions, but I was not ready to make all the concessions. I was in for a long, dreary time. The first six months were a study of the Fundamentalist mind. I learned . .

1. I had been selective in my choice of friends. They were Moderates before the word labeled us. Nearly all of them had gone long and deep in the theological education system (usually in our SBC seminaries). They did not use the vocabulary of Fundamentalism. They cared about evangelism, but they had broadened their reading of the Gospels. Like me, they were also into a mild form of ecumenism; the social agenda of the Gospels attracted us. Some people I met on the Peace Committee were consumed with growth and theological correctness. Several had a deep-seated suspicion of theological education.

2. My background built into me some self-doubt. Paul said "Now we see in a mirror, dimly, but then we will see face to face" (1 Cor 13:12a NRSV). I think he meant all our knowledge of God is partial in this life. On the Peace Committee I was in the company of people who were certain. They knew what God was like and what God wanted from us. And if anyone did not agree with their interpretations, that misinformed person was wrong. If the misinformed would not submit to correction, then he/she should be pushed to the margins of the company or excluded altogether. Not all held such dogmatic opinions, but the people who eventually controlled the Peace Committee did. They imposed their will on the group.

3. Historic Baptist ideas did not inform the Fundamentalist faction on the Peace Committee. As one of them said, "I'm a Baptist by convenience, not conviction." And I believed him. Baptists were born begging for freedom. No one can understand Baptist polity unless he or she bothers to read of the oppression that gave birth to Baptist

ideas. Because they were oppressed, English Baptists built a church system that gave maximum freedom both to individuals and congregations. I was a Southern Baptist, and it never occurred to me that I had to answer to some Southern Baptist creedal document before I could hold a policy-making place in Southern Baptist life. For most of the people on the Peace Committee, asking conformity to the Baptist Faith and Message Statement was reasonable, sensible, and should be required. That such conformity might squeeze out new insights from God never entered their minds. I see the value of denomination, and I am willing to take majority opinion into account. But ultimately, a Baptist answers to God, not a creed or an inquisitorial committee.

4. Fundamentalists emerged in opposition to modern thought systems. The Fundamentalist mind is pre-Enlightenment. One member of the committee said he believed God made the world in six twenty-four-hour days. To make a statement like that means this person has rejected a sizeable body of science. Evolution was considered of the devil. Education at any state university put faith at risk. That person put a pre-Enlightenment view of the world against all that is modern. For him, Christians were against and opposed to all that is modern. I'm looking at the world through a different lens. I'm trying to accept scientific insights, *and* I'm trying to hold on to basic Christian theology. Sometimes it is not a comfortable place to stand, but it seems to me the only place to be. I was not the only person on the Peace Committee who thought as I did. Talking to people who have a different worldview is hard; communication is nearly impossible.

## THE CAUSES OF OUR CONTROVERSIES

Our assignment was "to determine the sources of the controversies in our Convention, and make findings and recommendations regarding these controversies, so that Southern Baptists might effect reconciliation. . . ." For several meetings the discussion was about the controversies. What are they? What has caused them? In fall 1985, each member of the committee was asked to write a two-page paper on this question: "What Are the Major Theological Matters which I Believe Are at Issue among Southern Baptists Today?" I have copies of

those papers. More than half the papers include variations on the following ideas:

- The SBC has a basic theological document, the Baptist Faith and
  Message Statement. Teachers are expected to teach to the standard
  set by this statement. The possibility that the Baptist Faith and
  Message might become a creed was not a concern of the members of
  the Peace Committee.
- Those who teach in our schools now interpret the Baptist Faith and
  Message Statement "far different from what was in the mind and
  heart of those who first drafted these documents." The average
  Baptist has not changed; the seminary teachers have . . . and are not
  in touch with laity.
- Those who draw their salaries from agencies and institutions owned
  and operated by Southern Baptists have a theology that "is far more
  liberal than that of the majority of Southern Baptists who support
  them." The people who pay get to have the final say about what
  teachers teach. Adrian Rogers said of seminary teachers, "If we say
  pickles have souls, they will teach that pickles have souls."
- The right of private interpretation was suspect; it led to all kinds of
  mischief. Most members of the Peace Committee viewed private
  interpretation with suspicion; they considered it an academic way to
  defend liberalism.

So the first conclusion reached by our committee was this: our
controversy has been caused by theology. A second, and derivative,
problem is politics. But Fundamentalists were not greatly concerned
about politics and gave the subject short shrift (more on this later).

## Regarding Theology

Several theological issues surfaced, but Scripture and the inerrancy of
Scripture were always foremost. No other issue mattered like the
Bible. We wrangled over, discussed, and argued about the Bible. In his
paper about the causes of our controversies, Adrian Rogers wrote, "We
have views taught with reference to the Word of God in our colleges
and seminaries that are contrary to the deeply held convictions of the

majority of our Southern Baptist constituency." Rogers had a full-blown doctrine of inspiration. He also wrote in his paper, "There are those teaching in our institutions who do not accept the historicity of the first eleven chapters of Genesis, who eliminate much of the supernatural in the Scriptures, and make other accommodations in order to make Scripture more acceptable to the enlightened and sophisticated mind."

All the arguments for and against the theory of inerrancy were aired. We heard them all. We heard them again. And it went on and on. I felt sorry for the laity on the committee. It must have been a tedious exercise listening to preachers argue about a theory. Rogers was the chief spokesman for the inerrancy point of view. Jerry Vines, Ed Young, and Ray Roberts occasionally offered Adrian support. Most of the resistance to their arguments came from Bill Hull and myself. The way the discussion was framed put Rogers and his friends on the attack; they held the high view of Scripture. Hull and I were on the defensive because we were defending a view that most thought tended to liberalism. Often the glib phrase, "You don't believe the Bible" slipped into the conversation. It is irritating to hear yourself accused of "not believing the Bible" when you've spent your life trying to interpret the Bible rightly. But the charges never stopped.

There are good reasons not to use the word "inerrancy" to describe the Bible. They were given, but I don't remember anyone who was persuaded by them.

Charles Fuller did not unbalance the conversation; he gave both sides freedom to say their views. But Bill Hull and I were in a minority. People on the committee who declared themselves neutral would not dare vote against inerrancy. They knew the implications of that vote could affect their careers for the rest of their lives. And besides, it seemed that Bill and I were more liberal than most of them.

Frequently Adrian Rogers addressed me as "our liberal friend." He said it so often that it finally dawned on me what he was doing. By saying again and again that I was liberal, he was making me a liberal in the minds of the committee. By any reasonable measure, I am a fairly conservative Baptist. When compared to the Fundamentalist faction that was possessing the SBC, I was liberal. Compared to my opposition on the Peace Committee, the only intellectually honest place to be was on the left. But Adrian's "let's hear from our liberal friend" accomplished its purpose. By calling me liberal repeatedly, he diminished my effectiveness on the committee. Adrian knew what he was doing.

Neo-orthodoxy came in for a regular round of bashing. In his paper on the causes of the controversy, Jerry Vines wrote, "Neo-orthodoxy is an attempt to retain the heart of historic Christian orthodoxy and at the same time yield to the 'results' of radical biblical criticism . . . . neo-orthodox theologians use the conservative's vocabulary but not their dictionary." Fundamentalists on the committee believed the seminary teachers they opposed were neo-orthodox. They considered the teachers wicked, not true to the theology of the people who paid their salaries, and destructive of the faith of the students they taught. Several times Bill Hull and I tried to put Karl Barth and neo-orthodoxy in perspective. It was a giant step away from nineteenth-century European liberalism, a step back toward Christian orthodoxy. Peace Committee Fundamentalists never saw anything good in neo-orthodoxy. That theology had moved beyond neo-orthodoxy by the last part of the twentieth century did not move them either.

Once when discussing the Bible in a morning session, Adrian Rogers said, "I take the Bible literally. I know there are places in the Bible that use figurative language such as 'the land flowed with milk and honey,' but I always try to take the Bible literally." That afternoon I was in the company of Adrian Rogers and Jerry Vines. I referenced Adrian's statement about taking the Bible literally, and asked, "What do you do with those places in the New Testament that affirm slavery, like 1 Peter, Ephesians, and Colossians?" He hesitated a moment then said, "Well, I believe slavery is a much maligned institution; if we had slavery today, we would not have this welfare mess." I had never heard anyone speak a good word for slavery; I went upstairs and wrote it down. Rogers was saying he believed slaves should be obedient to their masters just as he believed wives should be obedient to their husbands. Such was the biblical literalism of the people who controlled the Peace Committee. No other issue was half as important as the inerrancy of the Bible. All other differences sprang from our differences over the Bible.

The issue of women in ministry was at the edge of our theological discussions. Fundamentalists were opposed to women serving in this way; we were for women in ministry. Neither side was open to negotiation; we simply disagreed. It was a train wreck.

Issues that would later surface in the Fundamentalist agenda, issues like the role of the pastor, separation of church and state, abortion, homosexuality . . . these were also at the margins of our discussion. I mention this to show how far the agenda of Fundamentalism has expanded since that time. For the Peace Committee, the main issue was the Bible.

The argument about the Bible was larger than a theory of inspiration. If one would not describe the Bible as inerrant, then that person was ineligible to teach, ineligible to be a trustee of an SBC institution, ineligible to write literature for the SBC's publishing house, ineligible to hold office in the SBC. And since the inerrantist party had prevailed at seven consecutive conventions by vote, anyone who was "on the fence" in the Peace Committee recognized the stakes. Conceding to "inerrancy" was a ticket to one's ambitions; refusing to use the word "inerrancy" condemned one to the margins of Southern Baptist life.

One day during lunch break, Adrian Rogers and I walked side by side toward a restaurant. He said, "Cecil, the position you are taking on this committee is not going to get you anywhere you want to go in Southern Baptist life." I thanked him for his interest in my career and replied, "Is it in your power to determine where I will go in Baptist life?" He turned aside my question, saying, "You know what I mean." And I did. As nearly as anyone, Rogers determined who went where in the division of the spoils when the takeover was accomplished.

Because of the Bible issue, theological education was always around the edges of our conversation. Fundamentalists wanted to control theological education. They had definite ideas about how it should be done. They were sure they knew the truth. The Bible was "truth without any mixture of error," and this applied to theology, ethics, history, and science. The Baptist Faith and Message supported them, and Herschel Hobbs (present on the committee) usually gave definitions of the intent of those who created the 1963 Baptist Faith and Message Statement that were friendly to Fundamentalists. If Fundamentalists could get control of the six Southern Baptist seminaries, then they could impose their theology on those who were studying to become pastors of Southern Baptist churches. In due time, the point of view of Fundamentalists would be the point of view of the average Baptist church. That process is in motion now, for the six seminaries are theirs.

An expectation of most people on the Peace Committee was that the views of most Southern Baptists should be the views taught in the seminaries. The idea that a plumber might not understand lower criticism was an idea that did not trouble them. For them, it was theology by poll. This line of thinking appeared so often in Peace Committee conversations that I began to telephone Russell Dilday, president of Southwestern Seminary. Russell was a friend, and Southwestern was just a few miles from my church. I tried to give Russell (and through Russell the other seminary presidents) some notion of their level of risk. Fundamentalists wanted professors who taught what they believed; a professor who did not mouth their views became disposable. I was not supposed to leak what the committee was doing; the further the meetings went, however, the less I cared for that rule. On a few occasions, I violated the gag rule to warn those who taught in our seminaries.

## Regarding Politics

Charles Fuller had a hard time moving the committee beyond the endless discussion of theology (meaning inerrancy). But on one cold morning in December 1985, an hour was set aside to discuss politics, for the committee had decided that politics was one reason we were in controversy.

Fuller opened the discussion by turning to Adrian Rogers and asking, "Adrian, tell us what you know about the politics of your side." Adrian replied that he was not aware of any Fundamentalist politics. "We are just a group of people who are of like mind; there is no political organization." Fuller did not accept Adrian's answer at face value. He pushed. Again the answer was a denial that a political structure supported the Fundamentalist position. That conversation went on for fifteen or twenty minutes. Fuller probed; Adrian denied.

Then Fuller turned to me and asked, "Cecil, tell us, do Moderates have a political structure?" I answered, "Yes. We have the best political organization I can put together." Then I told how we began our political activities in 1980. States were organized under the leadership of captains. We had meetings twice a year to select candidates, encourage each other, and devise ways to put our ideas before Southern Baptists. We talked about why we lost the last election and how we might win the next. I was as fulsome in my description of Moderate politics as Adrian was covert about Fundamentalist politics. The committee sat silently. Never was the ethic of the two groups more in stark contrast than that morning.

Two or three years after that conversation, Gary North interviewed Paul Pressler on a radio program he called "Fire Storm Chats." Pressler boasted about the method that won at the SBC. He said he had a job that let him travel several days a week; this allowed him to travel all over the South making the case that our seminaries were teaching heresy. He never tired of this work. The effect of Pressler's work (Paige Patterson did much the same work) was to create a network. He taught people how to do hard-nosed, secular politics—how to count and get their people to the annual conventions. The effectiveness of Pressler's work was clear for all to see in Houston in 1979. Gary North was proud of what Pressler had done and praised him. Pressler was the star of North's show that day.

What was denied on the Peace Committee came to light when Paul Pressler admitted to the Peace Committee that the Fundamentalists had an organized political framework. But Paul didn't have to tell the truth for anyone with half a mind to recognize that the people who were winning one election after another were organized. Fundamentalist foot soldiers took orders, packed halls, voted in block, came early, and stayed late. It was organized; there had to be political structure behind their behavior.

One side effect of the Peace Committee conversation on politics had far-reaching consequences. After that hour-long discussion on that cold December morning in Atlanta, we broke for lunch. I had a quick bite and then went outside in the cold to clear my mind. I was walking in the parking lot, round and round the hotel trying to relieve the tension of the meeting. Suddenly, Daniel Vestal was walking alongside me. He said, "Cecil, Adrian didn't tell the truth in that meeting this morning, did he?" I said, "Daniel, I don't believe he did." That was all we said. We walked in silence for a while, then went back into the afternoon meeting. That may have been the day Daniel began his journey away from those people and toward us. He was beginning to see through the smooth words, for underneath there was a lie.

## VISITING SBC INSTITUTIONS

Since some SBC institutions were accused of harboring heresy, the Peace Committee had to get at that heresy, document it, and recommend to the Convention ways to make wrongs right. To do this, several steps were taken.

- Notice was placed in Baptist state papers: any evidence of variation from the Baptist Faith and Message by any employee or institution of the SBC should be documented and sent to the Peace Committee.
- The Peace Committee was divided into visitation teams. Each would visit at least two SBC institutions with any accusations about those institutions in hand. The president and trustees of the institutions were given opportunity to respond (and defend). On my subcommittee were Winfred Moore, Adrian Rogers, and myself. Bill Crews was our chair. The four of us were to visit New Orleans Seminary and Southern in Louisville.
- When the visits were over, each subcommittee would give a judgment on the institutions they had visited. These reports/judgments might inform the final Peace Committee report to the SBC.

And so we went to our tasks. Bill Crews, Moore, Rogers, and myself went to Southern Seminary on January 9, 1986. Any complaint about Southern that had been received by the Peace Committee had been passed on to President Roy Honeycutt in advance. He had time to prepare a response/defense before our arrival. He was ready.

The meeting convened early in the afternoon. The setting was formal. On one side of a large table sat Southern Seminary president Roy Honeycutt, the chair of trustees, the vice chair of trustees, and the seminary lawyer. On the other side sat the four of us. Pleasantries were exchanged briefly; then we got to our work. One by one, about seventeen charges that had been made against Southern faculty members were answered. The answers were thorough. None was given short shrift. We took a break for dinner. President Honeycutt and his wife, June, entertained us in the president's home. After dinner we returned to our work. By 8:30 in the evening all of the charges against Southern faculty had been covered. The meeting should have been over.

When we thought we were finished, Adrian Rogers reached under the table and brought forth a briefcase filled with detail that he thought "proved" Southern faculty did not teach according to the Baptist Faith and Message Statement. There was an eight-inch stack of papers in that briefcase, and he began one page at a time, reading an accusation and questioning Honeycutt.

Some charges were brought by students who had copied or taped lectures; all were to the point that there was heresy at Southern. Honeycutt did not question what Rogers had done (though it was assumed all the charges he would be required to answer would be given to him in advance). Patiently the president answered. Rogers went on . . . and on . . . and on.

Time passed. About 10:30 in the evening, we adjourned to meet again at 8:30 the next morning. At 8:30 a.m., Rogers resumed his interrogation. The accusations were bottomless and repetitious. With the passing of time, Honeycutt's face became white; the blood went out of him. His answers were measured. Rogers: "How long have professors taught that Adam and Eve might not be real people?" Honeycutt: "I don't know. They were teaching that as a possibility when I came to Southern in the forties." His answers were not guarded; they were forthright. And Rogers went on and on. What began as questions became intimidation. The meeting grew tedious and tense.

After a couple of hours, I interrupted to say, "President Honeycutt, I am sorry for what is happening. We promised you advance notice on any charges. You are being called on to give impromptu answers. My apologies." None of this fazed Rogers. When I had made my statement, he resumed his questioning.

Another interruption came when the attorney for Southern tired of Rogers and said, "When do you plan to quit?" Rogers would give no definite time. He said his questions had to be answered. A suggestion was made that we might meet again at a later time. The attorney snapped, "No, we won't; we'll stay here until hell freezes over. We are going to be done with this." His patience was spent. And so was mine.

About 1:30 in the afternoon, after five hours of inquisitorial questioning, we adjourned. Adrian was about halfway through his eight-inch stack of papers. The four members of the Peace Committee retired to the Executive Inn, where we had lunch and our own discussion. Winfred Moore and I thought Southern's answers were more than adequate to clear them of any charge of misconduct or heresy. Bill Crews and Adrian Rogers remained convinced that Southern was out of bounds and ought to be corrected. Our votes were split; the Peace Committee would decide between us. That left no doubt which way the report would be heard; Winfred and I lost, and so did Southern.

The trip to New Orleans was a non-event. Adrian was a graduate of New Orleans; he was pleased with their work. Our visit was social, not substantive.

Other subcommittees brought their reports. Some cleared institutions of charges; others left institutions dangling. Three seminaries were under Fundamentalist suspicion: Midwestern, Southeastern, and Southern. The Christian Life Commission was left hanging because they had not come down firmly against abortion in all situations. The Foreign Mission Board was suspect because there were teachers at a seminary in Switzerland who had caught the eye of SBC Fundamentalists. The rest of the agencies were in pretty good shape.

# MODERATE EFFORTS TO FIND A MIDDLE WAY

Spring 1986 found the Peace Committee up against a deadline. In June the Southern Baptist Convention would meet. We had been commissioned to bring our report in a year; perhaps there could be a second year.

By now the members of the committee knew where others stood on issues. The Fundamentalists were clearly in a majority, for the pragmatists on the committee came down on the Fundamentalist side. Charles Fuller seemed committed to a report that would leave a place for Moderates; probably others were of the same mind. What would the Peace Committee bring to the SBC?

Between January and July 1986, several proposals were put before the Peace Committee. In condensed form, they were as follows:

1. Dated January 21, 1986, Bill Hull wrote "Pathways to Peace: Summary of a Proposal" for the Peace Committee. Bill identified three groups in the SBC. They were Moderates, inerrantists, and a middle group. "Discussions within the Peace Committee . . . reflect deeply held differences . . . ." The task of the Peace Committee was to write a report that would "honor our diversity without compromising our convictions."

Then Bill proposed that we redefine the Cooperative Program "to permit each church to give selective support to those SBC agencies which are believed to be undergirding its approach to evangelism and missions." Nobody would give money to a house they did not approve.

It was an idea that deserved more serious consideration than it got. The Peace Committee did not let Bill's idea live.

2. On February 3, 1986, I received a letter from Charles Fuller, chair of the committee. In that letter was a request: "I would like to ask that you consider drafting a short proposal, suggesting some of the possibilities we discussed in the last meeting about having one or two seminaries which represent the theological postures to the left and right of center" (I imagine Bill Hull's proposal was in response to a similar letter).

My proposal was much like Bill Hull's. "Divide our six seminaries into two groups. One group would have as a program assignment teaching the theology of the Right. The other would have the task of teaching the theology of Moderates." I suggested three schools for each. And I went further:

- No faculty member or administrator would lose his/her job.
- Trustees chosen for Moderate seminaries would be Moderate; trustees for Fundamentalist seminaries would be Fundamentalist.
- Administrators and faculty would be convictional about their assignments; Moderates would teach Moderates and Fundamentalists would teach Fundamentalists.
- "Selective support" would allow each church to decide which of the two theological tracks they would fund.
- The same model could be used in writing Sunday school literature. Create a line of literature that served the more conservative churches; create a set that served Moderates. Each church would buy what they wanted.

I titled my proposal, "Creating a Broad Denomination." Neither Bill Hull nor I presumed a division of the Convention; we were trying to make a way in which both sides could coexist. My idea received no more support than Bill's.

3. The third proposal came to the committee on July 28, 1986, at the Amfac Hotel, Dallas-Fort Worth Airport. Three Moderates (Norman Cavender, Winfred Moore, and Jim Slatton) gave these points:

- Pressler has won his campaign to take over the SBC. Fundamentalists now control.
- Peace requires dealing realistically with the issues that divide.
- Peace Committee's call for reducing political activity is vague; a peace plan must have agreed-upon terms. Moderates are willing to negotiate such.
- The SBC situation makes it impossible for Moderates to cease organizing and confronting. Fundamentalists are entrenched. Asking

Moderates to refrain from politics is asking them to accept the takeover and be silent about it.

- Ending political rallies does not address the problem. Fundamentalists have politicized all areas of the SBC. The Pastor's Conference is political; it is the "greased rut" to the office of SBC president. Evangelism conferences, schools of the prophets, revivals, etc.: all have become tools of political strategy. A peace plan has to deal with this.

- The SBC is huge and complex. To be involved in the decision-making process requires Moderates to use all forums (press and platforms) to answer the Fundamentalist movement. If Moderates stop doing this, they abandon participation in the SBC decision-making process.

- Moderates are compelled by conscience and led by God to speak up for what they believe is right. We believe the present course is disastrous to the SBC and wicked, for it is sinful to test cooperation and fellowship on the basis of a theory of biblical inspiration . . . a theory that has been made more important than the Lordship of Christ. Fundamentalists are maligning agency personnel, mutilating Baptist trust, turning education into a joke, violating consciences of others, and stagnating the intellectual life of the Baptist community.

- Politics is now ingrained in the SBC. It is even a part of Sunday morning sermons by TV pastors. Come to terms with it.

- The SBC controversy is not limited to the national Convention; it is already moving toward the state conventions. Moderates cannot be silent.

- We can agree to steps that will contain our politics and lift it to a civil level. Here are four proposals that might help:
    (a) The president of the SBC can depoliticize appointments to Committee on Committees by naming state presidents and WMU presidents to that committee. In return, Moderates will not run anyone against Rogers in 1987.
    (b) Depoliticize Pastor's Conference and SBC Forum. Put no one on the program who is identified with either side. All speakers would be required to refrain from references to the issues that now inflame us.

(c) Pressler and Patterson cease traveling around the country leading political meetings and promoting Fundamentalist candidates. Moderates would do likewise.

(d) Spokesmen cease attacking agency and institution personnel and attempting to intimidate faculties and administrations. Moderates are to practice restraint to the measure that Fundamentalists are.

The response to Slatton's reasoned argument came from Charles Pickering. He said, "The question is, Will you cease politics?" Slatton said, "That's what we have been proposing." Pickering said, "We don't need all that if everyone will agree to cease politics." Slatton replied, "You haven't heard anything I said; we can't cease politics by talking about it. We must do it in specific ways; that's what we are proposing." Pickering insisted Moderates just needed to stop politics and trust the Peace Committee. (I will say more on this meeting in the next section). So ended the most inclusive proposal brought by Moderates to deal with the SBC controversy.

## FUNDAMENTALIST REPONSES TO OUR SEARCH FOR MIDDLE GROUND

From childhood I was given an assumption: when contending parties seek a way to get along, the path to peace is a middle road. Not your way or my way, but a middle way where both of us make concessions for the sake of peace and for the strength that comes of mutual cooperation. My lifelong assumption was challenged on the Peace Committee. Already I've confessed that I am not unbiased in telling this story. So to cut through as much of my bias as I can, I'm going to let the Fundamentalists speak from transcripts of those meetings. I've chosen sections of the conversation that reveal the unyielding nature of Fundamentalist leadership.

1. At the April meeting of the Political Activities Committee, John Sullivan asked Pressler and Patterson about the single-party appointments by Fundamentalist presidents. This reply came from Patterson: "Dr. Stanley will name only those persons who are inerrantists. . . . I

am not for peace in the SBC if I have to compromise my convictions."
At the 1985 Southern Baptist Convention, about 45 percent of the
messengers voted in opposition to the inerrantist party, but we were
not to offend Paige Patterson's conscience. None of the 45 percent
would be represented in presidential appointments.

Toward the end of that April meeting, Paige Patterson asked me,
"Do you think it is a moral error and a heresy to believe in the
inerrancy of the Scripture?" I replied, "No." Then I turned the question around and asked, "Do you think it is a moral error and heresy
not to believe in the inerrancy of Scripture?" Patterson said, "Yes."
Then he added that I was a heretic. I had never been called a heretic
before.

2. In the July meeting of the Political Activities Sub-Committee, the
one where Cavender, Moore, and Slatton brought their proposal, these
exchanges took place:
- Cavender asked Adrian Rogers, "Do you have room in the SBC for
  my conscience?" Rogers gave a vague answer; so Cavender became
  specific. Three of the last six presidents of the Georgia Baptist
  Convention were from churches that had women deacons. Cavender
  noted that Charles Fuller's state (Virginia) also had many churches
  with women deacons. Cavendar asked Rogers if he would champion
  room for that spirit in at least one or two Southern Baptist seminaries. Rogers said he could not do that.
- Cavender said there were two understandings of Adam and Eve
  among us. "If you controlled five seminaries, would you champion
  one seminary to include our views on Adam and Eve?" Rogers said,
  "No."
- Cavender asked, "If you had 90 percent of all professors teaching
  your view, would you accept 10 percent representing ours?" Again
  Rogers said, "No."
- Cavender said, "In 1979 and 1980, you said, 'All we want is for our
  views to be represented and not made fun of.'" That was right and
  fair. That is the foundation for peace. The Peace Committee should
  work to see that the views of Fundamentalists are represented and

not made fun of. The Peace Committee should work to see that the views of Moderates are represented and not made fun of.

Rogers responded by charging Cavender, Moore, and Slatton with "setting pre-conditions. You are trying to do the work of the Peace Committee." And then he rejected the several proposals Cavender, Moore, and Slatton had brought. He went further. Everything from Moderates was unacceptable to him (at the time he was president of the SBC).

- Paul Pressler was asked if he would support a plan for fairness. He hedged his answer. Patterson answered for him: "Only inerrancy is acceptable anywhere." Patterson could not tolerate any Moderate views in agencies and institutions because of his conscience.

- Cavender asked Rogers if some plan of designated finances were arranged, "Would you allow us to support one seminary with our own money?" Charles Fuller interrupted to say that idea had been put before the Peace Committee and rejected.

Cavender persisted. "For the sake of discussion, if such existed, would you allow us representation in Southern Baptist life?" Rogers said there could not be even one seminary on that basis because it still left the problem of the mission fields. Cavender asked what that meant. Roger replied, "We cannot allow a Moderate seminary such as Southern because its graduates are totally unacceptable on the mission field."

This is the same Adrian Rogers who stood on the platform of the SBC and postured as a president who wanted to be fair and represent all Southern Baptists.

I have heard critics say, "Moderates were ineffective on the Peace Committee." It was not because we didn't offer fair, workable solutions. It was because the other side didn't have any intention of making peace. You can't make peace unless both parties want peace. I offered the committee a motion that would require the presidents to divide their appointments to the exact percentage of the vote in the presidential election that put them in office. The vote was a tie. Half the committee was not willing to require the president to be fair. Charles Fuller would not break the tie. John Sullivan was absent;

when he arrived he broke the tie in favor of my motion. And it was forgotten.

# A Motion that Made a Difference

At the July 28–29, 1986, meeting of the Peace Committee, a neutral member of the committee offered this motion:

> The Baptist Faith and Message Statement on Scripture has been interpreted in two primary ways. One is that Scripture is truth without mixture of error, only as it has to do with matters of faith and practice, and not necessarily on matters of science, history, and cosmology. The other is, Scripture is truth without mixture of error in all areas of reality.
>
> We as a Peace Committee have arrived at the conclusion that the percentage of the faculties of our seminaries, taken as a whole, does not equal the percentage of Southern Baptists who believe that Scripture is truth without mixture of error in all areas of reality.
>
> In order to correct that imbalance, we make the following recommendation:
>
> We recommend that the trustees of each seminary, working with the president, devise a plan that would result in a faculty in their own seminary more representative of Southern Baptists' interpretation of the Baptist Faith and Message Statement. (The above quotation is taken from the notes of Peace Committee secretary Martha Gaddis. She mailed meticulously detailed notes of the meetings to each member of the PC. This letter was dated July 30, 1986.)

Charles Pickering amended the above motion to include Herschel H. Hobbs's remarks as recorded in the proceedings of the June 9–11, 1981, Southern Baptist Convention in Los Angeles: "we reaffirm our historic Baptist position that the Holy Bible, which has truth without any mixture of error for its matter, is our adequate rule of faith and practice, and that we reaffirm our belief in 'The Baptist Faith and Message' adopted in 1963 . . ." (ibid.).

To accomplish the objective of the above motion, a method was suggested to the seminary presidents:

- Clearly state the two interpretations of the Baptist Faith and Message Statement on Scripture.
- Survey Southern Baptists for their interpretation of the Baptist Faith and Message Statement on Scripture.
- Survey the faculties of each seminary for their interpretation of the Baptist Faith and Message Statement on Scripture.
- Make adjustments within each seminary as needed over a period of time.

This motion came from one who had not declared himself on one side or the other. It was especially effective because of its source. Fundamentalists jumped on the motion as if it were a revelation from heaven. Jerry Vines thought it offered a special wisdom. Adrian Rogers agreed. Ray Roberts was pleased. Bill Crews liked it. John Sullivan spoke in favor.

In the way of the Peace Committee, our discussions did not follow a clearly marked path; we wandered from the motion. But before noon the author of the motion was asked to put his idea into writing for the consideration of the committee. After lunch the motion was debated for an hour and a half. Bill Hull and I did all we could to dissuade the committee from the motion. Our arguments ran like this:

1. Theology by poll of the laity will be a basic change in the way theological education has been done among Southern Baptists.
2. Whoever heard of doing education by poll? Does the preacher poll his congregation before he preaches on a controversial subject?
3. How often and on how many subjects will you poll Southern Baptists? If we are really going to keep our seminaries in touch with grassroots, then we are going to have to poll them on other issues, too.
4. You do not like it when the government imposes quotas. Now you want to press down a quota on the percentage of the faculty that holds a certain view on a controversial subject.

5. Is there nothing to be said for expertise? Does the person who pumps gas qualify to instruct the teacher of Old Testament? If a teacher studies a subject for thirty years, is it not possible that the teacher has come to see his subject in a different light from the fellow who pumps that gas, plows a field, or cuts hair at the beauty shop?

6. Is it possible for anyone to be "pre-critical" even if he/she declares himself/herself to be so. We all breathe the spirit of our age, whether we want to or not.

7. The route you are pursuing puts the presidents of the several seminaries in a precarious position. If they resist this motion, they are hiding liberalism. If they say it is a good idea, they make their faculty expose themselves to the slings and arrows of Fundamentalists.

The arguments used by the other side were few:

1. Every teacher ought to be willing to tell what he/she believes.
2. The people who pay the bills have the right to call the shots.

Adrian Rogers spoke for the motion. Here is what he said:

> This is the issue—it always has been—we come up to it and skirt around it and back off from it. We are scared to death of it. Are we going to say the Bible is inerrant in its cosmology, science and history whether or not we are pre-, post- or a-critical. Now that is the issue—are we gonna [sic] dance around it or face the issue?
>
> The motion as I understand it is not the preamble. The motion is that we recommend that the trustees working with each seminary president devise a plan which would eventually result in a faculty in their seminary more representative of Southern Baptists' interpretation of the Baptist Faith and Message Statement on Scripture. This is just saying that our professors who work for us must teach according to our beliefs. Now, that is a pussyfoot statement and yet we are afraid of it. It is time to fish or cut bait. (from Martha Gaddis's minutes of our meeting, July 28-29, 1986)

When the committee voted the results were as follows: 13 for the motion, 3 against the motion (Hull, McClelland, and myself), and 2 abstained (Poe and Hobbs). Robert Cuttino and Winfred Moore left the meeting early and therefore did not vote. Charles Stanley was not present at the meeting. Fuller, as chair, did not vote. If I had been a seminary president, I would have trembled at these words: "at this point we think this approach has merit . . . ."

I put myself in a seminary president's place. It looked like the work of the Peace Committee was beginning to zero in on me and my institution.

• The Peace Committee has visited my campus and they have a question about the way we are interpreting the Baptist Faith and Message Statement.
• Now the PC has a motion that will force my faculty to take a position that is unpopular with the Fundamentalist majority at the annual meeting of the SBC.
• Now, as seminary president, I face this question: Can I stand between our critics and my faculty and protect them?

The Fundamentalists on the Peace Committee were so focused on the seminaries that I broke faith with the rules of the Peace Committee and wrote a letter to the three seminary presidents I knew best. On August 1, 1986, I wrote Russell Dilday (Southwestern), Roy Honeycutt (Southern), and Randall Lolley (Southeastern). I explained exactly what had happened at the recent Peace Committee meeting. I gave the sense of the motion. Arguments pro and con were cited, and the names of those who voted for and those who voted against were called. I gave these presidents warning, for I thought the Peace Committee was at a turning point.

## GLORIETA AND RESIGNATION

Glorieta, New Mexico, is a lovely village some fifteen miles east of Santa Fe. In late October, the aspen leaves have turned and dropped. Winter's heavy hand has not clamped down on the mountains, but nights are cold. I liked to go to Glorieta; Broadway Baptist Church had a lodge there. Often I had gone there to get away from pastoral duty in Fort Worth to plan sermons and recharge my spiritual batteries in the quiet of the mountains.

Dot had never gone with me to a Peace Committee meeting. Since the two of us planned to stay in the Broadway Lodge, no extra expense would be incurred by her attending, and so she went. As things turned out, that was God's grace for me.

This meeting was different. Not only were the twenty-two members of the Peace Committee present, but all the agency heads and seminary presidents were there too. This meeting was not an option for any agency head; they had too much at stake in Peace Committee findings. More than fifty people were present. The meeting was called a "Prayer Retreat." We were supposed to be praying for peace in the SBC. I have the program before me as I write. More than previous Peace Committee meetings, this one was structured. If putting a meeting together with balance could bring about reconciliation, this one should have done it. Each session had worship, testimonies, and discussion. The two sides were given equal time. Everybody was wearing his or her best manners.

All of the above was window dressing. The memorable moment in the meeting came when Milton Ferguson, president of Midwestern Seminary, stood to bring a "statement" from the six seminary presidents. (Remember that three of the seminaries—Midwestern, Southeastern, and Southern—were under special observation. The Peace Committee had not cleared them. Remember the motion to poll Southern Baptists and poll seminary faculties. Now the larger context of the meeting comes into focus.)

Milton Ferguson began to read what has come to be called the "Glorieta Statement." I did not know it was coming. Though I had tried to communicate my concerns about the turns and twists within the Peace Committee, and though I had written these three presidents August 1 about the motion that would put them in harm's way, I still had been given no warning.

The seminary presidents' Glorieta Statement said, "We believe the Bible is fully inspired; it is 'God-breathed' (2 Tim 3:16), utterly unique. No other book or collection of books can justify that claim. The sixty-six books of the Bible are not errant in any area of reality. We hold to their infallible power and binding authority." When the presidents said the Bible was "not errant in any area of reality," they caved in to their Fundamentalist critics. They abandoned their friends and began trying to come to peace with their critics. The Glorieta Statement fairly reeked with words designed to appease Fundamentalists. They were begging Fundamentalists to get off their backs. And it worked . . . but not for long. Within a few years, the men who wrote the Glorieta Statement were forced from office or fired.

I sat within ten feet of Ferguson as he read his statement. His words were cutting the heart out of the Moderate movement. We existed to make space for serious theological education. The very people we had struggled for six years to protect were abandoning us and crossing over the line to snuggle up to their critics. I was devastated.

There was a break for refreshments. I went to Russell Dilday and asked, "Why have you done this? Do you know what this will mean to Moderates who have tried to defend you?" Russell dismissed my questions, saying, "Cecil, you are more trouble to us than those people are." When he made that remark, he inclined his head toward a cluster that included Adrian Rogers, Ed Young, and Jerry Vines. I was not prepared for his statement. I went back to the Broadway Lodge and Dot to process what was happening and collect myself.

I showed Dot the "Glorieta Statement." I told her what Russell Dilday had said. We talked late into the night. I'm not sure we slept at all. In the conversation, we talked of my resigning from the Peace Committee. There were three good reasons to resign:

1. The majority was going to side with the Fundamentalists. By now this had become clear.
2. The Moderate minority was not willing to come together and write a minority report. All Moderates were unhappy with where Fundamentalists were taking the committee, but the eight Moderates could not come together to make counter proposals. In

July 1986, I had called Moderates to my room at the Amfac Hotel
and tried to get us to agree on a Moderate agenda. Two hours of
conversation followed, but there was no consensus.

3. Going to Peace Committee meetings was becoming injurious to my
soul. I was angry, frustrated, and short-tempered when I came
home from our three-day meetings. By the time I got myself back
together, it was time to go to the next meeting. Dot thought resignation for the sake of my state of soul a good idea. She did not push
me; she simply stated what she saw the meetings doing to me.

During that long night, in the course of our conversation, I determined to quit the Peace Committee.

The next morning Dot and I went to breakfast. We chanced to sit
with Randall Lolley, a friend and president of Southeastern Seminary.
I asked him why the presidents wrote the Glorieta Statement. I don't
remember what he said. I do remember what I did. I lost my temper
as I banged my hand down on the breakfast table and said, "You didn't
tell the truth. You didn't tell the truth!" I wasn't surprised at what
Fundamentalists were doing. I was undone by friends who knew what
they had written was not so, but for the sake of buying time and space
from Fundamentalists had caved in and told a lie about the Bible.

Five years later I had Bruce Metzger at Broadway Baptist Church
to teach a Bible study. Dr. Metzger had been a New Testament professor at Princeton Theological Seminary. At lunch one day I asked Dr.
Metzger, "Is there any way I can honestly call the Bible inerrant?"
Since Dr. Metzger was chair of the international committee that trans-
lated the New Revised Standard Version of the Bible, he seemed the
right person to ask. Dr. Metzger reflected for a while, then said, "Well,
it certainly is not inerrant grammatically, and it is not inerrant histor-
ically. No, I don't think you can honestly say any Bible we have is
inerrant." The presidents of our seminaries knew what Dr. Metzger
knew, and they wrote the Glorieta Statement anyway. The first rule of
good scholarship is honesty.

Let me reiterate that I believe the Bible. I do not believe it is shot
through with errors. It is a book about God, a way to peace with God,
and the way to live in a way that is pleasing to God. When the Bible

speaks about these things, I take every word to heart. But there are times when the Bible is not internally consistent; at other times the numbers cited do not fit with parallel accounts of the same event. On immortality, I side with Jesus and Paul and against the view of immortality given in Ecclesiastes. It is for reasons like these that I do not use the word "inerrant." Pleas that the original autographs [long lost to us] are inerrant are foolishness. How can we discuss what we cannot examine?

Charles Fuller gave me time to say good-bye to the Peace Committee. I was so wounded from what the seminary presidents had done that my statement to the Peace Committee was disconnected. I had poured myself into Moderate politics for five years. I had given nearly eighteen months to the Peace Committee. I was defeated and tired. Fundamentalists didn't do me in. My friends did.

I've spent much time on this chapter. Several thoughts come to mind as I reflect on those frantic, tension-filled days:

1. As stated earlier, I have heard critics say, "Moderates were ineffective on the Peace Committee." The record shows we proposed fair ways to make peace and remain within the SBC. We were ineffective because the other side had no intention of being fair or making peace. You can't make peace unless both parties want to be peaceful.

2. Fundamentalists never presented any proposal to make peace . . . not one. Often we heard, "Trust the Peace Committee; trust the process. Stop your politicking." There Adrian Rogers sat, president of the SBC. He was telling us to quit politicking when he was elected three times by hardball politics that his side brought into the SBC. Fundamentalists made no proposals toward peace; they didn't need to. Each annual meeting of the SBC moved them one step closer to their goals. The Peace Committee was a public relations toy dangled before the messengers for a season.

3. When testifying before the Peace Committee, Fundamentalists were honest about where they intended to take the SBC and her institutions. When they stood before the SBC in annual session, they did not tell the truth. Before the SBC they said, "I want to serve all Southern Baptists; I want to be president of all Southern Baptists. I

will be even-handed in presidential appointments." When those same people spoke to us, they told us we would not be at the table in the SBC they were designing.

4. The Peace Committee was a smoke screen that hid what was really happening from the average messenger to the SBC. So long as the Peace Committee existed, there seemed a chance the controversy would go away. It made the fuzzy-headed "middle" in the SBC think something good might occur as a result. When Rogers told Cavender to "trust the Peace Committee," he knew exactly what he was doing. He was buying time to nail the coffin shut on Moderates in Southern Baptist life.

5. The Peace Committee was useless. The proposals put forward by Bill Hull and myself, by Cavender, Moore, and Slatton—they all came to nothing. Looking back on those frantic times, I am amazed at how little we changed anything. If the Peace Committee had never met, the SBC would be exactly as it is today.

After the Glorieta Statement, I went back to Broadway Church and tried to forget the Peace Committee and the Southern Baptist Convention. It was a difficult time.

Several times afterward, I became so depressed that I cried. I had been pushed out of my faith family, the one I had known since I was a boy. Blessedly, I had my church. Broadway people understood, sympathized, and supported. During that troubled, difficult time, they pastored me more than I pastored them.

Response to my resignation was surprisingly generous. Many friends wrote to thank me for my failed efforts to prevent a Fundamentalist takeover. Jim Flamming was given my seat on the Peace Committee. The final report of the Peace Committee came to the St. Louis convention in June 1987. It is a Fundamentalist document, but they threw one bone to Moderates: the Peace Committee report requested that SBC presidents be fair in their appointments. Nobody paid any attention to that recommendation, but they didn't intend to when they put it in the report.

I was damaged goods when I returned to Fort Worth after Glorieta. For a season, I had no place to hang my hat. Then the grace of God took over. I didn't so much forget what had happened in the SBC controversy as I was distracted from it by the good work we were doing in my church. It was God's way of moving me toward release from anger and pain and rejection and hypocrisy. I discovered the joy of seeing a church flower, grow, and serve. As my church became strong, I regained my spiritual balance. I was optimistic again. And then in 1992, when I was sixty-four years old, a door opened. An invitation was extended to me to move to Atlanta and become the first coordinator of the new Cooperative Baptist Fellowship. I was offered a new assignment at about the time most pastors retire. Maybe God still had work for me to do.

# Chapter 11

# CBF: PULLING MODERATES TOGETHER

The assignment I was given at the Cooperative Baptist Fellowship was unlike any task I had previously attempted. My job was to persuade individuals and churches either to leave the Southern Baptist Convention or split their loyalties by giving part of their missions money to CBF and part to the SBC. It was not an easy assignment, for Southern churches are Southern. They honor old ties and respect tradition. The story I will tell is not a history of the early years of CBF; that story is larger than my autobiography. I played a part in the first five years (1991–1996). With the help of Clarissa Strickland, I've pulled together minutes of those early meetings. I've read the stories that circulated in *Baptists Today* from that era. When my daughter first read this chapter, she said, "Dad, parts of this chapter sound like you were giving a report to the Coordinating Council." I suspect Genie is right; there is detail that does not make for easy reading. My goal in this chapter is to encapsulate what it was like to be coordinator of a fledgling group of Baptists who were building a new kind of Baptist body.

The Cooperative Baptist Fellowship is the major body of Baptists who pulled away from the Southern Baptist Convention at the end of the contest for control of the SBC (about 1990–1992). The story I've told to this point drops the SBC controversy at Glorieta, New Mexico, in October 1986. For the Cooperative Baptist Fellowship (CBF) to be born, a sizeable body of Baptists had to decide several things:

- The prospect of winning a Moderate victory in the SBC is lost, so the Fundamentalist "takeover" of the SBC will continue unchecked.
- Living with Fundamentalist leadership is more than we can bear.
- A new group holds my vision of what it means to be Baptist.
- There has to be a new way to do missions and theological education that does not offend historic Baptist sensibilities.

Between 1986 and 1990, ideas began to come to my mind that I never thought I would think. I began to consider separating from the Southern Baptist Convention. That idea was exactly the opposite of what I intended when I called friends to Gatlinburg, Tennessee, in September 1980. Then I was trying to divert the SBC from Fundamentalism. By 1988, I was pondering ways to pull together some part of the people who had been voting and losing with us at annual meetings of the SBC. Our ideas were endangered. If our understandings of Baptist ideas were to live, we had to create institutions that would perpetuate them.

As I relive those seminal days (1986–1990), several incidents come to mind. Though I did not recognize it at the time, these incidents were anticipating the birth of CBF.

- In summer 1986, there was a meeting of Moderates at Mercer University in Macon, Georgia. We had lost the contest for president of the SBC in Atlanta in June. At that Macon meeting, one part of the group said they did not want to continue to do politics. They wanted to create another organization. The SBC could go its way; they were pulling back. That group formed the Southern Baptist Alliance in February 1987 (now called the Alliance of Baptists). The Alliance still lives and is headquartered in Washington, D.C. It is not large, but it continues to have influence in Moderate Baptist life. The effect of this action was that several hundred people pulled out of the Moderate political effort after 1986. This decision reduced the already slim chances of Moderates to win back the SBC.
- In June 1987 at St. Louis, the SBC adopted the Peace Committee Report. It was a document written by Fundamentalists. Guidelines in that report inform hiring in SBC agencies until this day. One

must not only hold to the Baptist Faith and Message; one must hold to it as interpreted by the Peace Committee Report. One more piece of Fundamentalist canon law slipped into place.

- In June 1988, in San Antonio, the SBC adopted a resolution about the role of the pastor. That resolution declared the pastor "the ruler of the church." Fundamentalists were enlarging their agenda and securing the dominance of the pastor in congregational life. This resolution challenged basic Baptist teachings about congregationalism. Baptists are Baptists because they don't want bishops running their churches, but since little attention has been paid to church history, Southern Baptists were reverting back to the very system against which English Baptists had rebelled. This resolution helped some people step away from the SBC.

- In September 1988, Moderate Baptists gathered at Woodmont Baptist Church in Nashville, Tennessee (my brother's church). It was a sizeable crowd of about 800. The question before us was clear: Should we continue to contest Fundamentalists at the annual Southern Baptist Convention, or should we quit? The group could not reach a decision; some wanted to quit while others wanted to continue the struggle. Looking back on those days, all of us were struggling with "leaving home." We had been reared in the SBC. We loved the old SBC. We could not abide the Fundamentalist SBC. We were beginning to consider the idea of "leaving home" in our minds. It was not easy.

- The 1990 annual meeting of the SBC was in New Orleans. Moderates were still fielding a candidate. Our candidate that year was Daniel Vestal, a pastor who served on the Peace Committee as a neutral. But that experience changed Daniel. He came to be a committed Moderate. We gave him our best effort, but we only got 40 percent of the vote. As recently as San Antonio (1988), we had gotten more than 48 percent of the vote. This was the eleventh time we had fielded a Moderate candidate; we had lost every time. New Orleans meant that a good part of the Baptists who had been making a special effort to get to the annual meetings to vote against Fundamentalists had given up. They were staying home.

And there was more. At New Orleans, Fundamentalists made no attempt to be gracious. In fact, they were rude and overbearing. Once when a Moderate was making a point from a floor microphone that displeased the president, the president simply flipped a switch to turn off the microphone. The man was silenced; his ideas were not allowed before the house. Dot and I sat with Jim Slatton way up in the stands at the Superdome. All of us felt as if we were unwelcome guests at the party, and the president wished we would just go away.

After the presidential election, Fundamentalist leadership gathered at an outdoor cafe in the city and celebrated their victory. They knew we were defeated, and they made no secret of their elation. We had contested them for eleven years. We had lost, and they had won. We could stay in the SBC, but we would have no policy-making part in the life of the SBC. We were a tolerated, unwelcome presence. For me, staying in the SBC—under those conditions—was not an option.

As we drove out of New Orleans back toward Fort Worth, I said to Dot, "If you want to see the SBC, look in the rear view mirror. I will not be going to another convention." Dot said, "You are just discouraged; you will get over it." I replied, "No, honey, I mean it; I'll not be treated like that again."

I was not alone in getting the message that I was unwanted. Thousands of Moderates felt the same way I did. Fundamentalists had pushed us to a point where we were willing to consider leaving the SBC and creating something else. This feeling had to overtake a sizeable body of people for CBF to be born. We weren't going to be Southern Baptists any longer. It was not clear what we would be.

• Our fears of Fundamentalism were fleshed out between 1986 and 1990. Randall Lolley was forced to resign as president of Southeastern Baptist Theological Seminary. Appointments by Fundamentalist presidents had created a growing and threatening presence on the boards of all six seminaries. The Sunday School Board president, Lloyd Elder, was under pressure from Fundamentalist trustees. Shortly after the New Orleans convention (June 1990), two members of Baptist Press staff were fired. No longer would there be open reporting of news; the new Baptist Press would be a house-organ for Fundamentalists.

The events cited above had a cumulative effect. Not all Moderates were willing to quit the SBC, but the backbone of the Moderate movement had had enough.

# BIRTH OF CBF

The New Orleans SBC met in June. The next month (July 1990), about fifteen of us gathered in a conference room at the Amfac Hotel at the Dallas-Fort Worth airport. Daniel Vestal presided at our meeting; he had been our candidate at New Orleans and had handled himself well. The point of the meeting was this: We agreed that we were not going to field another candidate for president of the SBC. What were we going to do?

The meeting was not hurried or frantic. Carefully, thoughtfully, and prayerfully, the group came to the conclusion that we ought to hold a public meeting in August (in just six weeks) in Atlanta, Georgia. We reserved a motel that would accommodate 200; we had no idea who or how many would come. Oeita Bottorff of Dallas, a woman of unusual organizational skill, decided to put together a phone bank to call people and invite them to the meeting. She did, and she was amazingly successful. In about two weeks, we had to move the meeting to a larger venue that would house 600. In a few days, we canceled that venue, for we had promises from more than 1,000, then 2,000, that they would attend.

When the meeting convened, 3,100 Baptists were present. We had one thing in common: we were not going to remain in the SBC. What that organization had become was offensive to our understanding of what it meant to be Baptist. That's the one thing we agreed upon. The chair of deacons at Broadway Baptist Church went with me to that meeting; Dot stayed at home. I wish she had been there, for that Atlanta meeting was the most Spirit-filled meeting I've ever attended. No angry words were spoken. We did not bash the SBC. We simply said enough is enough. There has to be another and better way.

Daniel Vestal presided. A "Who's Who" of Moderate Baptist life attended. Out of the meeting came an Interim Steering Committee. About eighty of us were placed in that group; I was honored to be in such company. Our assignment was to create from nothing an organization (as yet unnamed), and come back to another meeting in Atlanta in May 1991.

And so we set to work. I have read the minutes of the Interim Steering Committee to refresh my mind. We met four times: October 11–13, 1990, at the Atlanta Airport Sheraton; January 17–19, 1991, at the Harvey Hotel, Dallas, Texas; March 7–9, 1991, at the Sheraton Hotel, Atlanta; and, our last meeting, May 8–9, 1991, in Atlanta just prior to the second general meeting when we presented our recommendations to the house.

I don't recall any group that was more talented or dedicated to task than the Interim Steering Committee. We were determined to do what we had been asked to do. But talent and dedication to task were not all that was in those meetings. We were through, finished, and done with the SBC, and that is what pulled us together. We were not agreed upon what the organization we were building would become. Some were from the Southern Baptist Alliance. Would the organization we were forming become an extension of the Alliance? And there were advocates for "causes." Would it become an advocacy group for women in ministry? Would the primary focus of the group be race relations? Would we become a denomination? If not a denomination, what would we be? How would we be different from the SBC? How would we be like the SBC? Where would missions fit into the organization we were creating? And what of theological education, for Fundamentalists controlled the six seminaries of the SBC? We knew what we were against; we were not agreed on what we were for, and, truthfully, that indecision still lurks around the edges of CBF.

The minutes tell the story of an infant organization rising from nothing:

• An offer of space to house an office was made and accepted.
• Authorization was given to open a bank account.

- Duke McCall (former president of Southern Seminary) and Grady Cothen (former president of the Baptist Sunday School Board) had, on their own initiative, opened a fund for any Baptist individual or church who wanted to divert their monies from the SBC to whatever Moderates were creating. They had gathered about $8,500 prior to October 1, 1990, and more was coming in all the time. Their intention from the beginning was that this money would move to whatever the Interim Steering Committee was creating. They called this holding account the Baptist Cooperative Missions Program.
- By the January 1991 meeting, there was discussion about hiring people to manage the money given to the holding fund. The fund had received more than $60,000 in the first fifteen days of January.
- The Interim Steering Committee was concerned about people who had been fired by Fundamentalists. We set up ways to distribute money to help people who had been fired. We called that fund the "Safety Net."
- Lawyers worked to get Internal Revenue Service approval for our organization.
- A constitution committee pieced together the framework of an organization. A budget was created. The officers who would preside over the organization were named and their jobs defined.
- Even before CBF was born, money was transferred from the Baptist Cooperative Missions Program account to Associated Baptist Press (a news service designed to give a more balanced statement of Baptist news). We were trying to help fragile, new Baptist entities make it even though CBF was not yet voted into existence.
- Missions was on our minds. We didn't know how it would work, but somehow, someway, the organization we were creating would do missions. Dotted throughout the minutes of those meetings are references to the Missions Task Team. At the March 1991 meeting, we were establishing a Missions Center. CBF was born with a heart for missions.
- Much discussion was directed toward the structure of the new organization. How many representatives would come from each state to a coordinating council? Who would choose these representatives? What would be the duties of the coordinating council? How could

we be sure women and laity would be fully represented? Did the representation fairly deal with geography?

All of this seems small now, but in those days we were trying to get it right. We had seen unfairness in our exit from the SBC. We wanted to make wrongs right. My chief contribution to the process came at the point of theological education. New seminaries were being born. The Southern Baptist Alliance had created a new seminary in Richmond, Virginia. That school opened her doors in fall 1991, with thirty-two students. President Herbert Reynolds of Baylor University was also considering the idea of a seminary at Baylor.

I made an appointment with President Reynolds and drove down from Fort Worth to ask him if he was serious about starting a seminary. Already he had reserved the name Truett Baptist Theological Seminary, but he had not finally committed himself to start the school. I said, "Mr. President, I'm on the budget planning committee of this organization we are creating. If you are going to start a seminary, I want to put Truett in the budget. Tell me what to do." He did not answer quickly. Then finally he said, "Go to Atlanta and put us in your budget." I called Ken Chafin, pastor of South Main Baptist Church in Houston. I told Ken what Herb Reynolds had said. The two of us went to Atlanta and put money into the budget of CBF for BTSR and Truett. Five percent of undesignated money given to CBF would go to BTSR, and five percent would go to Truett. Those percentages held for several years and were a real help to both schools in their early days. Several years later, when I was coordinator for CBF, I was called back to Waco and honored because CBF had delivered half a million dollars to Truett. The leadership of BTSR has been just as grateful. CBF still funds both those schools . . . and several more.

Walter Shurden was on the Interim Steering Committee. In winter 1991, he asked me to write my thoughts for a letter he was creating that would explain to the public why a new organization was necessary in Baptist life. I pondered his request for several weeks; then one Saturday afternoon I put to paper my reasons for a change in direction for Moderates. The "Address to the Public" explained and justified what we were about. "Buddy" Shurden edited and improved my thoughts. I'm proud of that piece. Buddy and I gave Moderate Baptists a reason for CBF, and it is still a good one. The "Address to the Public" was released at the Atlanta Convocation (see the full text of the "Address to the Public" at the end of this chapter).

In May 1991, more than 6,000 Baptists came to Atlanta again. The work of the Interim Steering Committee was submitted to the messengers. Our work was approved, and the Cooperative Baptist Fellowship was born. It had a name, a constitution, and a coordinating council to order its affairs. What the organization would do was largely undecided. As one wit put it, "We are having to fly this airplane while we put it together."

## THE CBF DECISION

Out of Atlanta came one motion that would change my life. The coordinating council formed a search committee for a coordinator for CBF. The coordinator would be a full-time job with an office in Atlanta. Jim Slatton of Richmond was chair of the search committee. That group worked through the summer and into the fall of 1991. In November, Jim called and asked if Dot and I would consent to a conversation about the job. We met with the committee and talked at length about what they wanted in leadership. I told them my ideas about what CBF ought to be. Apparently the search committee thought my vision for CBF and theirs was close enough, for in December 1991, the committee asked if they could recommend to the Coordinating Council that I be employed as the first coordinator of CBF. Dot and I had a decision to make.

It was not an easy decision. I was sixty-four years old and pastor at Broadway Baptist Church in Fort Worth. Things were going well at the church. In some ways I've never been more satisfied with the way a church I pastored was performing than with Broadway in 1991–1992. We had been there seven years; the first years were not easy, but slowly the old ship that was Broadway began to take on health and motion. Young adults were added; children were part of the church again. A strong staff was in place and working well together. Hard decisions were in the past; new buildings had been constructed.

The budget had grown from $1,400,000 a year to $1,900,000. Lay leadership of the church had asked me to stay beyond my sixty-fifth birthday. Broadway was a good fit for us, and the congregation was thriving.

My mother was in a nursing home, and her emphysema had progressed until she was constantly on oxygen. We could not leave while Mother was in that condition, for my sister was in Oklahoma City and my brother was in Nashville. I was a caregiver who had to stay with her. But in the providence of God, Mother slipped away on Christmas Day 1991. That reason for staying in Fort Worth was removed.

Dot and I took three days off and drove to Jefferson, Texas, for a time when we could focus on our decision: stay at Broadway or take the CBF job and move to Atlanta? Dot had always been hesitant to move, and change came hard for her. But in this case she was the one who was more intuitive than I. She saw that CBF was where I belonged, and she encouraged me to take the job. She knew I would be traveling much of the time, and that meant she would be alone, but she was for the move anyway.

I sought the counsel of three people besides Dot as I made the decision: my brother, Bill Sherman; Tom Graves; and Herbert Reynolds. Always my brother had my interest at heart; he would not let me make a mistake if he could help it. Also, Bill had been alongside me in the SBC troubles. He was aware of the temper of Moderate Baptists at that time and place. Tom Graves had been a professor at Southeastern Baptist Theological Seminary, a pastor in Charlotte, North Carolina, and had recently become president of the new Baptist seminary in Richmond. He knew what it was like to leave an old, established church and venture into the unknown of starting a "from scratch" seminary. When I told Tom why I had called, he said, "Oh, so they've asked you to jump off that cliff too!" Herbert Reynolds was president of Baylor University and a man of unusual judgment. He met with me at a cafe in Hillsboro, Texas, and we talked away a Saturday morning. His advice about CBF's prospects and how I might go about building the organization informed me the whole time I was at CBF. None of these advisors told me what to do; all of them gave good counsel and promised to do all they could to help me if I took the job.

A long time ago, back when I took the Chamblee Church (1956), I did not have a clue about what it meant to be the pastor of a church. But with the passing years I had become a pastor. At the prospect of giving up that kind of life, I was sad. The rhythm of the church year, the routine of building next Sunday's sermon, the close bonds that are formed when you walk with people through the marriage of a child or the death of a dear one . . . all of that would be gone. The coordinator of CBF is not a pastor; CBF would be a different kind of job.

The first Sunday in February 1992, I told the Broadway Church we would be going to Atlanta to take the CBF job. We had a month to say good-bye. It was a strange time to move. I was sixty-four, Dot was seventy-three, and we were off to build a new organization of Baptists. It's not the kind of work most people are doing at that age. The leaving was not all sadness; there was adventure in it. Could an old, established church pull away from the SBC? Would successful pastors of large churches risk leading their fellowships toward an unknown entity? My job was to pull together Moderate churches; would those churches let me in the door to make a case for CBF? These questions were in my mind as we left Fort Worth.

We did not move straight to Atlanta. Bud and Grace Brazil, dear friends from Asheville, had a condominium at Hilton Head Island, South Carolina. It was not in use during the month of March, and they offered us the place for the month. We went to Hilton Head, rested, and planned how we would get into the CBF job. During March, I called about thirty pastors from all over the Southeast. I asked them if I could come to their churches and make the case for CBF. Nearly all of those pastors had become friends during the SBC contest. Most of them said yes. I didn't begin the job with CBF until April 1, but during the month of March I planned a schedule that took me several months into the future.

# BUILDING CBF

On April 30, 1992, Herbert Reynolds, president of Baylor University, welcomed the General Assembly of CBF to Texas with these words: "We Texans are most grateful for your coming to the territory of blue-bonnets, pecan trees, longhorn cattle and friendly people. . . . There is a pervasive frontier and 'can do' spirit in Texas; thus, we join all of you in attendance at this budding fellowship with a great sense of anticipation and expectation."

Two days later Reynolds issued "the charge" at my installation. He said,

> First, we ask that you give us the enlightened servant leadership we so desperately need at this time in the history of Southern Baptists—and to give us a biblically sound, Christ-centered, and far-reaching flag to march under as we teach, preach, and minister in the name of Christ to a nation and a world in travail.
>
> Second, Cecil, we love you and we trust you to do the right thing, in all places and at all times. If we in the Cooperative Baptist Fellowship have to sacrifice truth and integrity to further our cause, then let us abandon the effort and look for other ways to serve our Lord Christ. We therefore charge you to lead us in taking the high road in all actions and in all relationships.
>
> Third, we charge you during your tenure to engage us in futuristic thinking and planning to develop domestic and global strategies for the twenty-first century. If you will give us early structure and directions for present-day ministry, and if you will give us a challenging plan for the future, then your years as our coordinator and leader will have provided the goals and road map we require to carry out the Great Commissions contained in Matthew 28:18-20.

I made notes as Reynolds spoke. Herb Reynolds helped me make my decision about going to CBF; he gave me a compass when I took office. I was blessed by his friendship and guided by his words.

## MISSIONS

From the beginning, CBF was into missions. April 1, 1992, came. Dot and I had not been able to sell our house in Fort Worth, so Dot returned to Fort Worth to wait for the house to sell. I was invited into the home of Tommy and Beth Ann Boland, old friends from Chamblee days. I lived with them for three months; that spared me living alone and provided great meals. Our house in Fort Worth finally sold and Dot joined me in Atlanta. We found a townhouse three miles from my office. She and I joined the Chamblee church and reconnected with old friends. Those old friendships were especially dear to Dot, for I began the life of an itinerant. One of the years I was at CBF, I attended the Chamblee church only two Sundays. I was gone; Dot needed the support those dear people gave.

The CBF office was modest in those days. I took MARTA (Atlanta's rapid transit system) to Decatur and walked down the hill to the little building. Inside I found two employees: Sandra Davey handled the money; Clarissa Strickland took care of everything else. Both were friendly and eager to help me, but they didn't know much more about what we were doing than I did. We did not stay in that cramped space long; I found other quarters for us at Mercer University's Atlanta campus. Mercer provided more space and access to I-85.

Something happened in fall 1991 that changed CBF. The Foreign Mission Board (FMB) of the SBC decided to pull their money out of a Baptist seminary in Ruschlikon, Switzerland. What the Foreign Mission Board did broke faith with European Baptists. The school had been given to European Baptists; the Foreign Mission Board had agreed to continue to support the school for several years. On a graduated scale, a little less money would be given the Ruschlikon seminary each year until European Baptists could adjust their modest budget to support the school. Then all of a sudden, because the Foreign Mission Board believed there was liberalism at the school, the money stopped on December 31, 1991. European Baptists had little money; what the Foreign Mission Board did threatened the existence of the school.

At Christmas 1991, Moderate Baptist churches gathered money and, in February 1992, delivered a check for nearly $241,000 to John

David Hopper, president of the Ruschlikon seminary (and an SBC missionary). Several of us joined John Hewett, moderator of CBF, as he presented that check to the Ruschlikon people, but that was not the end of the matter.

President Hopper wanted to solicit money from Southern Baptists to replace money taken from his school by the Foreign Mission Board. Hopper was told by the FMB he could not do that; basically, the FMB had taken promised money from Ruschlikon, then told Hopper he could not raise money to replace what had been taken away. It was a little like being asked to "make bricks without straw." Hopper and his wife resigned as missionaries of the Foreign Mission Board. Other Southern Baptist missionaries to Europe were embarrassed by the actions of the FMB. T. and Kathie Thomas resigned as the Hoppers had. The Hoppers and their colleagues asked CBF to appoint them as missionaries. CBF had a decision to make: Would we take on missionaries? Was our young organization ready for that kind of commitment? Maintaining a missionary couple in Europe in 1992 would cost about $100,000 a year.

The Global Missions Ministry Group recommended to the Coordinating Council that we appoint. A debate followed. There were eighty-plus people on the council. A few (perhaps fifteen) wanted CBF to focus on ethical and social issues, but most believed CBF's strongest investment should be in missions. The Hoppers and Thomases were appointed, and they were the first of a wave of Baptist missionaries in Europe who asked CBF to commission them. Because of the Foreign Mission Board's actions toward Ruschlikon seminary, CBF was pushed into missions a bit faster than the organization would have liked. From the Ruschlikon incident, a steady stream of requests came to my office from SBC missionaries. They wanted to resign their commission with the FMB and do missions with us. Several hundred SBC missionaries wrote to us asking for CBF sponsorship.

Within six months of my coming to CBF, more than twenty missionaries were in our employ. Jimmy Allen and Jean Bond were co-chairs of the Global Missions Ministry Group. As volunteers they were prodigal in the way they gave their time to the task, but Jimmy and Jean had their own lives. They were not in the Atlanta office all the time. Sometimes I was asked to speak for CBF to our European missionaries, and I was not qualified to do that. I had no experience as a missionary. CBF needed a supervisor for her missionaries, and we needed that person quickly.

A retired missionary, Grayson Tennison, helped us in the short run. The real answer to our problem came because of God's intervention (I don't use sacred language casually, in part because of how I saw it misused in the SBC conflict). CBF needed a known and trusted missions leader, and we needed someone our missionaries respected and would follow. Keith Parks was president of the Foreign Mission Board of the SBC for more than a decade. He was known and trusted by Moderate Baptists. He was and is a man of gentle temper; he tried to get along with the Fundamentalists who were being placed on his board. Keith was conservative, but not Fundamentalist; Fundamentalists correctly read his identity. They knew he was not one of them, so they wanted him out. Keith turned sixty-five in October 1992. Several months before his sixty-fifth birthday, he asked his board (now majority Fundamentalist) if he could continue for three years. They refused his request, so he had to leave the FMB at the end of October 1992.

What was happening to Keith was public knowledge. CBF began to court Keith to become our missions leader. We made our first contact with him in February 1992, before I began work at CBF. At a meeting of Global Missions leadership at River Road Church in Richmond, we decided that we would seek Keith. Jimmy Allen made a telephone call, I went to breakfast with Keith in Richmond. He was interested, but he was not willing to consider our job until he had finished his work at the Foreign Mission Board.

Keith and his wife, Helen Jean, came to the Fort Worth CBF General Assembly in May 1992. They were looking us over. Later Helen Jean told me she felt more at home in Fort Worth than she did at the SBC that followed in June. Her mission friends were at the CBF meeting. They were thinking about us, and I suspect they were praying about what to do. Our invitation dangled before them. Our missions involvement was growing larger every month; CBF needed Keith's help.

On Thanksgiving Day, three weeks after his retirement as president of the Foreign Mission Board of the SBC, Keith called me. Dot and I were living in the missionary house of the First Baptist Church of Chamblee, Georgia. I had earnestly prayed for help and for Keith, for I was in over my head when supervising missionaries. Keith said yes. I've always thought it was God's doing. He was exactly what CBF needed; he came to work February 1, 1993.

I had known Keith Parks since we were students at Southwestern Baptist Theological Seminary in the 1950s. We had been acquaintances, but not close friends. For nearly three and a half years we worked side by side at CBF. He knew what he was doing, and I left him alone. My job was to build CBF so Keith could do the missions task. He did his job well, and our working relationship became a friendship. He was head of the largest Protestant mission-sending organization in the world when he served with the SBC. He came to a start-up group; in the beginning he had no secretary and answered the phone himself. None of this discouraged him. When Keith came to CBF, Moderate Baptists knew we had professional leadership. Our missionaries were under the direction of one they trusted and were willing to follow. Keith's coming made my job easier and gave CBF enlarged credibility. God sent us the man we needed.

## BUILDING CBF

Twice during my tenure at CBF, we polled the people who came to the General Assembly. We asked, "What do you think should be the first work of CBF?" Then we listed missions, theological education, and ethical or social causes. The first poll told us 87 percent of the people present thought missions should be CBF's first work; in the second poll 86 percent said they wanted missions to be our first assignment. So doing missions was not only the choice of the Coordinating Council; it was the will of the people who supported CBF. I tell the missions story first because it influenced the way I went about my job. Appointing career missionaries is expensive and a long-term commitment for any institution. I was the one who had the job of going to churches and asking them to move monies they had been giving to SBC causes to CBF causes. If churches moved their missions money to CBF, then CBF was able to appoint more missionaries. I was CBF's salesman; I needed to go to the churches. Each morning I got up, shaved my face, put on my tie, and went out to persuade churches to fund missions through CBF. It was my job, and I believed in what I was doing.

Complicating my job was the tenacity of tradition in Southern Baptist life. The SBC was born in 1845. Many churches had been aligned with the Southern Baptist Convention for more than 100 years. Persuading those churches to move away from the SBC was like pulling teeth. Most ordinary church members were not aware of the changes that had happened in the SBC. They went to church to worship God. They wanted help rearing their children in the faith. They enjoyed singing in the choir. The SBC controversy had not touched their local church. Why should that church change her giving patterns? Besides, most pastors were afraid to tell their members about the controversy; it might divide their church. So getting the CBF cause in front of a church was not easy.

I spent time on the telephone asking pastors if I could come to their churches and make the case for CBF. To my pleasant surprise, I never ran out of pastors who were willing to put their careers on the line and allow me access to their people. Most weeks I worked in Atlanta. Then on Friday evening or Saturday morning I would go to the airport and fly away to tell the CBF story to another church. Sometimes, if my destination were near Atlanta, I would drive. The first year I was at CBF, Mark Brazil, the son of dear friends in Asheville, worked with me. He would drive, and I would rest or think about what I was going to say when we arrived at the next church. It became a routine. I preached on Sunday morning. On Sunday afternoon or evening I would talk about CBF. I had two "stump speeches." They were (1) Why Does CBF Exist? This speech was for laypeople who were not informed about the Fundamentalist takeover of the SBC. (2) What Does CBF Do? This speech was for people who knew why CBF existed, but did not know what we did with the money we collected. Obviously, this speech changed as CBF enlarged her mission and theological education investments.

Always at the end of my presentation I asked if there were questions. Most of the time the questions were straightforward, and it seemed to me they came from genuine curiosity. Occasionally I ran into a "plant," one who came to the meeting to ask questions with the intention of embarrassing or belittling CBF. The first year I was learning, and one of the things I learned was that critics asked several common questions:

- "Do you believe the Bible is inerrant?" The answer to that question was no. Then I would try to explain why I could not honestly use the word "inerrant" to describe the Bible. Only once did I get in trouble telling the truth about the Bible . . . and the trouble came from a pastor who knew I was telling the truth. He just didn't want me to say it out loud. The pastor didn't believe his laypeople could handle honesty about the text. But trusting laity is the Baptist way.
- "Are you for abortion?" No, I'm not for abortion, but sometimes an abortion is the best of very bad options. I've never advised an abortion, but there could be a situation where I would (this was exactly the same position taken by the Christian Life Commission of the SBC in the sixties and seventies).
- "Are you for homosexuality? Are you soft on homosexuality?" No, I'm not for homosexuality; the Bible uniformly says that homosexuality is not a God-approved way for us to practice our sexuality. But not all Christians are agreed on what the Bible says, and I am not appointed to speak for CBF churches. Each church has to study the Scripture and reach their own conclusion about how to relate to homosexuals who ask membership. For CBF to make a pronouncement at General Assembly and expect our churches to conform to our pronouncement would make us exactly like the SBC. Churches interpret the New Testament; CBF does not do it for them . . . and the SBC is not acting like a Baptist body when they press their resolutions down on the churches. One more comment: There is something pharisaic about the way the SBC has gone after homosexuality. Jesus did not beat up sinners; he tried to help them.

Slowly CBF gained strength. I was never sure whether it was because I was a good salesman for the organization or because the SBC was so offensive that reasonable people either had to gravitate toward us or become Presbyterians, Episcopalians, or Methodists. Either way, more and more churches came toward us. Growth was directly connected to expansion in missions. My job was to gather a group of giving churches so that our mission work could go forward. Sometimes I stayed awake at night thinking about my assignment. A pastor asked me, "What do you and Keith [Parks] do?" I said in half jest, "I raise money; Keith spends it." That was pretty close to the truth, and I found meaning and dignity in my assignment.

Even as churches began sending money to CBF, most of them instructed us to send the lion's share of their money forward to some agency of the SBC. We were faithful to their requests; thus, not nearly all monies sent to CBF stayed with CBF. Here's how that played out in those early years:

- In 1991, CBF received $4,517,000 from 391 churches. The churches and individuals who sent that money gave us specific instructions about how their money was to be spent. SBC agencies, especially the Foreign and Home Mission Boards, were targeted to receive 72 percent of the money. CBF had about $700,000 that was undesignated in 1991.
- In 1992, CBF received $7,152,000 from 841 churches. CBF was directed to  send  $3,275,000  to  SBC  agencies. That left $3,877,000 for CBF (54 percent of the monies sent to us).
- In 1993, CBF received $11,100,000 from 1,210 churches. The CBF portion of that money was $6,600,000 million. We were growing in size; better still, we were growing in missions.
- In 1994, CBF received $10,955,000 (all CBF money). The money came from 1,377 churches. (In June 1994, at the SBC in Orlando, the SBC decided they would accept no more money from CBF. I guess they thought our money was tainted. After summer 1994, money sent to CBF stayed at CBF.)

• In 1995, CBF received $12,314,490 from 1,450 churches. The pattern of growth was strong. By 1995, the number of missionaries had climbed to more than 100. We were doing what we set out to do.

This strange pattern of sending money to the SBC Foreign Mission Board through CBF instead of the Cooperative Program is a clue to the complexity of my task. Sending money to us to send to them was a mild way to protest what had happened in the SBC, and it would keep a preacher from facing trouble in his church.

The SBC decision to reject CBF gifts to their agencies is a window into the mind of Fundamentalists. I suspect they thought rejecting our money would cause churches to stop sending money to CBF, but it didn't turn out that way. Churches that sent money through us to SBC agencies had some feeling for CBF, else they would not have used us. The highhandedness of the SBC in rejecting CBF money offended those churches. CBF income increased, and best of all, what came to us stayed with us. Some churches left the SBC, but it was a slow process strung out over several years.

During those years I was encouraging, persuading, begging churches to think about what they were doing. *Baptists Today* invited me to write a column in every other issue of the paper. I've read the columns I wrote in 1992–1996. I wrote about churches making moral choices, suggesting that the decision to stay with or leave the SBC was a moral choice. Another column was about "Telling the Truth," for I did not believe our teachers were as liberal as Fundamentalists said they were. I tried to put myself in the position of a finance committee member who was being asked to decide between SBC or CBF; my article urged that finance committee member to move toward CBF. In a sense the job was contentious, but it was also a statement about Baptist polity. I thought (and still do) that the SBC had infringed on the rights of local churches in the Baptist Faith and Message Statement. They were making the SBC an organization that interpreted the New Testament for the churches. Baptist churches ought not give away that right to any convention or association.

Sometimes I spent a week touring a state. Bob Stephenson, a layman who cared deeply for Baptist principles, drove me around

Oklahoma for a week; we visited most of the CBF-friendly churches in the state. A week in Mississippi was a delight with people who believed in CBF there. In all these tours, efforts were made to persuade people who were unhappy with the turn of events in the SBC. I recall one man who said, "I don't like what they've done [Fundamentalists in the SBC], but I'm not sure I trust you." I suspect many who heard me were thinking what that outspoken man said. Dot and I spent three weeks telling the CBF story in Ohio, Indiana, Michigan, and Illinois. The crowds were small in those places, but we made new friends everywhere we went. CBF was gracious; any time Dot was able to travel with me, they paid her expenses.

For reasons not clear to me, geography and culture affected CBF support. From I-65 East (an interstate highway running from Louisville, Kentucky, to Birmingham, Alabama), CBF support was likely to be strong. From I-65 West to I-35 (an interstate highway going from Wichita, Kansas, to San Antonio, Texas), CBF support was spotty or nonexistent. The people in the region who supported us were courageous; pastors who opted for CBF were both rare and convictional. Tennessee is divided. East of Nashville, there is support for CBF; west of Nashville, the churches that supported CBF could be counted on the fingers of one hand. In Texas, if I stayed west of I-35, I had invitations, support, and encouragement. Those people were conservative, and they were determined in their independence. They did not want the SBC telling them how they had to believe. After telling the CBF story in First Baptist Church, Brownwood, Texas, I visited with Bryce Reid. He was a Baylor friend, a great churchman, and open to CBF. We lingered in the parking lot after church on a Sunday night. Bryce said, "Cecil, it looks to me like all this SBC fuss boils down to this: I don't want some damn judge in Houston telling me what to believe." Welcome to West Texas!

I've been asked, "Didn't you find that work repetitious and contentious?" I did find it repetitious, but in the main, it was not contentious. Most of the meetings were friendly. There was more curiosity than hostility. During those years, I met some great Baptists. They knew our polity. They knew what was wrong with both the theology and the polity of Fundamentalism. Often I stayed in homes instead of motels. I liked that. People told me their stories. They talked about when they became Christians. Others told of Baptists of another time and place who taught them what it meant to be Baptist. I recall the lady in Gadsden, Alabama, who rented a public hall at her expense; no Baptist church would allow our meeting. She spent her own money and got a crowd to morning and evening sessions so that I could tell the CBF story. She was sent to Meredith College a long time ago, and at Meredith she learned the Baptist way. I was honored to be in her company.

People who gave to CBF wanted to hear from CBF. Part of the time I was not traveling with a point of view to building CBF; I was reporting to the people who gave us money. Regularly I called the pastors of the churches who trusted CBF with large and regular gifts. I was building the CBF organization. This sounds so impersonal, but actually a strong organization was the key to doing the missions that excites people. A long time ago I got over my sophomoric hostility to organization. To do something good for God, I had to organize my resources . . . and I still think that way.

Organizing CBF was the other side of my job, but organization was not my private province. The Coordinating Council had much to say about the way CBF was put together. Sometimes I influenced them; I never controlled them. When I arrived at CBF, there were only three employees: Sandra Davey, Clarissa Strickland, and myself. When I left, there were twenty-five people working in the Atlanta office. There were hundreds of committee meetings. To create a new position required the consent of some part of the Coordinating Council. Council made policy; my job was to carry out their wishes. Once a year, staff leadership got together for reflection, evaluation of our performance, and planning the calendar. Officers came to Atlanta once a month; I was always there. Almost uniformly, the officers who led CBF were intelligent and wise, dedicated and generous with their time. Some of our best work was a result of their suggestions. This kind of work was the "bread and butter" of being the coordinator. Self-evaluation is always treacherous, but if I were grading my efforts at CBF, I would give myself a B+ on salesmanship. At best I was a C on in-house management.

Parts of my deficiencies in management were by design. There was a time when churches were open to CBF. They were dissatisfied with the SBC, and they were tired of the fussing. That was the time when those churches were open to a visit from me. I needed to "strike while the iron was hot." Without churches to support us, it didn't matter how we were organized. Without churches, CBF would be a house of cards. So I did what only I could do (the churches who could help us wanted to hear from the coordinator). I stayed on the road and told the CBF story. A fragment of my time was given to organizing and administering. Time has corrected what I left undone. My successor has improved CBF infrastructure. I left CBF after the Richmond General Assembly, June 30, 1996. There were almost 1,500 hundred churches sending money to us; all gifts totaled not quite $15,000,000 that year.

"Building CBF" would not end on the right note if credit were not given to staff. In four years and a little more, we added bright people to the staff. They were superior people who knew why they were Baptists, knew why CBF was born, were not consumed with anger about our split with SBC, and were willing to work. In the main we worked together well. We got CBF up and going.

It is hard to know exactly what God is doing. You can see where God has been more clearly than you can tell where God is going. As I write, I've been retired from CBF for eleven years. Eleven years is not long enough for the dust to settle in a serious study of history, but this is not a history of CBF. This is an autobiography of one person who was inside CBF when she was being born. I am biased, yet I believe God was in our efforts. I thought then and I still think that we were about God's business.

## RELATING TO OTHER BAPTISTS

CBF was a new body of Baptists. Other Baptist groups had to decide how they would relate to us. Representing CBF to other Baptists was not my assignment alone; always I was sitting alongside our moderator (and sometimes others). Here is a snapshot of our relationships with other Baptists.

## The Southern Baptist Convention

Already I've described the hostility of the SBC toward CBF. They saw us as liberal and competitive (we were growing at their expense). There was rarely a month at CBF that I was not defending CBF. A retired military officer in Virginia never stopped speaking ill of us. A layman from Missouri said we didn't believe the Bible and that we were liberal (critics used this word like a club to beat us over the head). If we were liberal, no Southern Baptist should have anything to do with us. So the drumbeat went on and on. It was tiresome. What they said was usually untrue, but if I responded, I was considered contentious because I answered. Most of the time I ignored them; sometimes I had to defend CBF. Misinformation had to be challenged in order for CBF to survive. This part of the job I did not enjoy.

The entire time I was at CBF, we were pulling away from the SBC. The break came in increments. One part of the separation is a story waiting to be told. On a Wednesday night in September 1994, I was in a church in Danville, Virginia, telling the CBF story. I returned to my motel and found a message from Paul Powell. Paul was president of the Annuity Board of the SBC. I had been investing my retirement in the Annuity Board since 1956; most of the people at CBF were doing the same. Paul said, "Cecil, I've just come from the Executive Board meeting of the SBC. I've been instructed to stop receiving money from CBF employees." I asked if this included our missionaries. He said that it did. I asked exactly when they would cut us off. He said, "We can take care of you until June 30, 1995." Blessedly, I had nine months to find help for our employees. (Paul Powell was and is a friend. It was not his idea to cut us off; he was doing what he was told to do. Many employees of the SBC were friendly to CBF even while they worked for the SBC. Some of them were at the ends of their careers; they hadn't much choice except to stay with the SBC.)

My problem was larger than it appears. Hospitalization, disability insurance, and term life insurance for CBF missionaries and Atlanta employees were carried by the Annuity Board. The money CBF employees had invested in the Annuity Board was not threatened, but the service was being withdrawn, and a replacement was hard to find.

How do you get hospitalization for a missionary serving in places like Asia or Albania?

Upon return to Atlanta, I called a meeting of the officers of CBF; they enlisted the help of a group of laypeople. That group worked for two months trying to solve our problem. The Internal Revenue Service has rules; we needed a church annuity program. That was the only way we could maximize the retirement benefits for clergy (which included missionaries). Giant insurance companies were willing to provide us a retirement program, but the cost of housing would not be tax-sheltered if the payout came from Hartford, Prudential, or Met Life. Another difficult piece of the puzzle was our size. We were not big enough to get the most favorable rates for service. We were not tiny; we were not giant. We were in between. And time was running out.

I was outside my area of expertise. The people who had trusted us with their careers were at risk. I was beginning to lie awake at night. At a December meeting of the special lay committee working on our problem, one of them said, "Why don't you call American Baptists? They have an excellent retirement program. See if they will help us." I had thought of that, but we had no connection with American Baptists and no grounds to make a claim on their service. But soon began our happy relationship with American Baptists.

## American Baptists

Early in December 1994, on a Monday morning, I called Daniel Weiss; he was general secretary of the American Baptist Churches. His offices were in Valley Forge, Pennsylvania. In some detail I told Daniel of CBF's predicament. I asked if there were a way CBF could come under the care of the Ministers and Missionaries Benefits Board of ABC. He said rules did not permit our coming under their care, but he would talk with their lawyers to see if a way could be found to accommodate us.

On Wednesday morning, two days later, Daniel called. He wanted me to come to New York for a conversation with himself and Gordon Smith, executive director of the Ministers and Missionaries Benefits Board.

So on a frosty morning a few days before Christmas 1994, Henry Huff, a retired lawyer from Mars Hill, North Carolina, who was on the Coordinating Council, and Keith Parks and I met at the Atlanta airport. We landed in New York as the sun came up. A cab took us to 475 Riverside Drive. Most of the day we spent with Gordon Smith and his people. When we left that afternoon, we had the outline of a plan to move all our people under the care of the M&M Board.

Daniel Weiss and Gordon Smith didn't have to help us. They could have cited times and places when the SBC had been highhanded and arrogant with American Baptists. None of this was in our conversation; they were using their resources to accommodate our need. I will ever be grateful to them, and again, God gave a fragile CBF just what we needed at the time we needed it. I slept better after that Christmas trip to New York.

CBF has teamed with American Baptists on a number of occasions since December 1994. Joint inner-city mission work in St. Louis, funding for Central Seminary in Kansas City, and overseas missions are all evidence of the connection between American Baptists and CBF.

## Alliance of Baptists

The Alliance of Baptists was born in February 1987; they were the first Baptists to break away from the SBC. In 1991, CBF was born. Since both of us came from the same stock (out of the SBC), it seemed the two groups might find a way to merge. Early minutes of CBF tell of efforts in that direction.

I met with the moderator of the Alliance in the home of my friends the Brazils in Asheville, North Carolina. We talked for more than two hours. Though we were agreed that we should leave the SBC, the Alliance wanted to remain a separate entity. CBF was much larger from birth than the Alliance. Our meetings attracted several thousand; theirs gathered several hundred. I asked if they had any interest in coming into CBF. The moderator finally said, "We don't trust you." I asked why. She said, "We don't trust you on the women's issue and ecumenicity." My reassurances on those subjects did not satisfy her. She wanted every church giving to CBF to have women deacons and be open to women in ministry. I responded that we were not likely to set requirements on our churches. What is the difference in CBF insisting that all supporting churches have women in leadership and the SBC insisting that everyone believe the Bible is inerrant? Congregations had to be left free to make their own decisions; they did not need CBF or SBC or the Alliance telling them what to do. My arguments did not persuade.

Later there was a meeting in Charlotte, North Carolina. The Alliance sent their moderator and Stan Hastey, who was coordinator of the Alliance. CBF was represented by the moderator (Pat Ayres) and myself. We talked for more than two hours. Would CBF and the Alliance merge? It became clear early in the meeting that both groups wanted to maintain their own identity.

The conversation then moved to other subjects. Stan Hastey said, "Would you people take the responsibility for funding Baptist Theological Seminary at Richmond? The Alliance does not want to be supporting institutions or missionaries. We want to be dealing with 'cutting edge issues.'" Since the Alliance had given birth to BTSR, I was surprised that they would want to withdraw support from their child. CBF has been a faithful supporter of BTSR, and the Alliance, though still friendly to BTSR, no longer funds the school.

Out of that meeting came this joint statement:

> Continuing the candid and constructive dialogue between the Cooperative Baptist Fellowship and the Alliance of Baptists, the joint group offers the following recommendations to the CBF Coordinating Council and the Alliance Board of Directors:
>
> 1. We agree on the continued existence of each group at this time.
> 2. We look with favor on every opportunity for cooperation, including:
>     a. Seeking means of making our annual meetings complement each other by moving toward common sites and dates beginning in 1994, and

     b. Exploring possibilities for common mission endeav-
       ors and offerings.
  3. We encourage the CBF to consult with and benefit from
     the experience of the Alliance in dialogue with other
     Baptist bodies and the larger Church. (Attached to the
     minutes of the CBF Coordinating Council, 9 September
     1992, Atlanta GA)

In 1987, when the Alliance of Baptists was born, I was sympathetic and joined. When CBF came along, I switched my allegiance to
CBF. The Alliance has chosen a path to the left of most CBF Baptists.
It's hard to pull Baptists together around a social cause; Herbert
Reynolds counseled me, "Cecil, build CBF around missions. That's
the cause Baptists will support." Herb Reynolds was right. Contacts
between CBF and the Alliance dwindled from that day in Charlotte.
There was no hostility; the two organizations simply had different
agendas.

## European Baptists

Since CBF's involvement in missions started in Europe, contact with
European Baptists was essential. Missionaries do not work in a
vacuum. Baptists have been a presence in most European countries for
a long time. The Foreign Mission Board of the SBC had put missionaries in several European countries for years. When division came to
the SBC in 1991, and when SBC missionaries were resigning their
commissions, the questions were: Who is this new CBF organization
that is willing to fund former SBC missionaries? Will European
Baptists partner with CBF in missions? These questions dangled.
Somebody had to go to Europe to explain why CBF existed and ask
European Baptists if they would work with us.

    In fall 1992, CBF sent Jimmy Allen, co-chair of the Global
Missions Task Force; Pat Ayres, moderator of CBF; and myself (Dot
went along at my expense) to a meeting of the European Baptist
Federation. That year EBF met in England because it was the 200th
anniversary of the birth of the Baptist modern missions movement
(William Carey went from England to India in 1792). I knew little

about EBF, and it was a steep learning curve for me. In nearly every European nation, there is a Baptist Union (their word for convention). Most of them were small. They were mildly curious about CBF. Who was this upstart Baptist body that had pulled away from the SBC? They allowed me to explain who we were and how we came to be. There was some sympathy for CBF, for the Foreign Mission Board had stopped funding a seminary at Ruschlikon less than a year before, and that was a direct blow to the school's limited budget. This little-known CBF had sent $241,000 to Ruschlikon (in February 1992). So we were not without some identity; we had helped them.

Now this new group, CBF, wanted to partner with them and send missionaries. Fortunately, they knew our missionaries and thought well of them. Our trip was successful; several Baptist Unions agreed to partner with us and welcome our missionaries. But not all. I recall the leader of the French Baptist Union saying, "We have eighteen SBC missionary couples working with us; if we partner with you, the SBC may withdraw them. I'm not willing to put at risk our connection to the Foreign Mission Board." Polity issues were not driving his decision; he believed the SBC could help him more than CBF.

Karl Heinz Walter was the leader of the European Baptist Union. He had watched the SBC controversy of the 1980s. He knew what was at stake, and he was a real Baptist. He did not want the SBC forcing doctrinal guidelines on European Baptists as a condition for missionaries or money. He smoothed our way and became a friend. Until this day, CBF and European Baptists work together.

Toward the end of 1995, after I had been at work for CBF about three-and-a-half years, I became very tired. The schedule did not allow for much rest. There had been brief breaks at Hilton Head Island or a trip to Madison, Wisconsin, to see our daughter and her family. But most of the time it was a steady, busy schedule: work in Atlanta during the week and travel on the weekend . . . usually to multiple churches. I liked the work; I loved the people. But I simply wore down. I was not sick; I was tired. In September 1995, I told the officers I would retire effective June 30, 1996, just after the CBF General Assembly in Richmond, Virginia.

There was another reason: Dot's health was becoming a question mark. Sometimes when I was away for days and she was alone, she came near depression. A psychiatrist helped her with anti-depressants during those days. It was not good that she be alone as much as my job required. She had encouraged me to take the CBF assignment; she was also ready for me to lay it down.

Though the officers of CBF had known of my plans, my resignation was not public knowledge until the January 1996 meeting of the Coordinating Council. Those last five months were long. A search committee was formed to replace me; they were at work. My calendar became a little lighter. I was not away from home every Sunday, and this was welcome. Retirement always brings mixed emotions. I knew it was time for me to cease my duties, but I was anxious about what would happen to CBF. I knew with my head that CBF would survive without me, but my feelings betrayed my head. I had been a part of the Moderate movement since 1980 (Gatlinburg); it had morphed into CBF. I had made the whole trip, and now the train would go on, but Dot and I would not be active players. Though it was not true, I felt as if CBF were my baby. The baby had grown, but the baby was not grown up yet. These were some of the thoughts that darted through my mind as I went to the Richmond General Assembly. About 4,000 registered for the Richmond Assembly. Pat Anderson was moderator. On Wednesday evening, Dot and I were honored at a banquet at the Richmond Marriott. It was a festive evening with several hundred present. Dot and I were showered with gifts and praise. In a sense, the celebration was about more than Dot and me or my retirement. It was a celebration of the maturing of CBF. No longer was CBF an infant organization that might make it. CBF was here to stay . . . a home for Moderate Baptists in the South. For several years CBF had struggled to get on her feet; now we were standing straight and strong. It was time for a party, and we had a good one.

My closing remarks to the General Assembly were both a report and a charge. Here are the points I presented:

- In all of 1995, 1,450 churches sent money to CBF. In the first six months of 1996, already we had heard from 1,435. We were still a growing organization.
- The percentage of the money we received divided like this: 90 percent came from churches, and 10 percent came from individuals. Of the money from churches, 70 percent of the money came from 200 churches. Our base was not large enough.
- I asked our people to tell the truth to each other; it is the only way we can come to trust. Trust was what we lost in the SBC controversy; it is up to us to learn to trust God and each other again.
- I asked them to reward sacrifice and service, to resurrect kindness and civility in their discourse.
- Finally, I asked them to have confidence in the younger generation that would soon come to CBF leadership.

And then I was retired. It had been forty years since I went as a young pastor to Chamblee. I was twenty-eight when I went to work, and now I was sixty-eight. Like all old people, I remarked at how quickly the years had flown by. Blessedly, I had reasonable health (the shadow of diabetes was on my horizon); now it was time for a different kind of life.

One postscript to CBF: At the Richmond General Assembly, Dot kept a heavy social and business schedule. She was honored in her own right at a luncheon. Our daughter and grandson came from Wisconsin for the occasion; Genie spoke in tribute to her mother in a tender, moving way. But there was a shadow over it all; Dot was a little disoriented by the schedule and all the people coming and going. This was not like her. I thought it a passing thing. I told myself that once we settled into a slower routine, she would be herself again. Actually, that disorientation in Richmond in 1996 was the first sign of Alzheimer's disease. I had not noticed little changes; our daughter, more observant than I, had been pondering what might be happening to her mother for several months. Retirement might not be exactly what I had hoped.

# ADDENDUM: "AN ADDRESS TO THE PUBLIC"

Cooperative Baptist Fellowship is a group of moderate Southern Baptists and ex-Southern Baptists. Born in August 1990 as a result of the fundamentalist-moderate controversy within the Southern Baptist Convention (1979–1990), it did not adopt the name "Cooperative Baptist Fellowship" until May 10, 1991, and after the adoption of the following document. Because the name of the organization originally proposed was the "United Baptist Fellowship," that was the term used in this document when presented to the Assembly. It has been replaced here by "Cooperative Baptist Fellowship," the name ultimately adopted for the organization.

Presented to the General Assembly as "information" on behalf of the "Interim Steering Committee," the document is the result of the work of two people, Cecil E. Sherman and Walter B. Shurden. Sherman's is the primary hand. A brief history of the document is found in the archives of the Cooperative Baptist Fellowship at Mercer University in Macon, Georgia.

Designed primarily to distinguish moderate Southern Baptists from fundamentalist Southern Baptists, "An Address to the Public" gives insight into what moderate Southern Baptists believe to be consistent with the Baptist tradition of freedom and responsibility. After providing a cursory background to the fundamentalist-moderate controversy, the document lists some of the major issues in the conflict. It then commits moderates to the building of a new organization that will embody Baptists principles and extend the missionary work of their people.

— **Walter B. Shurden** (from *The Struggle for the Soul of the SBC* [Macon GA: Mercer University Press, 1993], 309; used by permission from Dr. Shurden)

## An Address to the Public

(from the Interim Steering Committee of the Cooperative Baptist Fellowship, adopted May 9, 1991)

## Introduction

Forming something as fragile as the Cooperative Baptist Fellowship is not a move we make lightly. We are obligated to give some explanation for why we are doing what we are doing. Our children will know what we have done; they may not know why we have done what we have done. We have reasons for our actions. They are:

## I. Our Reasons Are Larger Than Losing.

For twelve years the Southern Baptist Convention in annual session has voted to sustain the people who lead the fundamentalist wing of the SBC. For twelve years the SBC in annual session has endorsed the arguments and the rationale of the fundamentalists. What has happened is not a quirk or a flash or an accident. It has been done again and again.

If inclined, one could conclude that the losers have tired of losing. But the formation of the Cooperative Baptist Fellowship does not spring from petty rivalry. If the old moderate wing of the SBC were represented in making policy and were treated as welcomed representatives of competing ideas in the Baptist mission task, then we would coexist, as we did for years, alongside fundamentalism, and continue to argue our ideas before Southern Baptists.

But this is not the way things are. When fundamentalists won in 1979, they immediately began a policy of exclusion. Non-fundamentalists are not appointed to any denominational positions. Rarely are gentle fundamentalists appointed. Usually only doctrinaire fundamentalists, hostile to the purposes of the very institutions they control, are rewarded for service by appointment. Thus, the boards of SBC agencies are filled by only one kind of Baptists. And this is true whether the vote to elect was 60-40 or 52-48. It has been since 1979 a "winner take all." We have no voice.

In another day Pilgrims and Quakers and Baptists came to America for the same reason. As a minority, they had no way to get a hearing. They found a place where they would not be second-class citizens. All who attended the annual meeting of the SBC in New Orleans in June of 1990 will have an enlarged understanding of why our ancestors left their homes and dear ones and all that was familiar. So forming the Cooperative Baptist Fellowship is not something we do lightly. Being Baptist should ensure that no one is ever excluded who confesses, "Jesus is Lord" (Philippians 2:11).

## II. Our Understandings Are Different.

Occasionally, someone accuses Baptists of being merely a contentious, controversial people. That may be. But the ideas that divide Baptists in the present "controversy" are the same ideas that have divided Presbyterians, Lutherans, and Episcopalians. These ideas are strong and central; these ideas will not be papered over. Here are some of these basic ideas:

### 1. Bible.

Many of our differences come from a different understanding and interpretation of Holy Scripture. But the difference is not at the point of the inspiration or authority of the Bible. We interpret the Bible differently, as will be seen below in our treatment of the biblical understanding of women and pastors. We also, however, have a different understanding of the nature of the Bible. We want to be biblical—especially in our view of the Bible. That means that we dare not claim less for the Bible than the Bible claims for itself. The Bible neither claims nor reveals inerrancy as a Christian teaching. Bible claims must be based on the Bible, not on human interpretations of the Bible.

### 2. Education.

What should happen in colleges and seminaries is a major bone of contention between fundamentalists and moderates. Fundamentalists educate by indoctrination. They have the truth and all the truth. As they see it, their job is to pass along the truth they have. They must not change it. They are certain that their understandings of the truth are correct, complete, and to be adopted by others.

Moderates, too, are concerned with truth, but we do not claim a monopoly. We seek to enlarge and build upon such truth as we have. The task of education is to take the past and review it, even criticize it. We work to give our children a larger understanding of spiritual and physical reality. We know we will always live in faith; our understandings will not be complete until we get to heaven and are loosed from the limitations of our mortality and sin.

### 3. Mission.

What ought to be the task of the missionary is another difference between us. We think the mission task is to reach people for faith in Jesus Christ by preaching, teaching, healing, and other ministries of mercy and justice. We believe this to be the model of Jesus in Galilee. That is the way he went about his mission task. Fundamentalists make the mission assignment narrower than Jesus did. They allow their emphasis on direct evangelism to undercut other biblical ministries of mercy and justice. This narrowed definition of what a missionary ought to be and do is a contention between us.

### 4. Pastor.

What is the task of the pastor? Fundamentalists argue the pastor should be the ruler of a congregation. This smacks of the bishops' task in the Middle Ages. It also sounds much like the kind of church leadership Baptists revolted against in the seventeenth century.

Our understanding of the role of the pastor is to be a servant/shepherd. Respecting lay leadership is our assignment. Allowing the congregation to make real decisions is of the very nature of Baptist congregationalism. And using corporate business models to "get results" is building the Church by the rules of a secular world rather than witnessing to the secular world by way of a servant Church.

### 5. Women.

The New Testament gives two signals about the role of women. A literal interpretation of Paul can build a case for making women submissive to men in the Church. But another body of Scripture points toward another place for women. In Galatians 3:27-28 Paul wrote, "As many of you as are baptized into Christ have clothed yourselves with Christ. There is no longer Jew or Greek, there is no longer slave or free, there is no longer male and female; for all of you are one in Christ Jesus" (NSRV).

We take Galatians as a clue to the way the Church should be ordered. We interpret the reference to women the same way we interpret the reference to slaves. If we have submissive roles for women, we must also have a place for the slaves in the Church. In Galatians Paul follows the spirit of Jesus who courageously challenged the conventional wisdom of his day. It was a wisdom with rigid boundaries between men and women in religion and in public life. Jesus deliberately broke those barriers. He called women to follow him; he treated women as equally capable of dealing with sacred issues. Our model for the role of women in matters of faith is the Lord Jesus.

*6. Church.*

An ecumenical and inclusive attitude is basic to our fellowship. The great ideas of theology are the common property of all the church. Baptists are only a part of that great and inclusive Church. So, we are eager to have fellowship with our brothers and sisters in the faith and to recognize their work for our Savior. We do not try to make them conform to us; we try to include them in our design for mission. Mending the torn fabric of both Baptist and Christian fellowship is important to us. God willing, we will bind together the broken parts into a new company in preview of the great fellowship we shall have with each other in heaven.

It should be apparent that the points of difference are critical. They are the stuff around which a fellowship such as the Southern Baptist Convention is made. We are different. It is regrettable, but we are different. And perhaps we are most different at the point of spirit. At no place have we been able to negotiate about these differences. Were our fundamentalist brethren to negotiate, they would compromise. And that would be a sin by their understandings. So, we can either come to their position, or we can form a new fellowship.

## III. We Are Called to Do More than Politick

Some people would have us continue as we have over the last twelve years, and continue to work with the SBC with a point of view to change the SBC. On the face of it this argument sounds reasonable. Acting it out is more difficult.

To change the SBC requires a majority vote. To effect a majority in annual session requires massive, expensive, contentious activity. We have done this, and we have done it repeatedly.

But we have never enjoyed doing it. Something is wrong with a religious body that spends such energy in overt political activity. Our time is unwisely invested in beating people or trying to beat people. We have to define the other side as bad and we are good. There is division. The existence of the Cooperative Baptist Fellowship is a simple confession of that division; it is not the cause of that division.

We can no longer devote our major energies to SBC politics. We would rejoice, however, to see the SBC return to its historic Baptist convictions. Our primary call is to be true to our understanding of the gospel. We are to advance the gospel in our time. When we get to heaven, God is not going to ask us, "Did you win in Atlanta in June of 1991?" If we understand the orders we are under, we will be asked larger questions. And to spend our time trying to reclaim a human institution (people made the SBC; it is not a scriptural entity) is to make more of that institution than we ought to make. A denomination is a missions delivery system; it is not meant to be an idol. When we make more of the SBC than we ought, we risk falling into idolatry. Twelve years is too long to engage in political activity. We are called to higher purposes.

## IV. Conclusion

- That we may have a voice in our Baptist mission . . . for that is our Baptist birthright
- That we may work by ideas consistent with our understanding of the gospel rather than fund ideas that are not our gospel
- That we may give our energies to the advancement of the Kingdom of God rather than in divisive, destructive politics . . .

For these reasons we form the Cooperative Baptist Fellowship. This does not require that we sever ties with the old Southern Baptist Convention. It does give us another missions delivery system, one more like our understanding of what it means to be Baptist and what it means to do gospel. Therefore, we create a new instrument to further the Kingdom and enlarge the Body of Christ.

# Chapter 12
# RETIREMENT YEARS

Retirement was not a goal throughout my career. Retirement was what came at the end of a life's work, and I was not sure whether I looked forward to it or dreaded it. Sometimes I thought retirement an unnatural state. It was not a normal existence; work and calling and mission were the goals of life. Retirement could be the end of what a life was about. The idea of retiring early never occurred to me. I spent eleven years of my life preparing to do ministry. Viewed in one light, retirement might be the end of what I had prepared to do, and I didn't want that.

Yet in summer 1996, it was time for me to spend more moments with Dot. The travel of CBF was wearing on my body; my absence from Dot was no longer desirable. Sometimes as I approached my last day at work, I wondered how I would fill my time. Other times I counted my anticipated income in retirement. Would there be enough for a decent living for Dot and me? Then there was concern for CBF. Was the young organization going to make it? I went to work for CBF when I was sixty-four; the people who hired me knew I would not be on the job twenty years. My job was to get CBF up and going. Had I done what I was hired to do? My questions about retirement were not answered when June 30, 1996, came. I would have to go into retirement the same way I had gone into ministry, gone into marriage, gone into CBF . . . by faith. I've given you a window into my mind as I laid down my job.

Our family had designed a reunion after my retirement. The Olympics were in Atlanta in summer 1996. Doug (Genie's husband), Genie, and Nathaniel (nine years old) scheduled time for us. We ordered tickets, and to our surprise we got most of the events we wanted to attend. We were "bed and board" for Genie and family; we took in the Olympics. World-class track and field is different from high school and college competition. This was obvious when I saw the women's trial meets in the 400-meter relay. The women were turning in better times than men did when I was in college. They were lithe and powerful. Olympic volleyball is different from pick-up games on the church lawn; we watched Brazil destroy a lesser team. We drove up to Athens, Georgia, to see a soccer match between Portugal and a South American team. Both teams had their fans, and the fans were about as entertaining as the game. What a way to begin retirement!

One other part of that magic summer still impacts my life. I had lived until I was sixty-eight without a computer. Doug and Genie thought that was immoral. With Doug's counsel, I bought a computer. Doug assembled it, and I was on my way into the modern world. Learning to use it was not as intimidating as I feared. Since then there has been a second- and now a third-generation computer. I will always be slow and clumsy at the computer; I was born into the wrong generation. But I can make the thing do what I need it to do. Were it not for Genie, Doug, and Nathaniel, I would not be as far along as I am in computer skills.

Everybody needs to retire to a task. The first task in my retirement was a part-time job at Baptist Theological Seminary at Richmond. BTSR needed someone to teach Baptist Heritage (a Baptist history and polity course) and Life and Work of the Pastor, a course designed to help young people figure out how they are supposed to act and what they are supposed to do when they go to work for a church. A happy combination of events opened the door to me to teach at BTSR.

Ron Crawford was pastor of First Baptist Church of Asheville (my church in a former time), *and* he was chair of the trustees at BTSR in 1996. Ron persuaded the Asheville church to pay my part-time salary at the seminary. The seminary was young; they needed financial help.

CBF had helped BTSR with gifts regularly; I was a friend of the school. Tom Graves, president of the school, was a friend. All these parts fitted together, and an invitation was extended to me to come to Richmond. I accepted.

Dot and I weren't sure we were a fit for BTSR. I had never been a teacher, and we had some reluctance about moving from Atlanta to Richmond. Our living arrangements were pleasant in Atlanta, and we had connections with medical care. To deal with our uncertainty, we made a temporary arrangement. Mark Brazil, a son of friends in Asheville, lived in our house in Atlanta. We took a student apartment at Union Theological Seminary (a Presbyterian seminary across the street from BTSR). It gave us a chance to "test the water" and see if we wanted to make a permanent move to Richmond. (I will comment about teaching later.)

During the year we lived in the student apartment, I was asked to preach here and there, but I took no interim assignments. My focus was on learning how to be a teacher. But in the back of my mind was a gift to Dot. A few times when we were talking about the things we would like to do in retirement, she said, "I wish we could go to Italy; I'm told it is lovely there." I filed that in my memory. All those trips with CBF had garnered me "frequent flyer" miles. I had enough to take Dot and me on her dream vacation. We arranged with my sister and her husband, Ruth and Roger Hamm of Oklahoma City, to join us, and in June 1997, we spent sixteen days in Rome, Florence, Venice, and Lake Como. Dot was in reasonable health; the disease that would later disable her was still at arm's length. She was forgetful, but she was able to take in the beauty, enjoy shopping, and see the galleries and antiquities that are Italy. It was a magic time for us. I nearly waited too late to take that trip. The Olympics and Italy: these were some of the luxuries of retirement.

## MAKING A LIFE IN RETIREMENT

I've done four things in retirement. Three of them are related to my career; the last falls in a separate category . . . becoming a caregiver for an Alzheimer's patient. The parts about ministry fell into place as if given from God.

## A Teacher

My first class was in fall 1996; eight students greeted me. I liked them. The class was "Life and Work of the Pastor." Preparing notes for a two-hour lecture required more work than I expected. That fall I stayed just one lecture ahead of the class. It is one thing to speak off the cuff about how to raise a budget or grow a Sunday school. It is another to put those ideas in order and present them to a class. One by one I labored on these lectures through the semester:

• The Character of the Pastor
• How Do You Talk to a Search Committee?
• The Political Side of Being a Pastor
• What Is a Church Supposed to Do?
• What Are the Vital Signs of a Healthy Church?
• One Way to Do a Wedding
• One Way to Do a Funeral

And the lectures went on and on (there were twenty-one). I was tired when the semester came to an end, but I knew I liked the students and I liked the work. I did not care for testing or grading; I was not sure of myself when doing it. I talked to other teachers and found they had misgivings about testing and grading too. Tom Graves (the president) and Tom Halbrooks (the dean) made my life easy. BTSR was a seminary born as a result of turmoil in the SBC. I was among people who understood what I had been about at CBF. BTSR was a good fit.

Eleven years have passed, and I'm still teaching at BTSR. Along the way I have occasionally taught an evangelism course (an elective). Each summer I assist Daniel Bagby with the first seminar for doctor of ministry students. That seminar is much like "Life and Work of the Pastor." Students are older and have some experience in church work. Often they have found church a difficult place; their churches were once larger. Now they are shrinking. The laity wants nothing to change, *and* they want their church to grow. It's hard to meet those conflicting expectations. If the church doesn't change, the church will not grow. If the pastor pushes change, he or she may risk being dismissed. Students are perplexed and sometimes discouraged. Dan Bagby and I are dealing with forty-year-old students who are wrestling with the question of whether or not they want to spend the rest of their careers as pastors. Two of my churches had to change to grow. My church experience is my qualification for the job of teaching these ministers.

The predicament I described in the previous paragraph is not isolated. Eighty percent of the Baptist churches in Virginia are either static or shrinking. Most of those churches want to live and grow. Too many seminaries are getting their students ready to be chaplains for dying churches. I have a life wish for the Church. Teaching is not just a job; it is a ministry to students who soon will be pastors. I want them to know what church work is like, "warts and all." And I want to give them some ways to cope, for I recall the times when I was a young pastor. I didn't know what to do to effect change. I met resistance from people who wanted church to stay as it "had always been." My job is to help that young minister have some success, feel a sense of accomplishment, and stay in the ministry. The "Life and Work of the Pastor" course has given me an opportunity to reflect on my years as a pastor, condense the experience of those years, and pass forward ideas that may spare my students pain and ease their way when they get a church of their own. In retirement I've become a teacher.

## A Writer

In 1992, soon after I had moved to Atlanta and CBF, Cecil Staton of Smyth & Helwys Publishing Company called. They were creating a new line of Sunday school literature for Moderate Baptist churches. Cecil had seen me teach the Bible on Broadway Baptist's *Window on the Word*, a half-hour Bible study featured by the old Radio and Television Commission of the SBC. He liked the way I taught the Bible on television, and so he asked me to write a commentary for adult Bible teachers. The invitation attracted me for two reasons:

• I had always been a promoter of Bible study in the Sunday school setting. Though some churches have deemphasized Sunday school, I think that is a mistake. Until people are involved in a small group at church, they are likely to slip to the margins of church. And I want Sunday school to teach the Bible rather than hop, skip, and jump from one current affairs topic to the latest hot social issue. Baptist churches need Bible-grounded laity to make congregationalism work.

• I was eager to demonstrate that Moderates take the Bible seriously. So often we had been put down with, "You don't believe the Bible." Cecil Staton was giving me a chance to open the Bible for teachers; if I believed the Bible, my writings would show it. So I agreed to write a commentary on the lectionary text chosen by an editorial board at Smyth & Helwys. I don't choose the texts; I write on what is assigned. For the first eleven years, I wrote nearly every lesson.

When Dot's illness came upon me, I had to ask for help. Then I had health problems that slowed me. Now I write some lessons in nearly every issue, but I'm not able to do all of them.

The commentaries have been well received. Circulation has grown slowly, and now I am often introduced in a new setting as "the fellow who writes the Sunday school commentary." Too many preachers retire and quit studying the Bible. When asked to preach, they just reach into a file and pull out an old sermon. I'm not sure that's good for the congregation who hears the sermon; I know it is not good for the preacher who delivers the sermon. The Bible is a resource for us all through life; when I quit working toward an enlarged understanding of the Bible, I atrophy in spirit.

William Barclay wrote a Daily Study Bible Series for the Church of Scotland; he stayed at it until he had written a commentary on the entire New Testament. His scholarship was sound, but the remarkable thing about Barclay was his writing style. Barclay did not write to impress his scholarly peers; he wrote for intelligent laypeople. He did not "write down" to them. He held their attention and helped them understand the Bible. I don't agree with all his interpretations (and I don't expect my readers to agree with all of mine), but I have always admired his ability to communicate. I wanted to write as well as Barclay. Sometimes as I write, I picture a teacher preparing a lesson.

The teacher is in a hurry. It is 5:30 a.m. on a Sunday morning; he or she is cramming for a 9:45 deadline. They don't need a long, rambling, "maybe this or that" discourse on a difficult text; they need a clear comment. They need something they can use. When there is debate about the interpretation of a text, I give the options and give my opinion.

Through the years I've been driven to texts I would never have chosen. The assignments have made me study the Bible in ways I would never have done had I not been writing. I'm grateful to Cecil Staton for asking me to write. It has been good for my soul. One part of what I do in retirement is write.

## An Interim Pastor

It was hard for me to leave Broadway Church and go to CBF. It had nothing to do with CBF. I had become a pastor, and the work of the church had become my life. During the CBF years, I visited several hundred churches. Some were struggling; others were thriving. I could not help observing and evaluating at each stop. What I saw in those CBF visits was God's preparation for my retirement.

I did not set out to become an interim pastor. The first year we were in Richmond, I preached here and there. No assignment lasted for more than two weeks. Then upon our return from the Italy vacation (summer 1997), I was invited to supply for Providence Baptist Church in Charlotte, North Carolina. The invitation was for only a few weeks; they were looking for another interim. I preached for them; they were pleased with my service. I was asked to return for more weeks, and then without commitment on my part or theirs, I became their interim. It was work I liked. I flew down to Charlotte each Saturday afternoon, preached at 8:30 and 11:00 Sunday morning, usually had lunch with church members, and flew back to Richmond. I was gone from Dot about twenty-four hours. We had just moved into the home we bought in the west end of Richmond; she was still able to take care of herself. The plan worked, and I was a pastor again. I enjoyed it.

Little did I know that the Providence church was the beginning of a string of interims. In the intervening ten years, I served about ten churches. There are some things an interim pastor can do, and some things have to wait for a permanent pastor. My first assignment in each place (though rarely verbalized) was to keep people coming to worship during the interim. I wanted to preach interesting, helpful sermons that made people want to come to church. Usually I had a chance to help with raising the budget. I found it difficult to enlist new members, for most prospects want to see who the new pastor is going to be before they join the church. But here and there I was able to sit with prospects and persuade them.

While an interim, I was not an advocate for CBF. When asked, I told them where I stood on SBC issues. But that was not my first work. I tried to preach Bible-based sermons that were meant to strengthen the Christian life of the audience. Actually, it was exactly what I did when I was the pastor of a church. Friends made in those churches keep in touch; often a card or brief letter is in my mailbox from people I met in an interim. Dot traveled with me until 2002. Her health was deteriorating. Always she was cared for tenderly. Someone would take her to the restroom, sit with her in Sunday school and church, and stay with her while I greeted people at the end of worship. After church, Dot and I found a restaurant, had lunch, then drove back to Richmond.

When Dot had to leave home and go into nursing care, I had good reason to continue doing interim work. The expense of nursing care is huge; my interim salary has helped meet Dot's nursing home costs for nearly five years now. So in retirement I've become an interim pastor.

Between teaching, writing, and being interim pastor, I've had a chance to be active in retirement. Having nothing to do is hard work, and thankfully, idleness has not come my way. Except for Dot's illness, retirement has been blessed.

## A Caregiver

What I am about to write is the story of my wife's descent into Alzheimer's disease and the effects that descent had on me, her caregiver. It is not from a medical journal; it does not pretend to be normative. This is what happened to us. If it matches the story of anyone else, then it might be helpful. Since so many people are beset by Alzheimer's, I will go into detail in the hope that our journey will shed some light on yours. It is not an easy road.

The CBF chapter closed in June 1996 with a suggestion that Dot was not well. What seems so clear now was unclear then. At my retirement, Dot was seventy-eight years old. A little forgetfulness at that age is not unusual, and since none of us wants to think the worst, I pushed away the idea that her confusion was anything of consequence. We spent the first year in Richmond in the student apartment. There was little housework to do. Dot spent her time cooking and going about with me. We invited students into our apartment, and she was her usual self, a gracious hostess. But one incident should have been a clue that she was not well. She was packing for her annual meeting with three women who were friends from her Sunday School Board days (1944–1949). It was their pattern to get together each spring for a three- or four-day visit. In 1997, the gathering was to be in Texas. Dot was to fly to Austin where a friend would meet her. Two weeks before she was to leave, she said, "I'm not going to get in a jam about packing this year. I'm packing now." I thought no more about her packing. She was taking care of it.

On the morning of her flight, I asked if her bags were ready. She said, "Oh my! I've got to pack." I was shocked. She had said she was taking care of packing. We needed to leave for the airport in ten minutes. In those minutes I tried to put the clothing and toiletries she would need into her bags. It was frantic. She made her flight, and she had a good time with friends. But what had happened lingered in my mind. How did she forget? She said she was packing days ahead. What was going on?

After the trip to Italy (June 1997), we sold our house in Atlanta and moved to Richmond. We had to buy a house and move into it. The move was not easy. Boxes came in the door. I began unpacking, but Dot seemed confused. She took a chair into the kitchen and watched me. Organizing her kitchen was not on her mind. A move is confusion, and confusion undid her. That was a first. In previous moves she had done more than her part.

Little changes began to creep into our lives. She could not keep up with her glasses, so we bought several pairs and left one pair in each room in the house. She could not balance her checkbook. It was left undone for months; then she asked me to do it for her. I began to notice that shopping was getting out of hand. We had several jars of peanut butter, too much Dr. Pepper, and the refrigerator was full of cheese. While doing the wash, she put washing powder into the dryer . . . after the clothes had been washed.

Always Dot did the cooking; I never learned. And why should I? She was so good in the kitchen; my job came after the meal. I washed dishes. She worked before the meal; I worked after. The routine was lunch at 12:30 p.m. There came a day when lunch was late; then lunch was forgotten. It was 1:15 and no lunch, nor was she preparing lunch. She had forgotten lunch.

It was not long before cooking fell to me (about 1999). I prepared breakfast and learned to make soup and sandwiches or a salad. We went out for one meal each day. This did not trouble Dot. One by one, I picked up the ordinary things she had done around the house. Washing, folding clothes, buying groceries, cooking (a generous term for what I did). Shifting these duties did not bother her. She went to bed soon after breakfast, would sleep until noon, eat lunch, and return to bed. About 3:30 each afternoon, she would wake and be reasonably alert. It was our pattern to play a game of Scrabble each afternoon at 4:00. Perhaps Scrabble would keep her mind active and postpone whatever was stealing her memory. She looked forward to our daily game, and so did I.

One incident did bother Dot. In 1999, she had two minor traffic accidents. Another time she went to the grocery store and got lost coming home, though she had made that trip often. A kind service station attendant drove her home. Her driving had become a risk both to herself and to others. I took her driver's license to the Department of Motor Vehicles and turned it in. She did not like that and argued at length that I was "being mean." She also said, "You are acting like my father, not my husband." There was a sense in which she was right, but I had no choice.

Then there were poignant times. She was self-aware . . . some of the time. One day she said, "Cecil, it looks like I'm losing my mind. I would not do this to you for anything in the world. It's going to be harder on you than it is on me." While sitting in the kitchen one afternoon, she said, "We've had a good marriage, haven't we?" She sensed that whatever she needed to say to me, she must say soon, for her mind was failing. She said she was glad we did our lives together. I slipped outside and wept.

Our daughter was the one who saw both of us more clearly than we saw ourselves. She set up an appointment for Dot with a geriatric neurologist at the Medical College of Virginia. The date was March 11, 2001. Dr. Peter Boling of MCV gently and thoroughly examined her nearly all morning. He went over parts of the examination twice. Genie and I sat with Dot throughout the whole process. I was amazed at her decline. She had masked her mental state. Boling asked her to tell him what day, month, and year it was. He asked her what time it was. She had a hard time getting the month of the year right, getting the time of day right. I had lived with her, and she had almost bluffed her way through each day. Though I lived with her, I did not recognize how much of her mind was already gone.

At the end of the examination, Dr. Boling had a nurse take Dot out of the room. He sat with Genie and me and said, "I am seventy percent sure she has Alzheimer's. You have one to two more years you can take care of her yourself. Then you will either need someone to come to your home and help you or you will have to place her in an Alzheimer's nursing home." I was grateful for the time, and the two-year prediction turned out to be uncanny in its accuracy.

The appointment with Dr. Boling didn't change our daily routine. I knew what her diagnosis was, but for the time being, my task was to live each day. I decided against telling her Dr. Boling's diagnosis; I could not see any good that would come of it. She was not insane. Part of the time she was intelligent and perceptive. Had I told her what the doctor had said, she would have gone to our medical dictionary and read about Alzheimer's disease. That would only lead to despair and perhaps depression. I did do one thing as a result of our visit to Dr. Boling. I applied for admission to Lakewood Manor, the Baptist retirement home in Richmond. When they learned Dot had an Alzheimer's diagnosis, we were turned down. Lakewood Manor did not accept people with an Alzheimer's diagnosis.

Dot had a lifelong habit of rising early in the morning. She would read her Bible, write a prayer for the day, and write in her journal. Reading those prayers and the journal is a window into her mind. On March 9, 2001, her prayer was,

> Father, my Heavenly Father, thank You for the many blessings You have bestowed on me. May I be of some use to You, if it be Your will. Evidently I get confused from time to time. I ask for Your Spirit to guide me in everything I do. As Cecil goes to Asheville, may he have a safe journey and be a blessing to those people. May I be guided by Your Spirit to the tasks You direct me to do. Bless Genie, Doug, and Nathaniel; how blessed we are by them. Thank You for the blessings You have showered on me. May I be a blessing to someone.
>
> Your long time daughter,
> DEHS

She was not out of her mind. She was self-aware. Her goodness seeps through every word. And especially at that time she wanted to be useful. It bothered her that she was not "doing something at the church." Several times she asked me to call our church and see if they could find a place for her to serve, any place. I gave evasive answers to her request.

In summer 2001, First Baptist Church of Asheville was without a pastor. They had decided against an interim; one speaker after another had taken the preaching assignment for two, three Sundays. Leadership of the church asked that I come and be both the preacher and administrator for about two months. Already the search committee had decided on Guy Sayles to be their pastor. He came the second Sunday in September; my job lasted until he came. Though it had been seventeen years since we lived among those people, we still had many friends in Asheville. Dot and I were put in a lovely hotel; our every need was met. I went to the church; old friends took care of Dot. We enjoyed meals with one family after another. Some days Dot struggled to keep schedule, but she enjoyed what amounted to a reunion. We came back to Richmond on a Monday, September 10. The next day Dot rested while I paid bills that had stacked up while we were away. I recall my surprise and shock when a neighbor shouted, "Cecil, turn on your TV." I did, and the 9-11 horror was being shown again and again.

By this time (late 2001), the Alzheimer's was more pronounced. I was afraid to leave Dot when I went to teach at the seminary, so I took her with me. She enjoyed being with the students. She would sit quietly in class, usually near the front. I would get a woman to take her down the hall; while she was away I told the class her condition. Women would go to the restroom with her. She did not always get her clothes buttoned or zipped just so when she left the restroom; the women would see that she was "back together." At class breaks students would hurry out and buy her a Coke, peanuts, or a cookie. She was given VIP treatment, for the students were tender and kind. I am grateful.

Twice she left the stove on and put us at risk of fire. She would not "stay put." Her motor skills were not impaired; she would go for walks in the neighborhood, but she could not find her way back home. Neighbors knew what was happening to us; they brought her back to our house.

Step by step she lost the ability to do basic things. She knew this was happening. I have her 2003 calendar before me as I write. Each day she wrote "Today" on the date; the last time she made that notation was March 19. She could not keep track of the days. Getting dressed requires that we put on our clothes in sequence. One day she put on her blouse first then the underclothes on top. It was funny . . . but it wasn't. In late 2002, my wife, who was always fastidious in her cleanliness, quit bathing. Of course I noticed and asked her to bathe. She said she did not need a bath. So began a running controversy: I was trying to talk her into taking a bath and she was refusing. Finally,

I had to bathe and dress her daily. She did not always approve of the way I went about it. Always I was amazed at how she could argue her point. She forgot so much, but when agitated, she could make her case like a lawyer. There were times when our lives were funny, sad, difficult, and wonderful. The good part was . . . we were together.

Christmas 2002, we flew to see Genie, Doug, and Nathaniel in Madison, Wisconsin. The aftermath of 9-11 made air travel more tedious. There were lines at the places where our bags and our persons were inspected. Of all people, Dot, now an eighty-four-year-old woman, was singled out and frisked like a criminal. Others were allowed to pass. Dot was randomly chosen for special scrutiny. It's a strange world!

Our visit to Madison was special. The season in Madison that year was the stuff of Christmas cards. On December 25, snow fell gently most of the day; the temperature did not get much above zero. We feasted and enjoyed each other. Dot was part of it all, but there were times when she could not follow the conversation. During a dinner conversation, our brains are hard at work. We are remembering, connecting, and forming new ideas to speak, and all of this is happening at the speed of light. Dot's brain would not allow such gymnastics. She would sit quietly, occasionally ask us to repeat a sentence, and often was at the margins. We knew it, and we hurt for her absence. Her body was present, but she was only half there. It is the way of Alzheimer's.

On New Year's Day 2003, we flew home. The flights were uneventful, but what followed wasn't. Between January 1 and March 22, Dot went into a precipitous decline. Much of the time she was almost passive. She wakened, ate, and went back to bed. Only for a few hours each day (usually in the afternoon) was she able to function. I was teaching at the seminary, but no longer could I take her with me. I hired a female seminary student to sit with her while I was away.

During those days River Road Church, Baptist, was without a pastor; it was the church Dot and I had joined when we moved to Richmond. Our friend, Jim Slatton, had resigned. I was asked to be the interim, and I was about to begin my duties. On a Tuesday, March 18, I went to the church for a brief meeting. I returned and found Dot in the front yard; it was a brisk, windy day. I asked her to join me in the car; I needed to go to the bank. She did. I parked the car in front of the bank, told Dot I would be gone only three to five minutes, and went inside. I was not in the bank any longer than three minutes. When I returned to the car, Dot was not there. The shopping center where the bank is located has an open parking lot. I looked for her, then went back into the bank and asked if they had seen my wife (they knew her). The answer was no. I began to look in the stores. Nowhere could I find a trace of her. The grocery story we used was near; I asked them to keep an eye out for her. The bank clerk and a woman from the store stopped their work and joined me in the search. An hour went by; then it was an hour and a half.

The mailman working his way through the shopping center heard me describing my wife to a shop owner. He had found her on his rounds, brought her to the grocery store, and then they began searching for me. I found her in the grocery. She had soiled herself and was afraid, for she knew she had been lost. I took her home, but she was not herself. She was loud and hyper. She would not go upstairs to the bath to clean up. She shouted at me in little barking sounds, noises that were more animal than human. This was not Dot at all; the disease had made her someone else. Finally I got her clean, but by now she was angry with me and the whole world.

I called my daughter in Madison. She listened to the noises Dot was making. Genie called Dr. Peter Boling in Richmond, the neurologist who had given us the Alzheimer's diagnosis, and asked that he call me. He did. When I picked up the phone, Dot was in full voice. Dr. Boling said, "I see you have a problem." He sent medicine to calm Dot.

A group of nurses put together a business they called "Mature Options." These nurses would come to your home, observe a person descending into Alzheimer's, and give advice on whether it was time to seek help or not. I had an appointment with one of those nurses that afternoon. The woman who came was in her fifties; she had been helping people like me for a number of years. I'm glad she came on the day she did. She saw Dot on a bad day, but she saw what I was dealing with. She wrote a five-page report recommending that I either begin searching for a person to come and help me in our home or seek a nursing care place. It was past time that I make some kind of change in Dot's care. That Tuesday was the hardest day of my life. I thought I had lost my wife. When I found her, she was not herself.

Genie came on Thursday after that awful Tuesday. We began visiting nursing homes that specialized in Alzheimer's care. Strangely, Dot had slept most of Wednesday; the medicine Dr. Boling sent sedated her. By Thursday Dot was almost herself again. Friday was a good day. Genie and I talked. Maybe Tuesday was an aberration, a horrible day that would not repeat itself. Saturday morning we went out, had lunch together, and came home. Genie planned to leave early Sunday morning; she wanted to get to bed early.

Dot went to our room. She dressed for bed. Then she thought she was not dressed right; she took off her gown and put on another. That process repeated itself for the next three hours. What began at 8:30 in the evening was still going on at 11:30, but by that time Dot was agitated and loud. We were slipping into Tuesday all over again. I called my son-in-law, Doug, who is a doctor. Genie and I described what was happening and let him listen to the noises Dot was making. Finally, Doug, Genie, and I decided it was time to take her to the emergency room. We chose the hospital at the Medical College of Virginia, the place where Dr. Boling worked. As we helped Dot down the stairs from our bedroom that late Saturday night, I recall wondering if Dot would ever enter our home again. She never did; it was the end of our life together. From that night Dot would be in one place and I in another.

Her care in the hospital was thorough. Dr. Boling supervised a team of doctors who examined her. They decided that she must not return home; Genie and I had to find an Alzheimer's care facility. We settled on Westminster-Canterbury Richmond; it is one of several retirement homes that offers full service—independent living, assisted living, and nursing care. There is a quiet, underlying Christian presence at Westminster-Canterbury. Episcopalians and Presbyterians founded it as a cooperative ministry.

On Monday, April 6, 2003, Jim Slatton joined me in the sad duty of taking Dot from the hospital to Westminster-Canterbury. I never dreamed that one day I would commit that beautiful girl I met in Dr. Price's office back in 1950, the girl I had married in Greer, South Carolina, to the care of a nursing home. Little did I know all I was saying when I stood before the preacher and vowed, "in sickness and in health, for better for worse, 'til death do us part." There was more to that promise than I knew. Dot was not "out of her head." Neither was she insane. At times she could connect ideas, events, and people in an almost normal way. But there were other times when her management required the full attention of people who knew more about Alzheimer's disease than I did.

The awful part of putting her in nursing care was her awareness. She wanted to know why I was putting her in a strange place. Again and again she asked, "Am I crazy? Why can't I go home? Please take me home." I felt guilty for not taking her home. One day through her Alzheimer's fog, she said, "Honey, do you remember that place we had with the pretty flowers in the backyard?" I said I remembered (she was describing our house in the west end of Richmond). "Can we live there again sometime?" I said, "I hope so, honey." I was dying inside.

A new routine developed from Dot's move to Westminster-Canterbury. Each afternoon I would drive the twelve miles to her, sit with her for a time, feed her dinner, and then return to the west end of Richmond. I chose to do her laundry; some days I took dirty clothes home with me; other days I brought clean clothes to her. A new doctor began experimenting with drugs that would suppress the outbursts that had prompted her leaving home. At first she was given too much of that drug; she slept nearly all the time. Then by trial and error, the dosage diminished. She takes just a little Zyprexa every other day. She doesn't go through the highs and lows she was suffering while at home, and she is monitored by people who know Alzheimer's.

Genie did not simply go back to Madison and leave us. For four-and-a-half years she has come from Madison to see her mother and me. She comes about every six weeks. I look forward to her coming; it always gives me a lift. In so many ways she, Doug, and Nathanial have been making this journey with us. They came when we celebrated our fiftieth wedding anniversary. They have gone out of their way to keep both of us in their busy lives.

This autobiography has said little about my brother and sister; mainly it has been about my work. But when hard times came, family ties surfaced. A pattern has developed. Each evening I get a call from my brother. Ruth calls and we talk at length at least twice a week. Fortunately, long distance telephone calls are inexpensive now. Bill and Ruth can talk to me without charge after 9:00 each evening. It is a rare evening when I do not hear from them. At first our conversations were almost exclusively about Dot. Now, with the passing of time, that awful move has receded into a part—not all—of the conversation. We talk about everything. Bill is a collector of funny stories; he brings me a new one nearly every day. The guys at Westminster-Canterbury want to meet Bill. He is the one who provides them a laugh at breakfast. Once a year Ruth, Bill, and I make time to get together. Ruth and her husband come from Oklahoma City to Nashville; I come from Richmond to Nashville. Bill and Veta serve as hosts, and we remember our parents, remember our childhood, remember wonderful times. We play games and become kids again. My brother Bill and Jim Slatton have become pastors to me. What began as a ministry to my need has now become a time that refreshes my spirit. Thank goodness for family.

When Dot was committed, I was interim pastor at River Road Church. But that does not describe what was really going on. They pastored me more than I pastored them. I tried not to bring my personal life into every sermon, but they knew what was happening. They did all a congregation can do to carry me through a difficult time. It has been a hard time, but God's grace has placed help all along the way.

The stress of caring for Dot wore on me. I was writing for Smyth & Helwys, teaching at BTSR (in winter and spring), doing interims, and caring for Dot and our house. I went for an early morning walk July 6, 2004. It was about 6:00 a.m. I had gotten only two blocks from our house when I noticed I was breathing hard and had a clammy sweat on my face. My arms felt odd. I recognized these as signs of heart trouble. I slowly retraced my steps to the house, and called a cardiologist from River Road Church; his wife answered. Dr. Charles Phillips had already gone to the hospital, but she would call him. She did, and he answered immediately . . . within two minutes of the time I hung up from talking to his wife. I described my symptoms, and he told me to get someone to drive me to Henrico Doctor's Hospital. I called Jim Slatton, who lived a mile away. Jim showed up at my door in less than ten minutes, drove me to the hospital, and shortly after 7:00 a.m. I was at the emergency room entrance. There was Dr. Phillips. He hurried me to an EKG machine and peered over the operator's shoulder while the results were printed out. He said in a flat, commanding voice, "You don't have indigestion; you have a heart problem. Give him aspirin, heparin, and knock him out." A nurse had been making an entry for medicines into my arm; quietly she whispered, "Now you are going to be a little sleepy . . . ." With that forewarning, one drop fell into my veins. The next thing I knew it was afternoon, and Dr. Phillips and Jim Slatton were standing at the foot of my bed. Dr. Phillips put three stents in my heart; they hold arteries open. In two days I went home; Genie came from Madison and cared for me. I was surprised at how weak I was after the procedure, but, as Dr. Phillips predicted, my strength returned in two to three weeks. In November 2004, I had angina, a sign that there was still blockage in the arteries in my heart. Dr. Phillips operated again, adding two more stents, and since then my heart has served me well. But the mild heart attack was a wake-up call.

There was an apartment available in the independent living section of Westminster-Canterbury. For twenty-two months I had made the twenty-five-mile round trip to visit Dot each day. I was tired of eating TV dinners alone in our house. I wanted to be nearer to Dot, to see her more than once a day. A move to Westminster-Canterbury would make that possible. So with Genie's help, I decided to sell our house and move to where Dot was. That would not be easy. There were eight rooms, an attic, and a two-car garage full of "stuff." It was the accumulation of a lifetime. I was moving into three rooms and two closets plus a small kitchen.

I had help. Carolyn Hartz is a realtor; she had sold us our house in the west end. With her help, our house was prepared for sale, and we received two offers only two days after it was put on the market. One was for our asking price; the other was $5,000 above our price. The house was sold; that was the easy part. Getting out was work. I had decisions to make. What part of these things do I need to take with me to Westminster-Canterbury? What part of what's left does Genie want? What part of what's left can be sold? I chose to give away the rest.

That division of goods went on for several weeks. The work of it was amazing, but I had help. Carolyn Hartz was a godsend. She went way beyond the call of duty. She knew the right people to get things done. Genie came several times to steady me in the process. A few people from River Road Church pitched in. It was a team effort, and on February 9, 2005, I was in an apartment at Westminster-Canterbury, just a four-minute walk from Dot. I'm glad I made the move, but it was hard on me. My weight was 159 the day I moved in; normally I travel at about 172. Thankfully, those pounds have been replaced.

Within six months of the time Dot checked into nursing care, she lost the ability to walk. Her motor skills left her. Since then she has lived in a wheelchair and the bed. Her ability to talk did not leave her so quickly. We often had conversations. They were circular; we said the same things over and over again. All through summer 2004, I would push her wheelchair to a shady place and she would enjoy the flowers. Each day she said the same thing: "Are we married?" I assured her that we were. Then she asked, "How long have we been married?" I said, "Fifty years." Upon hearing this she said, "That's a long time." The next day we repeated that brief conversation.

I tried to learn as much as I could about Alzheimer's disease. People who know say the things learned as a child are the things most likely to be remembered when the mind begins to fail. Taking this advice, I began to talk to her about things that happened to her when she was a little girl. All the stories she had told me over the past fifty years about her childhood, I tried to pull up and repeat to her. I talked of Pine Street School (her first elementary school in Spartanburg, South Carolina), about Southside Baptist Church (the church her family attended), about her mother and daddy, her sister, Helen. Sometimes she brightened and seemed to connect to what I was saying. Several times she said, "I want to go home to my mother in

Spartanburg. Will you take me?" (Her mother had died in 1963.) Usually I said, "It's a long way to Spartanburg; let's put that trip off a few days." That seemed to satisfy her. One day after asking to go home to her mother, she interrupted herself and said, "My mother's dead, isn't she?" I softly said, "Yes." Tears came to her eyes with the thought of her mother's death, but in thirty seconds the tears were gone. Such is the short-term retention of an Alzheimer's patient.

It was during this time that I began to sing to her. Usually we sit on a small love seat in her room. I put my arm about her shoulder, pull her close, and softly sing into her ear. The songs are either old hymns that she sang as a child, or they are love songs we knew in our courtship. The hymns mean the most to her. One night as I sang "Trust and Obey," she began to say the words with me. It was a small victory.

I had found her memory for a few seconds. Everything Dot has ever known is still stored in her mind. Alzheimer's has damaged the retriever; she can't pull that information up when she wants to. But the strange thing about Alzheimer's is that sometimes, for no apparent reason, the retriever will work again . . . for a moment. It's a baffling disease!

People who mean well have said to me, "Your wife is not suffering if she has Alzheimer's; you are but she isn't." I'm not sure that is true. Dot does have times when she ponders her condition. One morning in January 2006, I was feeding her breakfast. She had been in Westminster-Canterbury for nearly three years. She said, "Do you want me to die?" There was no antecedent to that comment. I had been talking about the weather, about oatmeal, and then she said that. I collected myself and said, "I come to you every day because I love you; I don't want you to die." She made no reply. But her question let me know there were times when she was self-aware and reflecting on her condition. That good mind is impaired, but it is not gone. The person I married is still inside, trapped by an awful disease we don't know how to cure.

After she had been in Westminster-Canterbury for about a year, her speech began to go. At first she slurred a word or did not finish a sentence. Then putting words together into a sentence became difficult. She began to speak in clipped phrases. Then Alzheimer's babble emerged. She would almost say a word, but she couldn't get it out. The first two words in a sentence were babble; then she would finish the sentence speaking normally. She recognized this speech change in herself, and she was frustrated. She would try to say again what she had garbled, and usually it wouldn't come out. Now most of her sounds are not words; they are attempts at words. Once in awhile, she can say something. The other day I came to her, and she surprised me by saying, "Hello, honey." It made my day.

Every day I sit with her on a sofa in her room, put my arm around her, and tell her I love her. I do this every day; often I do it several times a day. I don't know how much of what I say penetrates to her consciousness. What she is going through in this disease has to be a nightmare. When I tell her I love her, I am telling her that I am going to be with her, no matter what. She is not going to be abandoned; what I promised a long time ago in Greer, South Carolina, is a promise that still holds. The other day when I told her I loved her, she said, "I know." Not long ago when I said those magic words, she said, "Me too." I take it that she means she loves me too. That made me glad. Occasionally she softly, clearly says, "Thank you." Most of the time the disease has not changed her essential nature. I still love Dot. I don't know if the Dot I love is the Dot in my memory, the Dot of years ago, or the Dot I have, the Dot with Alzheimer's. Sorting out my mind is not a certain science.

Dot lives in an in-between world. She is not really alive in any meaningful sense, nor is she dead. She is in between. For at least five years, my wife has not been a wife, but she is alive and we are married. There are days when I talk to her and nothing comes back. She is not there; then, in another instant, there is a response. It is like a small shaft of light penetrating a dark room. I give thanks, but usually it is gone in a minute. The disease teases you, pulls you along, makes you hope . . . then takes hope away. It is cruel on her, and it is cruel on me. And it goes on and on and on. . . .

The preceding paragraphs may seem maudlin; some of you may be thinking that I am telling things that would be better left unspoken. But what I've told about Dot and me is the story of millions of people. In 2007, the American Alzheimer's Association reported that there are four-and-a-half million people suffering from Alzheimer's in America. That means there are at least that many caregivers. Half of the people who reach eighty years old are likely to develop the disease. A million husbands are praying that their wives will hear them say, "I love you." And only God knows how many women are longing to communicate with husbands who are in an Alzheimer's fog. What I've told you of our story is the story of so many people.

There is no happy ending to Alzheimer's disease today. Most people who suffer the disease do not die of it. They have a stroke or they come down with pneumonia or the women are taken by a urinary tract infection. But no one gets well. In the course of our marriage, we've had health problems. Alzheimer's is the first for which there is no cure, no relief. Learning that there cannot be a turnaround, that bad times cannot get better, has been one of the burdens of the disease. "Hope" is a sustaining word. When there is no hope of getting better, when every turn is a turn for the worse, then I am driven into my religion. Modern medicine can ease her way; it will not solve our problem. I have to look further down the road.

In September 2006, a urinary tract infection came upon Dot suddenly. In the evening I gave her orange juice and ice cream, and, as I fed her, she said, "I'm sick." I told the nurse what Dot said, and vital signs were checked. Nothing appeared amiss. But when I came to her the next morning at 8:00, she had a high fever and was breathing rapidly. Her face was flushed. It was a Tuesday, the day the doctor makes his rounds on the Alzheimer's floor. He came into her room, and I said, "What is wrong with Dot, and what we can we do for her?" He said, "My first suggestion is that you withdraw all medications and give her palliative care." I said, "That sounds like we are choosing to let Dot die. I'm not ready for that." He said, "She doesn't have much of a life now; it may be the best thing." I did not choose the course he suggested, but what the doctor said opened a conversation between Genie and me about what we might do the next time Dot becomes ill. That conversation is still in progress.

Death is out there. The subject has been on the table since that day we stood before Rev. O. K. Webb and promised to love each other "until death do us part." We were so young, so healthy, so full of life and ourselves that we gave little thought to death. C. S. Lewis was in correspondence with an English teacher in an American college. The teacher's wife was dying of cancer; the man was asking comfort from Lewis. The reply Lewis gave the man lingers in my mind. He said, "Death is the way a Christian marriage is supposed to end." That thought has often been on my mind. I don't know what is best for Dot. Her days are long; most of the time she is asleep. When she is awake, her life is the pitiful life of a nursing home. It is the best nursing home in town, but it is still a pitiful life. What to do? What is best? What is right? I don't have clear answers to questions I cannot avoid. It's a dreadful combination: age and Alzheimer's.

I've told the story of what is happening to us on the outside. There is another story: this illness has done something to the inside of me too. From infancy I've been programmed to be a Christian. I accepted Christian assumptions, and they have held me together my entire life. Those assumptions are more important today than when we were both healthy and living life to the full. Now we are diminished. We've gotten beyond our doctor's abilities to cure. The alternatives are despair and waiting until the end, or to hear and heed the advice of the Apostle Paul, who said, "So we do not lose heart. Even though our outer nature is wasting away, our inner nature is being renewed day by day. For this slight momentary affliction is preparing us for an eternal weight of glory beyond all measure" (2 Cor 4:16-17 NRSV). When I am thinking like a Christian, I choose Paul's outlook and try to make it my own. My faith teaches me how to die.

# EPILOGUE:
## REFLECTING ON MY LIFE

No autobiography takes the story to the end. I have more to do. But it seems appropriate that I reflect on my eighty years. For me, this is not like a teacher giving a grade on my own stewardship. Parts of my life have been public; people who witnessed some of it will make a more detached estimate of my service. Other parts have been religious; God will give the only judgment that matters. Yet there are observations that are mine:

## 1. I DID SOME THINGS RIGHT.

I was fortunate in the parents I was assigned. Not everyone is. They did their best to give me opportunities they never had. As a child, there were times when I did not understand my good fortune. That has changed. My father was tender, caring, emotional. My mother loved me as much as Dad did, but she showed her love in tough ways. She expected me to perform well in school. She set standards for me that I resented at the time, but down the road I realized they were necessary life skills. With the passing years I look more and more like my aged father. Any sense of humor I have came from him.

If ever I am purposeful and persistent, wise and prudent, honest and straight-thinking . . . I'm like my mother. Not everyone has that heritage. My parents were God's first gift to me, and one of His best. I'm glad I became a pastor/preacher. There were times when the frustrations of being the pastor discouraged me. I considered getting out of the ministry and into other work (I suspect most career pastors go through bouts of frustration that make them think similar thoughts). But I weathered those times and stayed with it.

Doing church work was the most satisfying and the most significant work I did. I got into people's lives. Some of them were moved toward God and have said so. People now fifty years old and in mid career thank me for something lost to my memory. They said I made a difference. Now I teach young people who are preparing to be pastors. I hope they stick with their calling too. I did not do everything right when I was a pastor, but I was about God's business. When I was about God's business, my life was enlarged and given dignity because of the nature of my work.

I'm glad I married Dot. We had a three-year courtship; she was concerned that I was nearly ten years her junior. Would that make for a mismatch and a difficult marriage? It didn't. She was a wonderful companion, but she was more. Her quiet goodness was a moral compass for me through uncertain waters. Not all pastors have a wife like Dot. She took the "pastor's wife" life and made it her calling. When a church got me, they got Dot too. She never worked outside the home after I went to Chamblee (September 1956). My work was her concern. Going to church was never a chore for her; it was her job just as it was mine. She read everything she could find about how to be a "pastor's wife." Before Alzheimer's came upon her, she would have been a good teacher about how to do the job. We never stopped being in love. Always it has been a marriage, not an arrangement. Late in life she said, "I want to thank you for not having a mistress . . . except the Church." She was all I needed.

Our daughter has been a grace note in our lives. She blessed us from birth. There were times when parenting her was a challenge, but either we (Dot and I) grew up or Genie did. Either way, it surely has turned out well. Now with our age, Genie is no longer our daughter; she is becoming our caretaker. She has done this willingly and gracefully. In so many ways I see Dot in the fifty-year-old Genie. She is a devout, devotional Christian. Her willingness to identify with causes that have moral content is like that of her mother. She cares about what people think of her, but that care does not order her life. Or, put another way, she is willing to take an unpopular position if she believes her faith drives her to it. Like most fathers, I'm proud of our daughter. Like most fathers, I wish I had spent more time with her when she was a child.

I was fortunate in the churches I served. Chamblee, College Station, Asheville (especially Asheville), and Broadway were right churches for Dot and me. Until I was halfway through the Asheville years, I was learning. I was green, unseasoned, and sometimes immature. Those people put up with my on-the-job training, helped me when I stumbled, and gave me time to grow. Not all pastors have been so lucky. I was forgiven and granted another chance. Some pastors have been dismissed for the same kinds of immaturity for which I was given a second chance. I wish I could take credit for making good choices in my churches, but mainly it was Providence, God's doing. That means it was gift, and I am grateful.

Along the way strangers became friends, and friends became almost family. I don't have hundreds of such people; I don't need hundreds. But now that age has come, I stay in touch with these friends. We have common memory banks; we can draw up stories from the past. When we do, time stands still, or maybe time goes into reverse. It is 1964, or 1980, or 1991, and I am again involved in causes and conflicts. The years fall away. Those stories give humor and substance to our friendships, and they give meaning to our lives. I'm not sure we set out to make friends; some people just fit, come close, share common convictions, and become friends. This is no place to name them. They know who they are, and they know how much I care for them.

## 2. AND WHAT OF MY PUBLIC LIFE?

I wish I had developed better relational skills. There were times when I was a pastor, involved in denominational strife, and establishing CBF when my relational skills did not serve me well. I came across as hard—right on the issue but uncaring of my opponent. With the passing years, I hope I've mellowed.

There are no regrets about the side I took in the SBC controversy (1979–1990). I believe we were right on the issues. There were times when I was right on the issues but wrong in the way I expressed myself.

It is difficult to be in controversy and not become controversial in temper. I opposed Fundamentalism in 1980, and I would do it again. It is a misrepresentation of the Christian religion. My opposition to Fundamentalism has not made me a liberal; in the present theological climate of Baptist life, such distinctions are hard to hold in proper place. But pandering to the popular mind, claiming to be an inerrantist by using all sorts of roundabout definitions, is neither honest nor helpful. Inerrancy is not intellectually honest. In an increasingly informed populace, Christian apologists must be scrupulously honest or they will not get a hearing. For the sake of the future of the Christian faith, we have to tell the truth about our sources, about Jesus, and about the Church. I've tried to be honest, and it got me in trouble with Southern Baptists. I might change some of the words I chose in debate; I would not change sides.

Sharp words were exchanged on the Peace Committee. Some of them were mine. I disagreed with Adrian Rogers. The effect of his convictions, and the way he went about institutionalizing them, put me out of the SBC (and thousands of others). My only regret about my part in resisting Fundamentalism is this: I wish I had been more effective. I have never known what to do with my anger about the meanness of Fundamentalism. That is unresolved until the present, and I see no prospect that it will be put to rest. That is a shadow in my mind, for my faith tells me that I am not to harbor anger against another . . . no matter what.

Sometimes I get out of character. I'm the pastor of a church again or I'm the coordinator of CBF. I don't like a direction that is being taken by leadership, and I want to correct them. That is the foolishness of age, and I get over it. I'm no longer in charge of anything. I don't know enough to sit in judgment on those who are. It is the way of those who are retired, who once were in charge but are no longer. I know my folly and try to keep my thoughts to myself, and most of the time I do.

I care deeply for the Church. It is troubling to me that so many Baptist churches (many of them Moderate) are not thriving. "Evangelism" and "enlistment" are words that have come into disrepute among some Moderates. A life wish for the church is not held by too many Moderates. I want Baptist ideas to flourish, and it seems to me those ideas are most threatened from within rather than from without.

## 3. COMING TO TERMS WITH LAST THINGS

I've been asked, "Are you angry that Dot has Alzheimer's disease?" I could turn the question inward and ask, "Am I angry with God for letting me have diabetes?" Not really. Do I wish things were still as they were years ago? Of course I do; all old people have that wish flit through their minds. But most old people have enough sense to see that we have had our run at life. We can say with the psalmist, "The lines are fallen unto me in pleasant places; yea, I have a goodly heritage" (Ps 16:5 KJV). Life is lived forward; there is no reversing time. Age is inexorable, relentless.

All my life I've been told there is life after death. At Easter I've preached about Jesus rising from the grave. At a thousand funerals I've quoted John 20 and 1 Corinthians 15. I believed what I said then, and age has not changed my mind. Sometimes I wonder about the afterlife. I don't know as much about heaven as I would like; I surely don't know as much as some preachers claim to know. There are occasions when I have doubts about immortality. An English pastor's wife wrote in her 2006 Christmas letter, "Now that I am old and death cannot be far away, I confess that I am having some doubts about immortality." Sometimes I do, too. But most of the time faith wins out over doubt, and I think like a Christian again. I've always believed that truth would prevail over falsehood and good stewardship would be rewarded in God's eternity. William Temple, Archbishop of Canterbury during World War II, was talking with his wife about life after death. He said, "There is nothing in the world of which I feel so certain; I have no idea what it will be like, and I think I am glad that I have not, as I am sure it would be wrong." And again Temple said, "For myself, I do cling to it [immortality] immensely. I do not mean that I want it for myself as mere continuance, but I want it for my understanding of life. . . . And moreover 'God is Love' appears nonsense in view of the world He has made, if there is no other" (F. A. Iremonger, *William Temple, Archbishop of Canterbury: His Life and Letters* [London:

Oxford University Press, 1948], 626). I quoted Temple because he spoke what I believe.

All of us want what Puritans called "a good death." Between now and that time I want to be useful, spend time in the company of family and friends, care for Dot until our marriage promise is finally kept, and bear witness to an abiding faith in Jesus Christ. I have found Christ faithful; my earnest prayer is that I will be found faithful. And so the road rises before me. I don't go into the sunset; that's not my state of mind. Using imagery from my childhood, "I'm Bound for the Promised Land." I'm Pilgrim, and I'm on my way toward the Celestial City.

*—Cecil E. Sherman*

Richmond, Virginia
October 2007